D1739256

Privileged Places

Privileged Places

Race, Residence, and the Structure of Opportunity

Gregory D. Squires
Charis E. Kubrin

LYNNE
RIENNER
PUBLISHERS

BOULDER
LONDON

Published in the United States of America in 2006 by
Lynne Rienner Publishers, Inc.
1800 30th Street, Boulder, Colorado 80301
www.rienner.com

and in the United Kingdom by
Lynne Rienner Publishers, Inc.
3 Henrietta Street, Covent Garden, London WC2E 8LU

Library of Congress Cataloging-in-Publication Data
Squires, Gregory D.
  Privileged places : race, residence, and the structure of opportunity / Gregory D. Squires,
Charis E. Kubrin.
     p.   cm.
  Includes bibliographical references and index.
  ISBN-13: 978-1-58826-449-7 (hardcover : alk. paper)
  ISBN-10: 1-58826-449-1 (hardcover : alk. paper)
  1. Housing—United States. 2. Race discrimination—United States. 3. United States—
Social conditions. 4. United States—Economic conditions. I. Kubrin, Charis Elizabeth.
II. Title.
HD7293.S656 2006
363.50973—dc22

                                                                                    2006011920

British Cataloguing in Publication Data
A Cataloguing in Publication record for this book
is available from the British Library.

Printed and bound in the United States of America

The paper used in this publication meets the requirements
of the American National Standard for Permanence of
Paper for Printed Library Materials Z39.48-1992.

5 4 3 2 1

Contents

Acknowledgments

Several people contributed to this book in a variety of ways, and we want to thank them all for their assistance: Lyndsay Boggess, Glenn Canner, William Chambliss, Samantha Friedman, George Galster, John Goering, Amanda Hazelwood, Anne Shlay, Shauna Sorrells, Stephen Steinberg, and Ron Weitzer. We also want to thank the Ford Foundation and the Open Society Institute of the Soros Foundation for their support.

—*Gregory D. Squires*
Charis E. Kubrin

1

Race and Place

The housing market and discrimination sort people into different neighborhoods, which in turn shape residents' lives—and deaths. Bluntly put, some neighborhoods are likely to kill you.
—John Logan 2003: 33

Real estate mantra tells us that three factors determine the market value of a home: location, location, and location. The same could be said about the factors that determine virtually any aspect of the good life and people's access to it in the metropolitan United States. Place matters. Neighborhood counts. Neighborhoods are not simply areas where people live, work, and play. They are "constellations of opportunities" (Pulido 2004: 86). Access to decent housing, safe neighborhoods, good schools, useful contacts, and other benefits is largely influenced by the community in which one is born, raised, and currently resides. Individual initiative, intelligence, experience, and all the elements of human capital are obviously important. But understanding the opportunity structure in the United States today requires complementing what we know about individual characteristics with what we are learning about place. Privilege cannot be understood outside the context of place.

The relationship between race and place has confounded efforts to understand and, where appropriate, alter the opportunity structure of the nation's urban communities. The racial composition of neighborhoods has long been at the center of public policy and private practice in the creation and destruction of communities and in determining access to elements of the good life, however defined. Place and race have long been and continue to be determinants of the distri-

1

bution of valued goods and services in metropolitan areas. Disentangling the impact of these two forces is difficult, if not impossible. But where one lives and one's racial background are both social constructs that, on their own and in interaction with each other, significantly shape the privileges (or lack thereof) that people enjoy.

In this book we explore the significance of place and race on two particularly important aspects of the good life: (1) access to housing and the financing that makes housing possible and (2) exposure to crime and the likelihood of being involved in the criminal justice system. We focus on these issues for two primary reasons.

First, they capture major incentives and disincentives for city living, thus fueling the uneven development of metropolitan areas and its associated social costs. (Uneven development refers to inequalities associated with a range of interrelated factors, including race, class, neighborhood, and industry). Homeownership constitutes the primary source of wealth for most families. The increasing value of housing in recent years has been a major attraction for city living, whereas crime, or at least fear of crime, remains a major deterrent. The value of homes in urban neighborhoods has increased substantially, and greater access to mortgage loans in many, though certainly not all, urban communities has made homeownership more accessible to more families. Between 2000 and 2004, home prices nationwide rose by 50 percent, with the largest increases occurring in cities along the East Coast and West Coast. In comparison, the Standard and Poor's 500 stock index fell by 17 percent during those years (Deane 2005; Andrews 2005). At the same time, suburban and nonmetropolitan areas continue to grow ever more rapidly, with fear of crime still constituting a primary reason many households choose what results in sprawling patterns of development.

A second reason for focusing on housing and crime is that many cities have made a significant comeback since the early 1990s in large part because of the increasing access to mortgage loans and the reduction in crime (Grogan and Proscio 2000). Since the mid-1980s, mortgage loans have been far more readily available to low-income borrowers, racial minorities, and residents of low-income and minority communities. Cities have also become safer than they were in previous decades, as indicated by a decline in violent and property crime (Federal Financial Institutions Examination Council 2003; Grogan and Proscio 2000). Given the salience of these two forces for shaping patterns of metropolitan development, it is critical to understand how they affect the quality of life for those who reside in the nation's population centers. Such understanding is essential to ameliorating the many social costs of uneven development. In this book we examine particular housing and crime issues that have emerged in recent years in urban policy debates and suggest how those debates can be advanced both for the enlightenment of urban scholars and the quality of life of the residents. We aim to shed light on persistent as well as emerging forms of inequality and propose steps to eradicate ongoing inequities.

In the area of housing, we consider housing mobility (e.g., minority access to predominantly white neighborhoods from which black and Latino families have long been excluded), predatory lending (an emerging form of exploitation that undercuts such mobility), and discrimination in the property insurance industry, which can deny the opportunity to own a home before a family even applies for a mortgage loan. Regarding crime, we examine the association between access to capital and neighborhood crime as well as determine how community influences offenders' successful reintegration into society after prison. Recidivism has long been the focus of much criminal justice research and policy. But its spatial dimensions—the highly concentrated neighborhoods from which offenders come and return to, often more than once—are just beginning to be understood. Housing and crime have their own complex social dynamics, but these dynamics feed into each other. We demonstrate how increased financing for housing and community reinvestment can ameliorate neighborhood crime rates and the uneven distribution of privilege generally.

The impacts of place and race are not inevitable. If place matters, policy does as well. Uneven development of metropolitan areas in the United States results directly from policy decisions made by public officials that shape actions taken in the private and nonprofit sectors. Policy decisions can be made to alter that pattern of development; in fact, some steps are being taken in that direction, as we note throughout the following chapters. Housing and crime are not the only areas where uneven development, fueled by public policy and private practice, shapes the opportunity structure confronting diverse groups, however. The following pages illustrate the applicability of this perspective to several walks of life (e.g., health, education, employment) before returning to the housing and crime focus in subsequent chapters. The significance of the broader race-place-policy perspective lies in the fact that it frames the opportunity structure across the board and provides the larger context for understanding the particular impact of housing and crime. One conclusion that applies across virtually all issues is that it is time to sever the linkages among place, race, and privilege.

These linkages are shaped by three dominant social forces: sprawl, concentrated poverty, and segregation, all of which play out in response to public policy decisions and the practices of powerful private institutional actors. This perspective emerges from what has been variously referred to as "the new urban sociology," "urban political economy" and other labels that place class, race, and relations of domination and subordination at the center of analysis. In general, this kind of analysis requires understanding how individual characteristics and choices (e.g., human capital, neighborhood preferences) and voluntary exchanges that occur via competitive markets are both framed and complemented by structural constraints in determining the distribution of valued goods and services. Specifically, it involves examining how land use practices, urban policy, the dynamics of race and class, and other social forces determine who gets what and why (Fainstein 2001; Fainstein and Campbell 2002; Feagin 1998; Gottdiener and Feagin 1988; Horan 1978).

The following discussion and the chapters in this book trace patterns of uneven metropolitan development during the post–World War II years, the social forces generating these patterns, their many costs, and potential remedies. We examine some of the contours of current policy debates and suggest directions for altering the inequitable opportunities confronting many residents of urban communities today. While focusing on housing and crime in the following chapters, we identify specific policies that already have been shown to ameliorate the linkages among place, race, and privilege. We also note potentially promising ideas for future initiatives. We assume that no outcome is preordained: severing these linkages is possible but not inevitable.

Race, Residence, and Uneven Development

> *Do the kids in the neighborhood play basketball or hockey?*
> —Anonymous insurance agent (Luquetta 2000)

The dominant forces of metropolitan development in the years after World War II are sprawl, concentrated poverty, and segregation (if not hypersegregation, or extremely high levels of separation of whites and nonwhites, as indicated by several different measures). Clearly, they are not separate, mutually exclusive patterns and processes. Rather, they are three critical underpinnings of the uneven development of place and privilege.

Sprawl has crept into the vocabulary of metropolitan development in recent years, with different observers offering diverse perspectives on its causes and consequences (Galster et al. 2001). Yet most would concur with Anthony Downs's observation that "Suburban sprawl has been the dominant form of metropolitan-area growth in the United States for the past 50 years" (Downs 1998: 8). Although there is no universal agreement on a definition of sprawl, there is at least a rough consensus that it is a pattern of development associated with outward expansion, low-density housing and commercial development, fragmentation of planning among multiple municipalities with large fiscal disparities among them, auto-dependent transportation, and segregated land use patterns (Downs 1999; Katz and Bradley 1999; Orfield 1997, 2002; Squires 2002).

A few numbers illustrate these spatial developments. Between 1950 and 1990, metropolitan areas grew from 208,000 square miles housing 84 million people to 585,000 square miles housing 193 million, so population increased by 128 percent, while the land on which residents lived expanded by 181 percent. Population density declined from 407 to 330 persons per square mile. During these years, the number of municipalities within metropolitan areas grew from 193 to 9,600 (Rusk 1999: 67, 68). And although some major cities have recently witnessed growth in their populations, between 1970 and 2000 the suburban share of the nation's metropolitan area population increased from 55.1 percent to 62.2 percent (US Department of Housing and Urban Development 2000: 63). This trend accelerated during the 1990s, when the suburban population grew by 17.7 percent, compared to just 8.0 for central cities (US Census Bureau 2001).

But people are not moving randomly. In general, income levels have been consistently higher and poverty levels lower in the suburbs. In 1960, per capita income in cities was 105 percent of suburban per capita income. By 1990 it fell to 84 percent, which is where it remained in 2000 (Cisneros 1993: 25; Logan 2002a: 4). Between 1970 and 1995, poverty increased in cities from below 13 percent to 20 percent while rising just slightly in the suburbs from 7 to 9 percent (US Department of Housing and Urban Development 1997: 32). During the 1990s, disparities between cities and suburbs remained virtually unchanged (Logan 2002a: 4), and concentrated poverty has grown in recent decades as well. Between 1970 and 1990, the number of census tracts in which at least 40 percent of the population was poor increased from under 1,500 to more than 3,400, and the number of people living in those tracts grew from 4.1 million to more than 8 million.

There were some positive developments during the 1990s, however. In that decade the number of tracts where the poverty rate reached at least 40 percent dropped to 2,510, and the number of residents dropped below 8 million (Jargowsky 1996: 30; 2003: 4, 20). A similar pattern was found using a 30 percent threshold. And conditions in those tracts improved. The share of adults without a high school degree, the share of families headed by women, and the share of households receiving public assistance declined, while the share of women who were working increased (Kingsley and Pettit 2003). But the 2000 census occurred at the peak of the economic boom of the 1990s, and most observers believe circumstances have deteriorated since then, although it is unclear by how much. There were gains, to be sure. How permanent they are remains to be determined (Kingsley and Pettit 2003: 10). Despite the progress of the 1990s, the number of poverty tracts and the population of those neighborhoods were higher in 2000 than in either 1970 or 1980. Concentrated poverty thus persists as a defining characteristic of urban communities in the United States.

The nonrandomness of sprawl is also reflected in the racial composition of city and suburban communities. Racial disparities between cities and suburbs and racial segregation in general persist as dominant features of metropolitan areas. Cities are disproportionately nonwhite, with over 52 percent of blacks and 21 percent of whites residing in central city neighborhoods, whereas suburbs are disproportionately white, with 57 percent of whites but just 36 percent of blacks residing there (McKinnon 2000: 2). Segregation, particularly between blacks and whites, persists at high levels, while Hispanic/white segregation has increased in recent years (Iceland et al. 2002a, 2002b; Lewis Mumford Center 2001a, 2001b). Although blacks account for about 12 percent of the nation's total population and Hispanics for about 13 percent, the typical white resident of metropolitan areas resides in a neighborhood that is 80 percent white, 7 percent black, 8 percent Hispanic, and 4 percent Asian. A typical black person lives in a neighborhood that is 33 percent white, 51 percent black, 11 percent Hispanic, and 3 percent Asian. And a typical Hispanic resident lives in a community that is 36 percent white, 11 percent black, 45 percent Hispanic, and 6 percent Asian (Lewis Mumford Center 2001a: 3). Thus, while racial minorities tend to live in relatively diverse neighborhoods, whites remain highly isolated.

As in the case of concentrated poverty, there have been some favorable segregation trends in recent years. Nationwide, the black/white index of dissimilarity has declined from .73 in 1980 to .64 in 2000 (Iceland et al. 2002a: 60). (A score of 1 would indicate total segregation, where every neighborhood is entirely black or white, and a score of 0 would indicate that each neighborhood has the same percentage of blacks and whites as the entire area.) Racial minorities increased their share of the suburban population from 19 percent in 1990 to 27 percent in 2000 (Frey 2001: 1). And between 1996 and 2001, the black homeownership rate increased by more than 4 percentage points (from 44.3 to 48.4 percent), compared to an increase of just over 2 percentage points for the nation generally (from 65.4 to 67.8 percent) (Joint Center for Housing Studies 2002: 31). But the suburbs remain segregated, and black/white segregation remains at high levels. Where segregation has declined, it has generally been in relatively small sunbelt communities with small black populations. In the older northeastern and midwestern industrial communities, traditional levels of segregation persist. Between 1980 and 2000, segregation declined by 6 percentage points in metropolitan areas where 20 percent or more of the population was black, compared to 12 points where they accounted for less than 10 percent of all residents. And in cities like New York, Chicago, Detroit, Milwaukee, and Newark, segregation scores were .8 or higher in 2000 (Lewis Mumford Center 2001a; Logan et al. 2004). City/suburban barriers have broken down somewhat in recent years, and levels of black/white segregation have moderated slightly. However, racial segregation remains a prominent feature of US metropolitan areas and, in conjunction with the concentration of poverty and growing economic inequality, results in increasing isolation of poor minority households.

If segregation is declining, albeit slightly, for blacks, it does not appear this has translated into their being able to move into better neighborhoods. The median census tract or neighborhood income for the typical black household in 1990 was $27,808, compared to $45,486 for whites, a gap of $17,679. By 2000 that gap had increased to $18,112. Perhaps more problematic, when looking at households with incomes above $60,000, similar patterns were observed. For example, in 1990 the typical black household with an income above $60,000 lived in a neighborhood where the median income was $31,585, compared to $46,760 for the typical white household in this income bracket, a gap of $15,175. By 2000 these figures were $35,306 for blacks and $51,459 for whites, creating an even larger gap of $16,152 (Logan 2002b: Tables 2 and 3). The same pattern holds for Hispanics, not surprisingly, given that in recent years, they have become concentrated in ever more segregated neighborhoods. Further confounding the intersection of place and race is the fact that in 2000, poor blacks and Hispanics were far more likely than poor whites to live in poor neighborhoods. Over 18 percent of poor blacks and almost 14 percent of poor Hispanics lived in such areas, whereas less than 6 percent of poor whites did (Jargowsky 2003: 10).

These neighborhood effects, of course, are felt by individuals and their families. At least since 1980, for example, median black and Hispanic family income has been approximately 60 percent that of white median family income (US Census Bureau 1999: Table B-4). But wealth disparities are far greater. While blacks earn about 60 percent of what whites earn, their net wealth is approximately one-tenth that of whites. These substantial wealth disparities persist even between whites and nonwhites who have equivalent educational backgrounds, comparable jobs, and similar incomes (Conley 1999; Oliver and Shapiro 1995). A number of factors contribute to these disparities.

Inheritance is one major contributor. Whites are more than three times as likely as blacks to inherit money, and among those who do, whites average $52,430 compared to $21,796 for blacks. These differentials do not take into account disparities in the amount of money children receive from their parents while they are still alive (Shapiro 2004: 67–71). These wealth disparities also reflect, at least in part, the fact that middle-class black families are more likely to have poor and working-class friends and relatives who look to them for financial support. And black middle-class neighborhoods are far more likely than white middle-class communities to be located in close proximity to poor neighborhoods, which black residents frequently pass through while commuting to work, going to the grocery store, and engaging in normal daily activities (Pattillo-McCoy 1999). Proximity to problematic neighborhoods also affects the value of homes and, therefore, further contributes to economic disparities.

Homeownership, in terms of the share of different groups who own their homes and the value of those homes, is another significant contributor to racial wealth disparities. Almost 75 percent of white families own their homes, whereas approximately half of black families do so (Joint Center for Housing Studies 2002a: 31). For blacks, home equity accounts for two-thirds of their assets, compared to two-fifths for whites (Oliver and Shapiro 1995: 106). Biases in the nation's housing and home finance markets have cost the current generation of blacks about $82 billion, with the disparity in home equity averaging $20,000 for those holding mortgages (Oliver and Shapiro 1995: 151, 171). Once again, place is a factor. Nationwide, racial composition of neighborhood affects appreciation in property values and wealth accumulation associated with homeownership, even after controlling for nonracial factors (e.g., characteristics of housing units, socioeconomic status of residents) that are associated with property values. Large concentrations of black and Latino homeowners, and in particular large increases in black representation, adversely affect the extent to which home values increase (Flippen 2004). The vast majority of the growing share of the nation's households that have become homeowners have experienced substantial growth in the equity of their homes. Such appreciation, as indicated earlier, is a major incentive for city living. At the same time, substantial racial disparities persist in homeownership rates and in wealth accumulation among those who do own their homes.

A large part of these gaps can be accounted for by racial discrimination and segregation in housing and financial service markets. A study of the 100 largest metropolitan areas found that black homeowners received 18 percent less value for their investments in their homes than did white homeowners (Rusk 2001). That is, for every dollar of income, blacks owned $2.16 worth of housing, compared to $2.64 for whites. For example, in Baltimore black homeowners had a mean household income of $41,466 and owned homes with a mean value of $69,600, so for every dollar of income they owned $1.68 worth of home. Whites had a mean income of $55,429 and owned homes with a mean value of $133,000. They owned $2.40 worth of home for every dollar of income. In determining the causes of variation in this "black tax" across the 100 communities, several factors were examined, including the size of the metropolitan area, economic inequality across neighborhoods, minority population, rates of homeownership among each group, and two measures of racial segregation (dissimilarity and isolation indices). David Rusk found that only the segregation measures were significant. The importance of place is also indicated by the success of efforts to relocate poor and minority households from low-income central city neighborhoods to middle-income suburban communities. Evaluations of the Gautreaux program in Chicago and early returns from the US Department of Housing and Urban Development's Moving to Opportunity (MTO) program have found evidence that students who relocate do better in school, engage in less delinquency, and experience improved health status and enhanced personal and family lives (Goering 2005; Goering et al. 2002; Goering and Feins 2003; Kling, Ludwig, and Katz 2005; Rosenbaum et al. 2005; Rubinowitz and Rosenbaum 2000).

The persistence of discrimination was documented in a nationwide housing study by the Urban Institute. The study found that black homebuyers encountered discrimination in 22 percent of their searches for rental units and 17 percent of their efforts to purchase homes. For Hispanics, the figures were 26 and 20 percent. Though this represented a substantial drop from the Urban Institute's previous study in 1988, it reveals continuing high levels of racial discrimination in the housing market (Turner et al. 2002b: iii–v; Turner and Ross 2005). And these figures represent a conservative estimate of the number of instances of discrimination that occur. The Urban Institute study focused on initial visits of homeseekers with managers of rental units and real estate agents. Follow-up visits and phone calls were not included. So, for example, the study did not capture what occurred when homeseekers followed up initial visits with subsequent requests for assistance or to make offers on a home. The study also did not examine discrimination in mortgage lending, property insurance, appraisals, and other aspects of the home rental and buying process. As the National Fair Housing Alliance noted, if a typical apartment search involves a visit to at least four or five units and racial minorities are encountering discrimination in one out of every four or five visits to a rental agent, it may be the case that black and Hispanic renters encounter discrimination virtually every time they move (National Fair Housing Alliance 2003b: 1).

At the same time, there is mounting evidence that many inner-ring suburbs are experiencing urban ills previously associated primarily with inner-city neighborhoods (Orfield 1997, 2002; Rusk 1999). So the growing presence of racial minorities in the suburbs in recent years makes the 1990s, as the title of one Brookings Institution report states, "A Decade of Mixed Blessings" (Berube and Frey 2002). Ethnic diversity may be growing in metropolitan areas, but neighborhood integration lags behind (Lewis Mumford Center 2001a).

The Costs of Spatial and Racial Inequality

These patterns are not just statistical or demographic curiosities. They correlate directly with access to virtually all products and services associated with the good life. Sprawl, concentrated poverty, and racial segregation target a host of problems and privileges in different neighborhoods and among different racial groups (Frazier, Margai, and Tettey-Fio 2003; Massey 2001; Massey and Denton 1993; Sampson, Morenoff, and Gannon-Rowley 2002). These "concentration effects" shape opportunities throughout life and across generations, as subsequent chapters show. This book focuses on housing and crime, but the linkages between race and place cut across virtually all areas of life. The following discussion illustrates just how pervasive these linkages are in shaping life chances for disparate groups.

Health disparities may constitute the most concrete disadvantages associated with the spatial and racial divide in urban areas, and they manifest themselves quite early in life. The black infant mortality rate in 1995 was 14.3 per 1,000 live births, compared to 6.3 for whites and Hispanics and 5.3 for Asians. More troubling is the fact that the ratio of black to white infant mortality increased from 1.6 to 2.4 between 1950 and the 1990s (Kington and Nickens 2001: 264–265). Overall, African Americans receive inferior care when being treated for more than two-thirds of the most important heath care problems (e.g., being advised to quite smoking, getting a lipid profile every two years for diabetics), and Hispanics receive inferior care for half of these measures (Agency for Healthcare Research and Quality 2004). Access to clean air and water, exposure to lead paint, stress, obesity, smoking habits, diet, social isolation, proximity to hospitals and other medical treatment facilities, and availability of health insurance all vary by neighborhood and all contribute to long-established disparities in health and wellness (Bullard 1996; Dreier et al. 2001: 66–82; Kington and Nickens 2001; Klinenberg 2002).

Recent research has documented that the environment can affect the fundamental development of the brain, which leads to variations in a range of intellectual, emotional, and social abilities. An ongoing controversial debate is the role of IQ, widely assumed to be inherited, in determining individual achievement (Herrnstein and Murray 1994). But as the National Academy of Sciences reported in *From Neurons to Neighborhoods*, the causal arrow points in both directions (Shonkoff and Phillips 2000). Intelligence no doubt influences achievement, but environment clearly influences development of the basic tool that drives intelligence, the human brain.

To illustrate the impact of place, in the Washington, D.C., area the affluent and predominantly white suburb of Bethesda, Maryland, has one pediatrician for every 400 children, whereas the poor and predominantly black neighborhoods in the District's southeast side have one pediatrician for every 3,700 children. And while the hospital admission rate for asthma in the state of New York is 1.8 per 1,000, it is three times higher in the Mott Haven area of the South Bronx (Dreier et al. 2001: 68, 70). That is hardly just an East Coast phenomenon. The predominantly black and Latino South-Central Los Angeles community has one primary care physician for every 12,993 residents, but a few miles away in the wealthy community of Bel-Air, the ratio is one to 214 (Brown et al. 2003: 14).

Education has long been regarded as the principal vehicle for ameliorating such problems. If education is to be "the great equalizer of the conditions of men—the balance wheel of the social machinery," as the Massachusetts educator Horace Mann anticipated over 150 years ago, that day has yet to arrive (Bowles and Gintis 1976: 23). Reliance on property taxes to fund public education nurtures ongoing inequality in the nation's schools that is explicitly tied to place. Though some communities have introduced equalization formulas, wealthier communities still provide substantially greater financial support for public schools, with a lesser tax effort, than poorer ones. Given the demographics of metropolitan areas, spatial inequalities are readily translated into racial disparities (Anyon 1997; 2005). After two decades of progress in desegregating the nation's schools, it appears that progress may have come to a halt in the 1990s or perhaps even have been reversed. In 2000, 40 percent of black students attended schools that were 90 to 100 percent black, compared to 32 percent of black students who attended such schools in 1988 (Orfield and Eaton 2003). The percentage of white students in the schools of the typical black student declined from more than 36 to less than 31 during these years. And the share of Latino students attending schools that were 90 to 100 percent minority grew from 23 percent during the late 1960s to 37 percent in 2000 (Frankenberg et al. 2003: 30, 33). John Logan has suggested that demographic changes rather than resegregation account for these patterns. That is, in public schools whites simply account for a smaller share of total enrollments, so students of all races are in schools that have higher minority enrollments. Yet, as Logan concludes, public schools remain highly segregated, and he also observes "Separate continues to mean unequal" (Logan 2004: 16). Continuing disparities result in fewer educational resources, less qualified teachers, higher teacher turnover, and ultimately lower educational achievement in low-income and minority communities (Frankenberg et al. 2003: 67).

If there is one single factor that most directly determines access to the good life, it might be employment. That is particularly true in the United States, where individuals and households depend far more on their jobs to secure basic goods and services than is the case with virtually all other industrialized nations that provide far more extensive social welfare services (e.g., national health insurance, child care, family leave) (Wilson 1996: 149–182). The importance of place and race have long been recognized by spatial mismatch theorists (Kain 1968, 1992, 2004), who posit that lower-income residents of poorer communities generally reside in or near central cities, whereas job growth has been greater in outlying suburban communities. Those most in need of employment, therefore, find it not only more difficult to learn about available jobs but more expensive to get to those jobs when they find one. That is particularly true for welfare recipients, who, in recent years, have come under increasing pressure to secure employment (Allard and Danziger 2002). Once again, this dynamic is not racially neutral. As of 2000, no racial group was more physically isolated from jobs than blacks, and those metropolitan areas with higher levels of black/white housing segregation exhibited higher levels of spatial mismatch between the residential location of blacks and the location of jobs (Raphael and Stoll 2002). Racial minorities tend to search for jobs in slower-growing areas; whites tend to search in faster-growing communities. The differences in the quality of these job searches is accounted for primarily by residential racial segregation, even after taking into consideration racial differences in social networks and search methods (Stoll and Raphael 2002).

Compounding these troubles are the "mental maps" many employers draw in which they attribute various job-related characteristics (e.g. skills, experience, attitudes) to residents of certain neighborhoods. A job applicant's address often has an independent effect, beyond his or her human capital, that makes it more difficult, particularly for racial minorities from urban areas, to secure employment (Tilly et al. 2001; Wilson 1996). Moreover, recent research has found that it is easier for a white person with a felony conviction to get a job than it is for a black person with no felony convictions, even among applicants with otherwise comparable credentials or where blacks had slightly better employment histories (Pager 2003). Such divergent employment experiences, of course, contribute directly to the income and wealth disparities described earlier. Employment opportunities also mediate the impact of place and race on the opportunity structure of urban areas. In general, employment influences access to a range of goods and services, including the neighborhoods where people live. And the neighborhoods where people live also influence their employment opportunities. In short, employment is an important piece of the race-place-privilege equation.

Another critical quality of life factor is access to and the cost of financial services. In recent years a two-tiered financial services marketplace has emerged, with conventional lenders (e.g., commercial banks, savings institutions) concentrated in outlying urban and suburban areas and so-called fringe bankers (e.g., check cashers, payday lenders, pawn shops) in central city neighborhoods (Caskey 1994, 2002; Sawyer and Temkin 2004). And the latter are big business. Today check cashers process approximately $60 billion in checks annually, and they charge 2 or 3 percent of the check's value, generating fee income of more than $1 billion every year (Sawyer and Temkin 2004: 9). Often, however, the fringe bankers are financed by, or are partners with, mainstream financial services corporations, including household names like Citibank, Bank of America, and Wells Fargo Bank (Fisher 2005).

Between 1975 and 1995, the number of banking offices in low- and moderate-income areas declined by 21 percent, even as they increased by 29 percent overall (Avery et al. 1997: 55). That withdrawal created opportunities for fringe institutions to become major players in those markets. Check-cashing businesses increased from 2,151 to 5,500 between 1986 and 1997 (Leonhardt 1997: 84–86) and then to 22,000 in 2003 (Fisher 2005: 1). A case study of Milwaukee, Wisconsin, found that in 1996 there were two banks for each check-cashing business in the city's economically distressed neighborhoods (as determined by the Milwaukee Comptroller), compared to ten banks for each check casher elsewhere. In predominantly African American neighborhoods, there was one bank for each check-cashing business, compared to fifteen banks in predominantly white areas. In Hispanic neighborhoods, there were two banks for each check casher, compared to eight banks in non-Hispanic communities. Equally problematic, there was just over one bank per 10,000 households in African American areas, compared to six in Hispanic neighborhoods and almost eight banks per 10,000 households in white areas (Squires and O'Connor 1998: 131–132). A study of payday lenders in North Carolina found that African American neighborhoods had three times as many stores as white areas, and this ratio persisted even after controlling for neighborhood income, homeownership, poverty, unemployment, education level, and other socioeconomic characteristics (King et al. 2005). Access to mainstream financial services, however, is not simply a matter of location. Where conventional branch banks are located nearby, they still do not effectively market to low-income and minority households, thus creating a vacuum that fringe bankers fill (Sawyer and Temkin 2004).

Areas served by fringe bankers pay for that "service." One study of banking customers in New York City found that a check-cashing customer with an annual income of $17,000 would pay almost $250 a year for services that would cost just $60 at a bank (Moskowitz 1995: 9). The Federal Reserve Bank of Kansas City reported that a family with a $24,000 annual income would spend $400 for services at a check casher that would cost $110 at a bank (Lunt 1993: 52). The California Reinvestment Coalition found that a typical user of check cashers and payday lenders spends about $1,000 more annually than such services would cost at a mainstream bank (Fisher 2005: 2). Families without bank accounts pay as much as $15,000 over a lifetime in fees for basic financial services to check cashers and other fringe bankers (Stegman et al. 2004: 5). In addition, subprime and predatory lending has grown dramatically in older urban and minority communities, increasing the cost of housing for residents of those areas, while conventional prime loans remain the norm in most metropolitan areas. A particularly severe family and community cost has been a dramatic increase in foreclosure rates that cost many poor and working families their life savings (Immergluck 2004; Immergluck and Smith 2004a, 2004b; Renuart 2002).

As indicated earlier, exposure to crime—and fear of crime—may be a primary determinant of the quality of life for most families and a major deterrent to city living among many who choose to live outside the nation's cities. If indices of serious crime have gone down in recent years, crime remains concentrated in central cities and selected inner-ring suburbs. For example, in 2000, the estimated violent crime victimization rate per 1,000 people in urban areas was 35.1, compared with only 25.8 in suburban areas (US Department of Justice 2001). And in 2002, for every 1,000 people, seven urban, four suburban, and three rural residents were victims of an aggravated assault, with urban residents being robbed at about four times the rate of rural residents. Many of these incidents, of course, involve repeat offenders. A recent Bureau of Justice Statistics study of 272,111 prisoners released from prisons in 1994 indicated that 68 percent were rearrested within three years for a new crime (Langan and Levin 2002). Race also enters the picture. Surveys of twelve cities in 1998 found that black residents in urban areas experienced a higher rate of violent crime than urban whites in a majority of cities (US Department of Justice 1999). Likewise, minorities, and particularly African Americans, recidivate at higher rates than whites (Gendreau et al. 1996: 575).

Tense police-community relations exacerbate crime problems for racial minorities. Ironically, the communities most in need of police protection—poor minority communities—are also those in which many residents view the police with most ambivalence. This stems, in part, from a recognition that color counts as a mark of suspicion that police officers use to justify their actions—stopping, questioning, patting down, arresting, and so forth. Such practices cause residents who might otherwise assist police to avoid them, to decline to cooperate with investigations, to assume dishonesty on the part of officers, and to teach others that such reactions are necessary (Anderson 1999; Kennedy 1997; Kubrin and Weitzer 2003). In an age when race is used for purposes of calculating suspiciousness (what some refer to as racial profiling), it is no surprise that residents of poor minority communities distrust the police. Research on police behavior supports residents' perceptions. Unwarranted police stops, verbal and physical abuse, and racial bias toward residents of disadvantaged communities continue to strain minority residents' relations with the police (Weitzer 1999).

Crime, of course, reflects and reinforces several quality of life factors, including homeownership rates, job opportunities, access to retail and commercial businesses, family life, and many others. For example, Richard D. Alba, John R. Logan, and Paul E. Bellair (1994: 412) find that owning a home enables residents to live in safer communities. According to their study, homeowners reside in communities where violent crime rates are nearly 250 (per 100,000) units lower than in communities where renters reside, controlling for a range of socioeconomic factors. In other words, the concentration of crime does not simply reflect the concentration of individuals prone to criminal activity but various neighborhood characteristics as well (Sampson et al. 2000). Once again, racial segregation is a critical culprit. Segregation tends to concentrate poverty and a range of social problems long associated with older urban communities, including crime (Massey 1995; Peterson and Krivo 1993).

Perhaps most problematic is the impact of uneven development on children and how the proverbial vicious cycle recreates itself over time. In addition to the impact of unequal educational opportunity noted above, the neighborhood effects literature has demonstrated links between neighborhood characteristics (like poverty and inequality) and teenage pregnancy, high school dropout rates, and delinquent behavior (Fischer 2003: 690). Patterns of privilege emerge early in life, persist throughout the life cycle, and recreate themselves in subsequent generations.

More provocative is the evidence that all parts of metropolitan areas are adversely affected by sprawl, concentrated poverty, segregation, and uneven development generally. Central city per capita income correlates with suburban income. Consequently, as cities do well, so do their suburbs. Conversely, where city income declines, so does suburban income. And regional economies with relatively large city/suburban income disparities grow more slowly than those communities with lower levels of inequality (Dreier et al. 2001: 36). Once again, race enters in. According to the National Research Council, high levels of racial segregation lead to a 3 to 6 percent decline in metropolitan level productivity while increasing the costs of policing a disadvantaged group that believes it has been unfairly denied opportunities (Bollens 2002: 634).

In many cities, racial differences in poverty, employment opportunities, wages, education, housing, and health care, among other things, are so strong that the worst urban contexts in which whites reside are considerably better than the average context of black communities (Sampson 1987: 354). The tragedies surrounding Hurricane Katrina illustrate all too vividly how these costs can be so devastatingly concentrated. Unfortunately, they reflect policies and practices that long predate this particular storm, with costs that far exceed those experienced in the Gulf region in 2005 (Reed 2005; Dreier 2006). Robert J. Sampson and William Julius Wilson (1995: 42) assert that in not one city over 100,000 in the United States do blacks live in comparable circumstances as do whites when it comes to the basic features of economic and family organization. A depressing feature of these developments is that many of these differences reflect policy decisions that, if not designed expressly to create disparate outcomes, have contributed to them nevertheless. The upside is that if policy contributed to these problems, it likely can help ameliorate them as well.

How Policy Matters

Inequality has long been explained primarily in terms of varying levels of human capital that individuals bring to various markets, particularly the labor market. Human capital consists primarily of a combination of skills, experience, and education (Becker 1964). More recently, the role of culture, attitude (e.g., work ethic), and other attributes individuals bring to the market have been noted as contributing to the varying rewards people receive (McWhorter 2000; Mead 1992; Murray 1984). But the basic model prevails whereby individual buyers (e.g., employers) and sellers (employees) enter into voluntary exchanges in the labor market, with each trying to maximize their "utility." Inequality of place also has been explained in terms of individual characteristics and voluntary market exchanges. It has long been argued that individuals or households make voluntary choices, based on their financial capacity, in selecting their communities when they "vote with their feet" by moving to those areas offering the bundle of services for which they are willing or able to pay (Tiebout 1956). But individualistic models of labor market inequality have been challenged by institutional theorists in economics, who identify a number of structural characteristics of those markets that impede consummation of individual, voluntary exchanges (e.g., race and gender discrimination; internal and dual labor markets; labor law, including minimum wage statutes; union activity) (Holzer and Danziger 2001). Likewise, urban scholars have noted the role of public policies and institutionalized private practices (e.g., tax policy, transportation patterns, land use planning) that serve as barriers to individual choice in housing markets and contributors to spatial inequality in metropolitan areas (Dreier, Mollenkopf, and Swamstrom 2001; Fainstein and Campbell 2002; Feagin 1998; Orfield 1997, 2002; Rusk 1999). These exclusionary practices amount to structural barriers that block racial minorities from being able to exercise their individual preferences in the housing market.

Individuals do make choices, of course. Many households select their neighborhoods on the basis of the services, jobs, cultural facilities, and other amenities that are available within the constraints of their budgets. Critical for many households is a dense network of families, friends, and other social ties that bind them to particular locations. Even the most distressed neighborhoods, including some notorious public housing complexes, can have a culture, social organization, and other attributes that residents want to retain (Fullilove

2004; Rae 2003; Suttles 1968; Venkatesh 2000). Particularly in diverse urban communities, what appears to outsiders as the minutiae of everyday life takes on important symbolic significance to local residents. In what she referred to as the "sidewalk ballet," Jane Jacobs described how seemingly minor daily rituals of life—neighbors unlocking their businesses to start a new day, young children marching off to school—deliver the important message to local residents that "all is well" (Jacobs 1961: 50, 51). Community, defined in many different ways, attracts and retains residents of all types of neighborhoods.

But, again, these choices are made in a context shaped by a range of public policy decisions and private practices over which most individuals have little control. Those decisions often have, by design, exclusionary implications that limit opportunities for many, particularly low-income households and people of color. It is precisely because of the history and ongoing reality of economic and racial exclusion that many find their family, friendship, and other social ties in distressed neighborhoods. And it is the conflict and hassles that racial minorities face outside their communities that lead some to choose a segregated neighborhood for their home, even when they could afford to live elsewhere. As an accountant who lived in a black suburb of Atlanta stated in reference to her neighborhood:

> There are not any white people around here staring us in the face and trying to prove we don't matter. So much goes on at the job that we have to endure, the slights and the negative comments, and feelings that we're unwanted. When I have to work around them all day, by the time I come home I don't want to have to deal with white people anymore. (Fullwood 1996: 204–205)

Choice matters. Individual tastes and talents count. But all too frequently such decisionmaking is framed and limited by a range of structural constraints. Individuals exercise choice, but those choices often do not reflect what is normally understood by the term "voluntary."

If suburbanization and sprawl reflect the housing choices of residents, these are choices that have been influenced by explicit public policies and private practices. Suburbia has been sold as much as it has been bought (Judd 1984). Creation of the long-term thirty-year mortgage (and more recently, even a forty-year mortgage) featuring low down payment requirements, the availability of federal insurance to protect mortgage lenders, federal financing to support a secondary market in mortgage loans (e.g., Fannie Mae and Freddie Mac) that dramatically increases the availability of mortgage money, tax deductibility of interest and property tax payments, and the proliferation of federally funded highways created sprawling suburban communities that would not have been possible without such public largesse (Jackson 1985).

The federal government's underwriting rules for Federal Housing Administration and other federal mortgage insurance products and enforcement of racially restrictive covenants by the courts, along with overt redlining practices by mortgage lenders and racial steering by real estate agents, virtually guaranteed the patterns of racial segregation that were commonplace by the 1950s. Redlining refers to the practice of refusing to provide financial services or providing them unequally, based on the neighborhood in which the borrower lives, independent of the risk posed by that borrower. Steering involves directing homebuyers to certain neighborhoods based on race. For example, racial minorities are often shown homes in predominantly minority or integrated areas, whereas whites are shown homes in white communities. Concentration of public housing in central city high-rise complexes (many of which are now being torn down) reinforced the patterns of economic and racial segregation that persist today. Most suburban municipalities passed exclusionary zoning ordinances that mandated minimum lot size and maximum density requirements for housing developments (often prohibiting construction of multifamily housing), thus complementing federal policy (Hays 1995; Hirsch 1998; Ihlanfeldt 2004; Jackson 1985, 2000; Massey and Denton 1993; Polikoff 2006; Rusk 1999; Yinger 1995).

Government policy has also encouraged the flight of businesses and jobs from cities to surrounding suburban communities and beyond. Financial incentives, including infrastructure investments, tax abatements, and depreciation allowances favoring new equipment over reinvestment in existing facilities, have all contributed to the deindustrialization and disinvestment of urban communities. The pursuit of reduced taxes, fewer government regulations, and workers willing to accept lower wages has also encouraged the flight of business from cities viewed as high-cost areas to other regions of the country, and to other nations altogether, that present capital with lower costs (Bluestone and Harrison 1982, 2000). In order to "meet the competition," local officials often believe they must provide incentives to businesses that they cannot afford and that undercut their ability to provide traditional public services for less privileged communities more dependent on those services (Barnekov and Rich 1989; Reed 1988). Research has generally failed to demonstrate that these incentives encourage new investment or employment or target development to economically distressed communities (Peters and Fisher 2004). Often, incentives are offered, but little effort is made to ensure that recipients meet the terms and conditions (e.g., job creation goals) they promise to meet. And, frequently, such expenditures are offered for development that would have occurred anyway (Barnekov and Rich 1989; Ellen and Schwartz 2000; LeRoy 1997, 2005; Lynch 2004). As one observer noted, "Subsidizing economic development in the suburbs is like paying teenagers to think about sex" (Wray 1999). The end result is often an unintended subsidy of private economic activity by jurisdictions that compete in a "race to the bottom" in efforts to attract footloose firms and mobile capital, starving traditional public services—like education—for resources in the process. A downward spiral is established that further undercuts the quality of life, including the business climate, and deindustrialization becomes both a cause and consequence of uneven development.

Place, Privilege, and Policy

The following chapters examine in greater depth the dynamics of housing (including housing finance) and crime in shaping the opportunity structure and quality of life in metropolitan areas. For decades, crime has been a major issue for cities. In a 2002 survey conducted for the Fannie Mae Foundation, a nationally representative sample of adults was asked what community factors were most important when they thought about places to live. The safety of the neighborhood was the most frequently cited factor. Economic conditions and quality of available housing came in second and third (Hart and Teeter 2002: 11).

Crime has long been a major concern of families, particularly those with children or those who reside in central city neighborhoods. Although crime has decreased over the last decade, reductions have not occurred in all cities or neighborhoods. And fear of crime continues to haunt residents. In 2000, for instance, 40 percent of whites and 47 percent of blacks reported that they were afraid to walk alone near their homes at night (BJS 2001: 120). Crime and fear of crime may explain why many have left, why suburban sprawl has taken place, and why it has taken such exclusionary forms. Most big city mayors recognize that urban revitalization and the future of both their political careers and their cities depend on addressing the problems posed by crime. Indeed, increases in the size of police forces are higher in mayoral and gubernatorial election years (Levitt 1997). As indicated earlier, in recent years several cities have experienced a rebound and safer streets have been a major contributor (Grogan and Proscio 2000), but budget-busting prison and criminal justice expenditures indicate there is far to go. Crime remains a central challenge to the nation's cities.

Affordable housing and the state of the local economy constitute additional challenges. Economic conditions for most households are determined by their income and wealth, and home equity has been a major source of wealth. For half of all homeowners, more than 50 percent of their wealth is accounted for by the equity they have in their homes (Joint Center for Housing Studies 2002: 7). A second critical factor in the rebound of some cities has been greater access to affordable credit, particularly for home loans (Grogan and Proscio 2000). As with the fight against crime, however, much remains to be done to address prevailing racial inequities, particularly those associated with residence. As noted earlier, housing constitutes a larger share of household wealth for minority than for white households, but the value of typical homes in all white neighborhoods is well over $100,000, compared to half of that in communities where blacks exceed 30 percent of the population (Flippen 2004: 1536).

The place-race nexus is explored in our examination of selected housing and crime-related issues that have been the subject of heated policy debate in recent years (e.g. bank and insurance redlining, predatory financing practices, crime, recidivism). We focus on the interplay of race, place, and policy and how the structure of opportunity evolves, particularly on key issues of housing and crime. In the chapters that follow, we present empirical research that documents the relationship between access to capital and various aspects of the good life. For example, we show how access to mortgage loans affects homeownership for minorities and minority neighborhoods generally. More to the point, we demonstrate how policy has shaped inequities in the housing market but can also ameliorate them. Specifically, we present evidence that fair housing policy has facilitated the movement of minorities into traditionally inaccessible white neighborhoods. We also show how the availability of home mortgage loans affects neighborhood crime rates. Perhaps more importantly, we demonstrate how access to financial services and policies that support increasing access to those services have reduced neighborhood crime rates.

Racially discriminatory mortgage lending practices have long constituted barriers to homeownership and wealth accumulation for racial minorities. But in recent years the federal Community Reinvestment Act (CRA), which prohibits redlining; other fair lending rules; and organizing efforts by community groups across the nation all have increased the share of loans going to minority applicants and minority neighborhoods. Chapter 2, "Accessing Traditionally Inaccessible Neighborhoods," addresses the question of whether such policy changes have enabled nonwhite families to find homes in predominantly white neighborhoods that have traditionally been closed to them. After examining lending patterns in 101 large metropolitan areas, we found that in communities where a relatively larger share of mortgage loans are subject to the CRA, blacks and Latinos are more likely to purchase homes in white neighborhoods, where home values are higher and other neighborhood amenities are more readily available. At the end of the chapter, we offer recommendations for revising federal fair lending requirements to increase their impact.

At the same time that mortgage loans have become more available for residents of minority and low-income communities and other traditionally underserved markets, it appears that subprime and predatory loans have begun to fill part of that void. Such practices are costly for many households, often leading to foreclosure and the loss of a home along with the life savings that were wrapped up in the home. Entire neighborhoods are adversely affected, including households and businesses not directly caught up in a predatory loan. Chapter 3, "Predatory Lending: The New Redlining," examines the role of exploitative lending practices in undercutting revitalization efforts in such communities and efforts to eliminate predatory practices.

Property insurance, which is essential in securing a mortgage to purchase a home, has received far less attention than other forces that have created and perpetuated dual housing markets in metropolitan areas. Yet, as Chapter 4, "Racial Profiling, Insurance-Style," demonstrates, insurance redlining has been a critical institutional underpinning of that duality in metropolitan housing markets. This chapter also offers recommendations for what the industry, regulators, and residents can do to ameliorate racial discrimination and increase availability of property insurance in urban communities.

Housing values and crime, of course, are not mutually exclusive. And, as indicated above, crime rates constitute a critical determinant of the quality of life for residents in any neighborhood. One issue that arises is whether, or to what extent, investment in housing reduces neighborhood crime. Chapter 5, "How Home Mortgage Money Reduces Crime," finds that increased levels of mortgage lending are associated with lower crime rates, even after taking into consideration poverty, unemployment, racial composition, and other factors long known to be associated with crime. Community reinvestment proposals are offered to further combat crime and increase housing values in central city neighborhoods.

Community characteristics like affordable housing, employment opportunities, and social services matter for all residents, but particularly for those returning home from prison. Given the unprecedented numbers of inmates leaving prison and returning to communities today, the issue of prisoner reentry is at the forefront of domestic public policy. Chapter 6, "Residence and Recidivism," explores how recidivism among former offenders is linked to the neighborhoods to which they return. We also show how race affects the linkages among place, privilege, and recidivism and discuss how these connections can be severed.

In the conclusion, "Race, Place, and the Politics of Privilege," we identify ways to undo the connections between place, race, and privilege. One of the researchers who participated in Russell Sage's recent multicity study of urban inequality concluded: "Race is woven into the fabric of residential and industrial location choices, of hiring and wage determination, and of the human perceptions that underlie all these processes" (O'Connor 2001: 28). That is one tapestry that needs to be unraveled. If policy is largely responsible for getting us where we are today, policy can help us pursue a different path tomorrow.

Notes

Portions of this chapter, as well as Chapter 7, draw on material published as Gregory D. Squires and Charis E. Kubrin, "Privileged Places: Race, Uneven Development, and the Geography of Opportunity in Urban America," *Urban Studies* 42 (2005): 47–68. http://www.tandf.co.uk.

2

Accessing Traditionally Inaccessible Neighborhoods

I love Puerto Ricans and Negroes
As long as they don't move next door.
              —Phil Ochs, 1965 (cited in Meyer 2000, vii)

In no area of public life have race and residence been more explicitly utilized as criteria for dispensing privilege than in the nation's mortgage lending markets. Historically, virtually all participants in these markets (e.g., insurers, appraisers, lenders) have literally drawn lines on maps to identify areas that would not be eligible for their products and services or would be eligible only under more onerous terms and conditions. More subtle practices have perpetuated white privilege in recent decades (Jackson 1985; Yinger 1995). But a combination of new laws and law enforcement, community organizing and advocacy, and related activities has begun to turn a tradition of redlining into an effective social movement for reinvestment. In addition to making credit more readily available in older urban neighborhoods, particularly those with large minority populations that have long been underserved by mainstream financial institutions, it also appears that racial minorities are more able to access predominantly white neighborhoods from which they traditionally have been excluded. In this chapter we examine how recent policy initiatives, particularly the federal Community Reinvestment Act (CRA), have helped nonwhite households purchase housing in white neighborhoods that have long been denied to them.

This chapter was written with Samantha Friedman.

Community Reinvestment: The Civil Rights
Movement in the Post–Civil Rights Era

In response to decades of redlining and racial discrimination in lending, particularly in home mortgage lending, Congress passed the
CRA in 1977, prohibiting redlining.[1] This federal law has led to more
than $4.2 trillion in new loans to economically distressed areas since
it was enacted (National Community Reinvestment Coalition 2005a:
1). Traditional banking practices had long denied credit to low-
income communities and racial minorities throughout metropolitan
areas. One consequence was that minority families seeking to buy
homes were restricted in their ability to do so, particularly in white
neighborhoods.

Recent research has established that the CRA is meeting its
objectives. Credit is more readily available in low- and moderate-
income communities; racial minorities have greater access to credit;
and scholarly research has established that the CRA has been, at least
in part, responsible for these gains. Stronger enforcement of the CRA
and related fair lending laws, in part due to pressure by community
groups, along with market forces, have resulted in an increase in conventional home purchase lending to low- and moderate-income borrowers from 19 percent of all loans in 1993 to 29 percent in 2000.
Lending to blacks grew from 3.8 percent to 6.6 percent in those
years, and lending to Latinos increased from 4.0 percent to 6.9 percent (Avery et al. 2005a; Board of Governors 2000; Joint Center for
Housing Studies 2002b; Litan et al. 2001; National Community
Reinvestment Coalition 2001a: 9). A question that arises is whether
minorities have been able to access traditionally inaccessible white
communities and, therefore, the amenities generally associated with
such communities (Cashin 2004; Massey 1985). That question is the
focus of this chapter.

In 1995 regulations implementing the CRA were revised to
slightly alter the spatial emphasis of the CRA. Under the revision,
loans to low- and moderate-income borrowers, regardless of the economic status of their neighborhoods, are evaluated for CRA purposes.
So lenders are now evaluated in terms of their lending to low- and
moderate-income borrowers as well as their lending in low- and moderate-income neighborhoods. Because black and Latino households
are more likely than white households to occupy the lower end of the
income distribution, as described in the last chapter, the revised CRA
evaluation criteria may indirectly increase the ability of minority

homebuyers to purchase homes in predominantly white neighborhoods. The following pages reveal that the CRA has, in fact, nurtured minority home ownership in those traditionally inaccessible neighborhoods.

To date, little research has specifically explored how lending policies and practices in general and the impact of the CRA in particular may be linked to the access that minority homebuyers have to white neighborhoods. Many studies have explored the CRA's influence on the economic status of neighborhoods within which these groups of homebuyers settle, rather than on the community's racial/ethnic composition (see Haag 2000 and Joint Center for Housing Studies 2002 for reviews of this literature). The studies that do focus on the racial/ethnic composition of neighborhoods examine redlining and the denial rates for racial/ethnic minority applicants and for borrowers in predominantly minority neighborhoods (see Ross and Yinger 2002 and Turner and Skidmore 1999 for reviews of this literature).

Only one study, to our knowledge, has documented the extent to which blacks apply for loans in predominantly white neighborhoods, but it does not explicitly examine how, if at all, the CRA affects the prevalence of such applications (MacDonald 1998). Several studies have explored the effect of neighborhood racial composition on mortgage lending, but again without determining the impact of CRA and how it affects nonwhite access to white neighborhoods (Dedman 1988; Munnell et al. 1996; Squires and Velez 1987).

A separate demographic literature has examined mobility. A number of studies assess the residential mobility of blacks into nonpoor and suburban neighborhoods (South and Crowder 1997a, 1997b; South and Deane 1993), but only one considers black mobility into white neighborhoods (South and Crowder 1998a). However, the study focuses on blacks who are both renters and homeowners and pays no attention to the impact that federal policy such as the CRA has had on access to white neighborhoods.

Given the paucity of research on the effects of policy in this area, we have conducted an empirical analysis of this issue. The results of that investigation follow, along with detailed policy recommendations for increasing the opportunity for minority families to buy homes in white neighborhoods and, consequently, further break down the linkages among race, place, and privilege. This chapter is the first attempt to systematically examine the effect of fair lending policy generally, and the CRA in particular, on the access that black and

Latino homebuyers have to predominantly white neighborhoods. It is important to evaluate such policies for two main reasons. First, little is known about the factors that may be dismantling the dual housing market. Second, little is known about the effect of federal housing policy on the mobility underlying residential patterns, despite the fact that a key theoretical perspective, the place stratification model, deems such policy as central to the residential outcomes of minorities (South and Crowder 1998b). Until such policies can be incorporated into analyses of residential patterns, little progress will be made in identifying the continuing causes of segregation and, conversely, the factors that facilitate minority access to traditionally inaccessible neighborhoods.

To address this issue, we use data from the 2000 Home Mortgage Disclosure Act reports (HMDA) and from the 2000 census. We examine the impact of the CRA on minority access to predominantly white neighborhoods in large metropolitan areas with substantial black and Latino populations. Using descriptive analyses, we examine the proportions of minorities who purchased homes in predominantly white neighborhoods in metropolitan areas in which a relatively high share of loans are made by CRA-covered institutions, compared to areas where relatively fewer loans are made by such lenders. Using multivariate analyses, we then determine whether the proportions of blacks and Latinos buying homes in predominantly white neighborhoods are higher in metropolitan areas where a greater share of loans is covered by the CRA than in metropolitan areas where a relatively lower share of loans is covered by this statute, controlling for relevant socioeconomic factors.

Minority Access to Predominantly White Neighborhoods

We draw upon a combination of perspectives on segregation and residential mobility to explain variation in minority access to predominantly white neighborhoods. One perspective, derived from the spatial assimilation model (Massey 1985), the classic human ecology model (Hawley 1971), and the housing availability model (South and Crowder 1997b), suggests that minority access is a function of economic and ecological factors. These perspectives view minority access as related to a group's own circumstances (e.g., income, wealth, personal preferences) in conjunction with local housing market opportunities. Thus, these explanations focus on passive forces, ignoring how the power dynamic within society shapes groups' access. Because of these commonalities, we label these approaches the economic/ecological perspective.

The economic resources possessed by minority groups are central to this perspective. It is presumed that access to largely white neighborhoods is desirable because of the greater privileges associated with such neighborhoods. As minorities progress upward socioeconomically, they are increasingly able to obtain better housing and related amenities (Cashin 2004; Massey 1985). Thus, metropolitan areas with larger shares of affluent minorities should have a larger proportion of minorities residing in predominantly white neighborhoods than metropolitan areas with fewer affluent minorities.

Another important factor from this perspective is the supply of housing. As Scott J. South and Kyle D. Crowder (1997b) note, high vacancy rates in a metropolitan area indicate more housing opportunities for those who want to change residences and should, therefore, be linked with minority access to predominantly white neighborhoods. Variation in the level of owner-occupied housing units across metropolitan areas also will be important in determining minority access because it is another way to gauge access to the supply of potential housing available to homebuyers.

The ecology and population size of metropolitan areas also matter according to this perspective. Larger areas generally display higher segregation levels between minorities and whites and thus afford minorities less access to white neighborhoods than is the case in smaller areas (Farley and Frey 1994; Massey and Denton 1987). Although racial/ethnic diversity is usually greater in larger metropolitan areas, there are more traditional "natural areas" of settlement for racial/ethnic groups, creating higher segregation levels and ultimately less access.

A second perspective is the place stratification model (Alba and Logan 1992; Logan and Molotch 1987). This model maintains that a hierarchical ordering exists among groups within society and that more advantaged groups use their power to maintain social and physical distance from the least advantaged groups. This power is often manifested in various forms of discriminatory actions, which effectively constrain minority choices within the housing market (Massey and Denton 1993; Turner et al. 2002a, 2002b; Turner and Ross 2005; Yinger 1995). Unlike the economic/ecological perspective, the place stratification model focuses explicitly on the conscious efforts of powerful actors in shaping residential patterns of minority and white populations.

According to this perspective, the racial/ethnic composition of the metropolitan area is important in explaining minority access to predominantly white neighborhoods. Areas that have higher levels of residential segregation typically offer fewer opportunities for minorities to move to white areas. Segregation is indicative of the long-standing operation of a dual housing market (perhaps now a tri-housing market) where whites and nonwhites are steered to separate neighborhoods, and blacks and Latinos constitute separate markets. The place stratification model suggests that segregation results from whites using power to maintain their distance from minorities (Massey and Denton 1993). The size of the minority population is negatively related to minority access to predominantly white neighborhoods from this perspective (South and Crowder 1997b). Where there are relatively larger minority populations, whites are more likely to feel threatened by these out-groups and therefore may engage in discriminatory practices (Blalock 1967; Stearns and Logan 1986).

Finally, areas with larger suburban populations are likely to have lower levels of minority, particularly black, mobility into white neighborhoods (South and Crowder 1997b). As indicated in the previous chapter, suburban communities historically have used restrictive covenants, land-use regulations, and zoning ordinances to restrict the in-mobility of minorities (Farley and Frey 1994; Gotham 2002; Jackson 1985; Massey and Denton 1993). According to this perspective, such policies have impeded and continue to constrain minority access.

Although informative, neither approach takes into account policies designed to facilitate access to predominantly white neighborhoods. Although agency is key to the place stratification perspective, its focus is on actions that restrict, rather than encourage, minority access. The CRA and its implementing regulations constitute one set of the latter kind of political activity. An important question is whether minority access to traditionally inaccessible neighborhoods is due to improvements in their socioeconomic status or to better enforcement of the Fair Housing Act and a reduction of discriminatory barriers generally.[2] At the same time, debate remains as to whether the persistence of segregation in many metropolitan areas is due to minorities' poorer socioeconomic circumstances or discriminatory constraints that they face within the housing market. Despite the importance of federal housing policies in shaping minority residential patterns, virtually no research has tested the impact of such legislation on racial residential mobility (see South and Crowder 1998b for an exception). Failure to incorporate these policies into our research hinders our understanding of the causes of segregation specifically and the linkages of place and race generally.

The CRA, particularly at this critical point in time, provides an opportunity to examine the connections among place, race, and policy. By focusing on such legislation, we can make an explicit link between fair lending and fair housing policy with homebuyer mobility and the public understanding of racial/ethnic inequality in general. During the 1990s, changes in the regulatory framework of the CRA, in conjunction with an expansion of enforcement powers granted under fair lending legislation and community-based advocacy, might have opened up more housing opportunities for minorities in white neighborhoods. However, legislation passed in 1999 and subsequent CRA regulatory "reform" (discussed below) may undermine the law's potential. Before explaining the linkages among the CRA, fair lending policies, and minority access to predominantly white neighborhoods, we review the CRA and related fair lending policies and briefly discuss the research that has been done on the effectiveness of the CRA.

Federal Housing Policies and Minority Access to Traditionally Inaccessible Neighborhoods

A Review of the Legislation

Passage of the CRA (12 U.S.C. §§ 2901–2908 (2001)) in 1977 was motivated by concerns about redlining—the lack of credit in inner-city neighborhoods, along with evidence that the unavailability of credit was due at least in part to racial and ethnic discrimination. Its enactment was part of a larger effort to promote fair lending. Three other major pieces of legislation preceded the passage of the CRA: the Fair Housing Act of 1968 (FHA), the Equal Credit Opportunity Act of 1974 (ECOA), and the Home Mortgage Disclosure Act of 1975. Prior to this legislation, government at all levels, along with private financial institutions and other providers of housing-related services, were actively involved in discriminating against minorities rather than in combating discrimination (Gotham 2002; Jackson 1985; Massey and Denton 1993).

The CRA requires all federally regulated depository institutions to be responsive to the credit needs of the communities they serve, including low- and moderate-income neighborhoods. The act mandates that bank regulatory agencies (e.g., the Federal Reserve Board, Federal Deposit Insurance Corporation, Comptroller of the Currency, Office of Thrift Supervision) evaluate how effectively lenders meet these credit needs and take their CRA performance into account when they apply for changes in their business practices (e.g., to purchase or merge with another institution, open or close a branch office). The act also allows third parties to challenge applications made by lenders. Regulators can approve, deny, or temporarily delay consideration of the application. Although applications are rarely denied, it is less unusual to delay consideration and request that the lender attempt to resolve the differences with the challenging party. Such delays can be costly and, therefore, provide incentives for lenders to negotiate reinvestment agreements in order to have the challenge removed.

The impact of the CRA in its early years was restricted in part because it did not give clear guidelines to regulators on how to evaluate bank performance. The focus on process (e.g., whether chief executive officers were involved in CRA planning) rather than performance (e.g., distribution of loans) limited enforcement. One aspect of the legislation that appeared to have an impact was the threat of third-party challenges. Financial institutions realized that challenges could pose delays in the application approval process and therefore could be quite costly. In many cases, community groups did challenge such applications, which encouraged lenders to negotiate reinvestment agreements that would result in those organizations dropping their challenges (Joint Center for Housing Studies 2002b).

Enforcement of the CRA was strengthened significantly in the 1990s. In 1989 Congress passed the Financial Institutions Reform, Recovery, and Enforcement Act (FIRREA), which amended the CRA by changing the rating system used by regulators, requiring public disclosure of these ratings, and directing regulators to make detailed written CRA evaluations publicly available. Essentially, regulators were required to report whether the financial institutions under their purview were effectively meeting the credit needs of the communities they served, consistent with safe and sound banking practices.

One of the most important changes to the CRA came in 1995, when federal banking regulators promulgated a new regulation revising CRA enforcement procedures so that they focused on lender performance in meeting the credit needs of the communities they serve.

Until that point, CRA exams had focused on *how* these institutions did business and not on the actual *results* of their activities. Put simply, the new rules required examiners to evaluate three elements of lender performance—lending, investment, and service—with lending as the most important (for details on the 1995 regulations, see the Joint Center for Housing 2002 and Schill 2002). In addition to making the focus of CRA evaluation outcome-based, the 1995 regulations slightly altered the spatial emphasis of the act. Under the lending test, loans could be counted for CRA credit if they were made to low- and moderate-income areas or to low- and moderate-income borrowers, regardless of neighborhood socioeconomic status. That is the precise regulatory change that could be responsible for increased minority access to predominantly white neighborhoods.

More recently, however, changes have been made that indirectly affect the CRA and may undermine the progress of the 1990s. The Gramm-Leach-Bliley Financial Services Modernization Act (GLBA), passed in 1999, allows securities firms, banks, and insurance companies to merge and to enter into each others' lines of business with fewer restrictions than in the past. Independent mortgage banks, insurers, and other providers of financial services not covered by the CRA increased their mortgage lending activity and did so, therefore, outside the purview of CRA. In addition, several banks shifted their mortgage activity to mortgage banking affiliates and nontraditional lenders within their holding companies, in part because such entities are also not covered by the CRA. Only depository financial institutions within these conglomerates are covered by the act. Preliminary evidence suggests that the GLBA is already slowing the earlier progress in lending. Commercial banks and savings institutions, which formerly made the vast majority of mortgage loans, now make approximately one-third of all home loans. Independent mortgage banks, insurance companies, and other institutions not covered by the CRA, including most predatory lenders (to be discussed in Chapter 3), now occupy a far more significant part of this market (Insurance Information Institute 2002: 29).

In early 2005 the Office of Thrift Supervision eliminated the mandatory service and investment tests under the CRA. Later that year, the Federal Reserve Board, Office of the Comptroller of the Currency, and Federal Deposit Insurance Corporation replaced these two tests with a new community development test for lenders with between $250 million and $1 billion in assets, further weakening the statute. The impact, if any, of these changes remains to be determined

(Board of Governors of the Federal Reserve System 2005; National Community Reinvestment Coalition 2005b).

The Impact of the CRA on Lending to Minorities

As indicated earlier, there is now substantial evidence that CRA is having the intended impact. In a review of CRA-related research, the Brookings Institution found that in the 1990s, home purchase mortgage lending to low-income and minority households and neighborhoods increased faster than home purchase mortgage lending generally (Haag 2000). The US Department of the Treasury reported similar findings, with the greatest increases coming after implementation of the 1995 performance-oriented regulation. In addition, the Treasury report found greater increases in communities where there had been at least one CRA agreement signed by a lender with a community group (Litan et al. 2001). Alex Schwartz (1998a, 1998b) drew similar conclusions in a nationwide study comparing the lending record of financial institutions that signed CRA agreements with those that had not. Raphael W. Bostic and Breck Robinson (2002) found that the number of conventional home purchase loans going to low- and moderate-income and minority borrowers and areas increased significantly in urban counties with the introduction of new CRA agreements, though these effects were most pronounced in the first two years the agreements were in place. The Federal Reserve Board also reported that CRA-related lending was profitable for the vast majority of covered lenders, though not quite as profitable as other home lending (Board of Governors of the Federal Reserve System 2000). And the Joint Center for Housing Studies found that CRA-regulated lenders made a higher share of their loans to lower-income people and communities and to minority markets than did unregulated institutions, that this effect was most noticeable in the assessment areas of CRA lenders (areas where lenders have branch banks and their loans are most closely scrutinized), and that the CRA has had a direct impact on these patterns (Joint Center for Housing Studies 2002: 135–136.)

However, as noted in Chapter 1, significant levels of racial discrimination persist in the mortgage lending market. Statistical analyses of application denial rates and the distribution of loans across communities, along with paired testing or audit studies, confirm that racial minorities are more likely to be denied loans, offered fewer options when credit is made available, and provided less information about financing options than similarly qualified white applicants

(Munnell et al. 1996; Ross and Yinger 2002; Turner et al. 2002a, 2002b; Turner and Ross 2005). Much progress has been made, but much more remains to be achieved.

Linking Federal Fair Housing Policies to Minority Access

Even as research has documented the CRA's overwhelmingly positive impact on minority lending, less attention has been paid to the racial/ethnic composition of the neighborhoods within which minorities ultimately settle. This lack of research reflects the fact that the main focus of the CRA has been economic rather than racial. Moreover, until 1995, financial institutions could not fulfill the lending test mandated by regulators by lending to borrowers outside low- and moderate-income communities. Now that the spatial requirement of lending has been relaxed, there is the potential for this legislation to improve minority access to predominantly white communities and the presumed associated wealth accumulation benefits. In support of this possibility, the Joint Center for Housing Studies (2002b: 23) found that between 1995 and 2000, 66 percent of the growth in CRA-eligible home purchase lending was accounted for by mortgage loans made to lower-income borrowers in higher-income neighborhoods.

This change to the CRA regulatory framework provides a unique opportunity to assess the impact of public policy, the role of powerful private institutions, and the impact of nonprofit community organizations on minority access to traditionally inaccessible neighborhoods. The CRA requires that depository institutions under the act's purview respond to the credit needs of low- and moderate-income borrowers and communities—markets that are disproportionately nonwhite. Although the legislation and its implementing regulations have focused on the economic status of borrowers and communities, there is little doubt that the act has strongly encouraged depository institutions to comply more effectively with fair lending laws. From the outset, the CRA was established to combat redlining in mortgage lending, and since its inception, it has been unclear to many policymakers exactly how the CRA is independent from fair lending legislation (Schill 2002). The fact that community groups have been able to participate in the regulatory process also has blurred the lines between the objectives of CRA and fair lending legislation. Many community groups have successfully negotiated CRA agreements with financial institutions that require lenders to service the needs of low- and moderate-income borrowers and communities as well as minority borrowers and communities (National Community Reinvestment Coalition 2002b; Sidney 2003; Squires and O'Connor 2001).

In light of the additional scrutiny that CRA lenders undergo and the overlap, if not confusion, between CRA and fair lending requirements, it is plausible that one additional outcome of CRA would be increased access for minority borrowers to white neighborhoods. Although the focus of CRA has been on lending to low- and moderate-income communities rather than lending to minorities and minority communities, the legal and public relations pressure has focused more on fair lending and discrimination issues than traditional redlining.

The greater scrutiny of CRA lenders takes many forms. The lenders undergo regular CRA exams by their federal regulatory agency in which the distribution of their loans becomes a matter of public record. Community organizations utilize leverage provided by the law to challenge and change lending behavior. The media often report on CRA exams, lender-community conflict and partnerships, and related activities of these financial institutions. And race is the issue that gets the most attention. The most visible regulatory actions have been taken by the US Department of Justice, which has settled several discrimination complaints against major mortgage lenders (Lee 1999). Newspaper headlines have focused on racial disparities, if not racial discrimination, in lending activity (Dedman 1988, 1989; Malveaux 2003). Community groups, including fair housing and community reinvestment organizations, have highlighted racially discriminatory practices in their challenges and reinvestment agreements (National Community Reinvestment Coalition 2003; Sidney 2003). Consequently, CRA lenders may well have developed more effective nondiscriminatory lending policies and practices. Minority borrowers who had the capacity to purchase and the interest in locating in suburban communities may well have been among the first that such lenders attempted to reach in their fair lending initiatives. Such qualified minority borrowers may be the ones who have been most egregiously underserved in the past and among the relatively easier households to finance for CRA and fair lending credit.

How CRA Affects Minority Access

The preceding discussion suggests the following possible relationships. The tenets of the economic/ecological perspective maintain that the economic circumstances of minorities and the structure of metropolitan areas will be important in shaping minority access to predominantly white areas. We expect that in metropolitan areas with more affluent minorities, higher vacancy rates, and greater shares of owner-occupied housing, minority homebuyers will have greater access. The overall population size of the metropolitan area, however, will be negatively associated with minority access.

In light of the disparities presented in Chapter 1 and consistent with the place stratification thesis, we expect that minority access will be shaped more by discrimination than by macroeconomic forces of supply and demand or ecological factors. High levels of minorites and segregation within metropolitan areas will impede minority access. Minorities in metropolitan areas with large suburban populations also will be less likely to buy homes in white neighborhoods.

Given our focus on public policy, the key variable in our analysis is the proportion of loans within the metropolitan area that are made by CRA-covered institutions. We expect that in regions where larger shares of loans are made by such institutions, minority homebuyers will have greater access than in areas where relatively fewer loans are covered by CRA institutions. We expect the effect of the CRA-related measure to hold, even after controlling for applicant income, population size, and related factors.

The Research Strategy

The analysis draws on two principal data sets. The first is the 2000 Home Mortgage Disclosure Act reports, which contain detailed information on each mortgage loan application submitted to most mortgage lenders, including depository institutions, mortgage banking affiliates of these institutions, and independent mortgage bankers and brokers. Since 1993, these institutions have been required to supply the following information on all loan applications: the race, income, and gender of the applicant; the state, county, and census tract of the property included in the application; the type and purpose of loan applied for; and the disposition of the application. For each loan, HMDA also contains information about the agency regulating the financial institution where the loan application was filed. Annual HMDA reports are required of banks, savings institutions, credit unions, and other for-profit mortgage lenders with a significant presence in any metropolitan area (e.g., a branch bank). Banks, savings institutions, and credit unions must report if their assets total more than $32 million (a figure adjusted annually according to the consumer price index). Other for-profit mortgage lenders must report if their assets exceed $10 million or they made 100 or more loans (Federal Financial Institutions Examination Council 2003).

HMDA has become a principal data set for mortgage lending research in recent years. Virtually all redlining and related studies use HMDA data in the analyses (Hillier 2003: 141). According to Federal Reserve Board economist Glenn Canner, approximately 80 percent of all home purchase mortgage loans are captured by HMDA. Most of the excluded loans are originated by smaller lenders who do not meet the threshold reporting requirements, and these loans tend to be outside metropolitan areas. HMDA is clearly the superior publicly available data set, and it is a reliable source for mortgage lending in urban communities. As Canner observed, HMDA "is the best we have" (Canner 2003). (For more detailed information on HMDA see the website of the Federal Financial Institutions Examination Council, http://www.ffiec.gov/.)

We restrict our analysis to conventional loans originated to purchase one- to four-family homes because we are primarily concerned with single-family homebuyers.[3] The analysis does not include loan applications that were denied or not originated for any reason or loans for home improvement, refinancing, or multifamily housing.[4] We also utilize 2000 census data. HMDA contains the census tract identification number for the property included in each loan application, making the link between census and HMDA data relatively straightforward.

Our unit of analysis is the metropolitan area.[5] The access that minority homebuyers have to predominantly white neighborhoods reflects metropolitan-level phenomena. Their choices, as a group, are guided by the actions of members of the banking and real estate industries, particularly as they relate to federal policies such as the CRA, the supply of housing, the demand within the market, and the ecology of the metropolitan area. We are specifically interested in whether and how differences in CRA coverage across communities relate to minority access and are less concerned with explaining variation across individual minority homebuyers within metropolitan areas in terms of where they reside. That variation is more likely due to individual- or household-level characteristics, which cannot be controlled for using HMDA data, than to macrolevel phenomena within the housing market.

The central dependent variables in our analysis are the proportions of conventional home purchase loans originated to blacks and Latinos in predominantly white neighborhoods.[6] That is, among blacks and Latinos who received home purchase loans in 2000, we attempt to account for the share of these families that purchased homes in white neighborhoods. In order to determine whether the property is located in a predominantly white area, we use 2000 census tract data. Predominantly white neighborhoods are tracts in which non-Hispanic whites comprised at least 90 percent of the population, consistent with previous research (Ellen 2000).

After classifying predominantly white census tracts, we aggregated the data to the metropolitan level. Thus, for each area, we know the proportion of all home-purchase loans given to blacks, Latinos, and whites moving into properties in predominantly white neighborhoods. We eliminated loan applications that did not have a valid census tract identification number (of 3.07 million applications, 3.06 million, or 99.6 percent, had valid tracts identified). Following Douglas S. Massey and Mary J. Fischer (1999), we focus on large metropolitan areas with sizable shares of minorities and include all US areas with a population of at least 500,000 and 5,000 or more blacks and Latinos. This results in a sample of 101 municipalities containing 72.1 percent of the nation's non-Hispanic blacks and 77.3 percent of all Latinos. It comprises the entire universe of metropolitan areas in the United States with which our analysis is concerned.[7]

The key variable is the nature of the regulatory and fair lending climate in the metropolitan area, measured as the proportion of loans in 2000 within the area that were originated by CRA-covered institutions. Loans made by institutions monitored by the following regulatory agencies were considered to be CRA-covered: the Office of the Comptroller of the Currency, Federal Reserve System, Federal Deposit Insurance Corporation, and the Office of Thrift Supervision. This classification is consistent with previous research (Canner 2002). Other lenders, those not covered by the CRA, are regulated by the US Department of Housing and Urban Development and the National Credit Union Administration.

Recalling that the economic/ecological perspective suggests that economic capacity influences minority access to white neighborhoods, one measure of that capacity is the average income for white, black, and Hispanic mortgage loan applicants, which is aggregated from the HMDA loan-level data. For all metropolitan areas, we measure the economic resources of each racial/ethnic group by using the average income for that group of applicants.[8] We employ two other measures to capture housing supply, which likely affect minority access: the proportion of occupied housing units that are owner-occupied and the homeowner vacancy rate, defined as the number of vacant units "for sale only" within the metropolitan area, divided by the sum of owner-occupied housing units and vacant units "for sale only" (US Census Bureau 2002a, 2002b: Appendix B, 66). A final variable reflective of the economic/ecological perspective is the population size of each metropolitan area, which allows us to test the assertion that in large areas minorities will have less access to predominantly white neighborhoods than in smaller ones.[9]

According to the place stratification perspective, segregation constitutes one of the main factors affecting minority access. Consequently, we calculated dissimilarity indices between black and white homeowners and Latino and white homeowners for our sample.[10] To our knowledge, no one has computed measures of segregation among homeowners, but because our study is focused on this subset of the population, it is instructive to do so to more accurately control for the opportunities that recent homebuyers may have to move into white neighborhoods. Interestingly, in fourteen of the fifteen largest metropolitan areas, the segregation between black and white homeowners was greater than that between black and white renters (see Table 2.1, columns 5 and 6). Moreover, in twelve of the fifteen areas, dissimilarity indices were above 60, considered the "high" segregation range (Massey and Denton 1993). For Latinos, however, in only five of the fifteen largest areas was segregation from whites higher among homeowners than among renters, and in only four of the fifteen metropolitan areas did the dissimilarity indices rise above 60 (columns 7 and 8).

To further determine whether racial/ethnic composition impedes minority homebuyer access to predominantly white neighborhoods, we create measures of the proportion of black, Latino, and white people living in each area. We expect that in areas with more minorities, there will be less access. For each group-specific analysis (e.g., black analysis, Latino analysis), we employ the corresponding racial/ethnic measure. A final measure is the proportion of the population residing within suburbs in each metropolitan area. As stated earlier, according to the place stratification approach, this proportion may be negatively related to minority access because of discriminatory policies historically adopted by many suburban governments.

We perform descriptive and multivariate analyses to examine the

Table 2.1 Black/White and Latino/White Dissimilarity Indices for the Population in Owner- and Renter-Occupied Housing Units in the Fifteen Largest Metropolitan Areas

Metropolitan Area	2000 Population (1)	Percent Owners Among			Dissimilarity Scores			
		Blacks (2)	Whites (3)	Latinos (4)	B/W Owner (5)	B/W Renter (6)	L/W Owner (7)	L/W Renter (8)
Los Angeles–Long Beach, CA	9,519,338	40.06	63.80	41.01	72.92	65.87	63.52	64.25
New York, NY	9,314,235	29.63	54.14	16.08	85.08	81.62	60.21	67.12
Chicago, IL	8,272,768	46.71	80.30	52.91	83.92	77.54	62.42	58.71
Boston, MA	6,057,826	35.83	73.20	25.04	67.68	60.29	54.82	57.58
Philadelphia, PA	5,100,931	57.50	81.72	52.19	76.58	68.94	62.43	61.52
Washington, DC	4,923,153	53.31	77.56	47.06	63.97	62.31	45.80	52.69
Detroit, MI	4,441,551	55.18	83.83	57.44	87.99	80.58	43.33	55.26
Houston, TX	4,177,646	48.58	75.96	50.54	69.62	64.51	56.03	56.49
Atlanta, GA	4,112,198	52.26	80.83	36.46	65.79	61.10	40.11	52.76
Dallas, TX	3,519,176	46.21	74.20	45.10	62.37	56.72	53.52	55.82
Riverside, CA	3,254,821	50.41	73.95	61.58	46.61	42.68	44.33	41.49
Phoenix, AZ	3,251,876	48.43	76.82	54.23	44.20	38.28	53.96	49.90
Minneapolis, MN	2,968,806	38.13	82.75	44.04	60.03	53.58	42.20	50.95
Orange County, CA	2,846,289	41.17	72.12	41.72	35.29	38.61	54.83	55.51
San Diego, CA	2,813,833	33.83	65.64	40.61	60.80	48.83	52.70	51.27

Source: Census 2000, authors' tabulations.
Note: Blacks/B=all blacks; Whites/W=non-Hispanic whites; Latinos/L=Latinos, regardless of race.

proportions of blacks and Latinos who purchased homes in predominantly white neighborhoods. For comparison, we also examine white homebuyers and the proportion of all three groups that purchased homes in racially integrated and predominantly minority neighborhoods. We then examine the proportion of blacks and Latinos who bought homes in predominantly white areas in metropolitan areas where a relatively high proportion of loans are made by institutions covered by the CRA, compared to areas where relatively fewer loans are made by such lenders. Finally, we utilize multivariate regression to determine whether the findings hold, controlling for relevant socioeconomic factors.

The Research Findings

To what extent do white and minority homebuyers locate in predominantly white areas, relative to racially integrated and predominantly minority neighborhoods? Table 2.2 begins to answer this question. The table shows the average proportion of conventional home purchase loans originated to black and Latino homebuyers in predominantly white neighborhoods. It is evident that whites are more likely than blacks and Latinos to have purchased single-family homes in predominantly white neighborhoods. Column 1 of Table 2.2 shows that, on average, 40 percent of whites purchased single-family homes in predominantly white neighborhoods, compared to only 12 percent of blacks and 22 percent of Latinos, figures in line with statistics presented in the previous chapter.

Interestingly, on average, a higher share of white homebuyers purchased homes in racially integrated neighborhoods than was the case for minority homebuyers. Although at first glance the figure for whites seems high, it is actually quite reasonable because integration could involve whites living with Asians or Latinos, not necessarily blacks. With respect to predominantly minority neighborhoods, on average, recent black and Latino homebuyers are significantly more likely to move there than recent white homebuyers. Almost twice as many blacks as Latinos move to predominantly minority neighborhoods (see column 3), but at the same time, about half as many black as Latino homebuyers are able to purchase homes in predominantly white neighborhoods (see column 1).

Table 2.3 begins to explore how the distribution of blacks and Latinos across white neighborhoods is affected by the level of CRA

Table 2.2   Average Proportions of Conventional Home Purchase Loans Given to Homebuyers by Racial Composition of the Census Tract

Average Proportion of Homebuyers	Predominantly White (1)	Racially Integrated (2)	Predominantly Minority (3)
	Racial Composition of the Census Tracts		
Total	.3696	.3359	.1407
White	.4012	.3662	.0869
Black	.1160	.2446	.4201
Latino	.2236	.2707	.2808
N	101		

Source: HMDA 2000 and Census 2000/1990, authors' tabulations.
Note: N = number of cases.

Table 2.3   Average Proportion of Conventional Home Purchase Loans Originated to Homebuyers in Predominantly White Census Tracts, by CRA Coverage Level

	At or Above Median-Level CRA Coverage	Below Median-Level CRA Coverage
Total	.5079	.2341
White	.5402	.2648
Black	.1518	.0809
Latino	.3036	.1452
N	50	51

Source: HMDA 2000 and Census 2000/1990, authors' tabulations.
Note: N = number of cases.

regulation within metropolitan areas. Again, we examine whites for comparison. We divided the 101 metropolitan areas into two groups, one at or above and the other below the median share of area loans covered by the CRA. We compare the average proportion of conventional home purchase loans originated to homebuyers in predominantly white tracts across these two groups. With respect to the CRA coverage indicator, we tailor it to be racially and ethnically specific, so we calculated the proportion of loans made to whites, blacks, and Latinos by CRA coverage across areas.

The main finding from Table 2.3 is that CRA appears to be having an impact on the residential location of minority homebuyers. On average, in areas where a relatively larger share of the loans were made by CRA-covered institutions, 15.2 percent of black homebuyers settled in predominantly white neighborhoods, compared to only 8.1 percent of blacks in areas with lower levels of CRA coverage.[11] Therefore, black homebuyers living in areas where a greater share of loans are made by CRA-covered institutions appear to have more access to white neighborhoods than black homebuyers living in areas where a relatively lower share of loans are made by such institutions. The same pattern is evident for Latinos and whites.[12]

More detailed examination of individual metropolitan areas reinforces this finding. Table 2.4 reveals similar information for areas that are above the seventy-fifth or below the twenty-fifth percentiles of CRA coverage. For example, metropolitan areas like El Paso, Fresno, and San Antonio have among the lowest proportions of loans made by CRA-covered institutions and, consequently, no black or Latino homebuyers living in predominantly white neighborhoods. In metropolitan areas like Buffalo, Albany, and Milwaukee, however, which have relatively greater proportions of loans made by CRA-covered institutions, minority homebuyers have greater access to predominantly white neighborhoods.

In general, it appears that metropolitan areas with low proportions of loans originated by CRA-covered institutions tend to have less residential segregation (e.g., El Paso, Las Vegas, Riverside). Areas with a greater share of loans made by CRA-covered institutions, however, tend to be those with historically higher levels of segregation (e.g., Buffalo, New York, Chicago). Perhaps if residential segregation was comparable across all areas, the level of CRA coverage would have an even greater impact on minority access.

We now turn to the results of our multivariate analysis, which evaluates the impact of CRA coverage on minority access, controlling for other important variables. Table 2.5 reports the results of multiple regression models predicting the proportion of conventional home purchase loans originated to blacks, Latinos, and whites in predominantly white neighborhoods.

Models 1 through 3 of Table 2.5 present the results for the proportion of black, Latino, and white homebuyers, respectively. The results in row 1 reveal that CRA coverage continues to have a substantial and positive effect on the residential location of minority homebuyers, controlling for other variables. For blacks, a 10 percentage point increase in CRA coverage results in a 2 percentage point

Table 2.4 Proportion of Conventional Home Purchase Loans to Black and Latino Homebuyers in White Census Tracts in Selected Metropolitan Areas

Metropolitan Area	2000 Population (1)	Proportion of CRA Coverage (2)	Proportion in Predominantly White Census Tracts Blacks (3)	Latinos (4)
Below the Twenty-Fifth Percentile of CRA Coverage				
El Paso, TX	679,622	.5053	.0000	.0000
Fresno, CA	922,516	.5053	.0000	.0000
San Antonio, TX	1,592,383	.5092	.0000	.0000
Las Vegas, NV	1,563,282	.5701	.0017	.0103
Sacramento, CA	1,628,197	.5767	.0092	.0444
Houston, TX	4,177,646	.5943	.0046	.0084
Dallas, TX	3,519,176	.5977	.0197	.0299
Riverside, CA	3,254,821	.6171	.0000	.0002
Albuquerque, NM	712,738	.6236	.0557	.2112
Orlando, FL	1,644,561	.6597	.0226	.0296
Above the Seventy-Fifth Percentile of CRA Coverage				
Buffalo, NY	1,170,111	.7531	.1906	.4423
Baltimore, MD	2,552,994	.7544	.0889	.2721
New Haven, CT	1,706,575	.7740	.1153	.1857
Cincinnati, OH	1,646,395	.7845	.1931	.7483
Kansas City, KS	1,776,062	.7853	.2137	.4365
New York, NY	9,314,235	.7894	.0126	.0332
Chicago, IL	8,272,768	.7896	.0336	.0815
Toledo, OH	618,203	.8152	.1802	.4925
Albany, NY	875,583	.8158	.3571	.5517
Milwaukee, WI	1,500,741	.8163	.0923	.2796

Source: HMDA 2000 and Census 2000/1990, authors' tabulations.

increase in the share of black homebuyers who move to predominantly white neighborhoods. For Latinos, a 10 percentage point increase results in a 5 percentage point increase in the share of Latino homebuyers locating in white neighborhoods. Model 3 reveals that CRA coverage also has a positive effect on white home purchases in white neighborhoods, although the magnitude of the effect is not much larg-

Table 2.5 Multiple Regression Models Predicting the Proportion of Conventional Home Purchase Loans to Homebuyers in White Neighborhoods

Variable	Blacks (1)	Latinos (2)	Whites (3)
Level of CRA Coverage	0.2311	0.5251	0.6000
	(0.1291)	(0.2260)	(0.2073)
Dissimilarity Index	0.1244	−0.5275	0.7685
	(0.1025)	(0.2619)	(0.1271)
Proportion:			
Black/Latino/White[a]	−0.6934	−0.4690	0.9977
	(0.1278)	(0.1802)	(0.1267)
Mean Applicant Income[b] (logged) ·	−0.2398	−0.1221	−0.3582
	(0.0629)	(0.1237)	(0.0994)
Homeowner Vacancy Rate	−1.0026	0.7358	−6.0458
	(2.6038)	(5.0434)	(3.4740)
Proportion in Owner-Occupied Housing	0.2773	0.5039	0.0941
	(0.1910)	(0.3497)	(0.2726)
Proportion in Suburbs	0.0629	0.0408	0.0046
	(0.0675)	(0.1161)	(0.0861)
Population Size (logged)	−0.0039	0.0020	0.0094
	(0.0171)	(0.0304)	(0.0239)
Intercept	0.7896	0.2203	0.2573
	(0.3660)	(0.6855)	(0.5134)
R^2	0.456	0.461	0.836
N	101		

Source: HMDA 2000 and Census 2000/1990, authors' tabulations.

Notes: Standard errors are in parentheses. N = number of cases.

a. The group referenced depends on the race- or ethnic-specific model being analyzed. For example, for the black models, it refers to proportion black.

b. The applicant income referenced depends on the race- or ethnic-specific model being analyzed. For example, for the black models, it refers to the average of all black applicants' incomes.

er than for Latinos. That may reflect the fact that in areas with a greater share of CRA coverage, there is more of a history of racial prejudice and discrimination. Therefore, whites would be more likely to move to predominantly white neighborhoods. Fair housing and community reinvestment activity has been concentrated in the Midwest (Cloud 2004), reflecting the relatively greater discrimination in those communities.

Given the CRA impact on whites as well as blacks and Latinos, the extent to which the law is affecting aggregate measures of segregation is unclear. But these findings clearly indicate that it facilitates black and Latino access to white neighborhoods and the wealth accumulation benefits generally associated with such neighborhoods. Again, where a greater share of loans are accounted for by CRA lenders, a larger share of minority homebuyers move into predominantly white neighborhoods that traditionally have been denied to these families.[13]

As reported below, we find modest support for some tenets of the economic/ecological perspective. Models 1 and 3 show that average incomes of black and white applicants have negative effects, respectively, on black and white homebuyer location in predominantly white neighborhoods. Although this finding is contrary to our expectations, further analysis reveals that it may not be so contradictory. In bivariate analyses (not shown), we find that the average income of blacks and whites in the metropolitan area is negatively related to their location in predominantly white neighborhoods. What this likely means is that in regions where black and white homebuyers have higher incomes, they are less likely to buy homes in predominantly white neighborhoods than in those regions with lower incomes because it is probably more expensive to buy homes in the former areas.

Regarding indicators related to housing supply, the proportion of owner-occupied housing units has a sizable impact on the mobility of nonwhites and a negligible impact on white mobility. A 10 percentage point increase in the homeownership rate results in a 3 percentage point increase in the share of black homebuyers and a 5 percentage point increase in the share of Latino homebuyers who move to predominantly white neighborhoods. For whites, it results in only a 1 percentage point increase. Other housing supply measures have less of an impact on homebuyer access to predominantly white neighborhoods. The homeowner vacancy rate has a negative effect on black and white location in white neighborhoods, contrary to our expectations, although it has a more substantial impact on Latino location. Population size has a minimal effect on location for all racial groups. The relatively minimal effects of these variables, taken together, may well reflect the impact of key political and institutional factors not explicitly accounted for by this perspective.

Given these findings, how well does the place stratification perspective explain homebuyer access to white neighborhoods? Interestingly, the level of segregation has no substantial impact on black access; instead, it is the proportion of blacks that has a substantial and negative effect. For example, a 10 percentage point increase in the share of blacks within a metropolitan area decreases the proportion of black homebuyers in predominantly white neighborhoods by 6.9 percent. With respect to Latinos, both segregation and the proportion of Latinos are negatively related to Latino access. A 10 percentage point increase in the Latino-white homeowner dissimilarity index and in the share of Latinos within a metropolitan area decreases the share of Latino homebuyers in predominantly white neighborhoods by 5.3 and 4.7 percent, respectively. Not surprisingly, for whites, segregation from blacks and the proportion of whites in the metropolitan area are positively and substantially related to white homebuyer location in predominantly white neighborhoods. For all groups, the proportion of the population living in suburbs has little impact. Taken together, the results indicate the significance of important institutional actors on racial/ethnic group access to white neighborhoods.

In sum, several factors account for minority access to white neighborhoods. Household income and related socioeconomic factors matter, but so do politics and policy. In this case, the policy that appears to matter is the Community Reinvestment Act. That is, the share of mortgage loans covered by the CRA influences the share of blacks and Latinos residing in predominantly white neighborhoods, even after socioeconomic and demographic variables are accounted for. As CRA coverage increases, so does minority access.

However, we recognize that other policy-related factors may be operating. Non-CRA lenders may have directed more of their lending to minority neighborhoods, leaving CRA lenders with a greater share of the market in white communities. That may reflect, in part, the role of predatory lenders who target minority communities for these exploitative practices, the focus of the following chapter. Structural differences between CRA and non-CRA lenders may also play a role. The CRA covers most depository institutions, but not credit unions or mortgage bankers and brokers. Perhaps these structural differences contribute to the findings. Our findings also could not establish that it was CRA lenders who actually made the loans to minority borrowers in white areas, but there is evidence that the CRA has had a "halo effect." That is, the CRA appears to have influenced the lending practices of many lenders not directly subject to its jurisdiction (Shlay 1999). The available evidence, therefore, suggests that the CRA has favorably affected the ability of minority households to purchase homes in traditionally inaccessible communities.

Policy, Place, and Housing Privilege

Our central finding is that minorities are more likely to purchase homes in predominantly white neighborhoods where a greater share of loans are made by CRA-covered institutions. Although it has not led to significant changes in aggregate measures of segregation, it has provided homeownership opportunities for minority homeowners in communities from which they traditionally have been excluded. Our multivariate analyses revealed, most importantly, the impact of CRA coverage on minority access, even in the presence of relevant control variables. Although factors such as the share of owner-occupied housing units and population size emphasized by the economic/eco-logical perspective affect minority access, it is clear that segregation, the presence of dual housing markets, and other political factors high-lighted by the place stratification perspective matter as well. The independent effect of CRA on minority access reinforces the impor-tance of policy and politics in shaping the racial demography of urban communities.

Theoretical Implications

Our results are most consistent with the place stratification perspec-tive. They also reveal the need to bring policy-related variables into the study of the racial/ethnic demography of metropolitan areas. The racial/ethnic composition of an area has a significant negative effect on minority access to predominantly white neighborhoods, indicating the persistence of a dual housing market whereby whites and white-controlled institutions use their power to maintain spatial and social distance from racial minorities and related concrete racial economic disparities. But this is a complex puzzle. If policy matters, it remains difficult to parcel out the extent to which specific policy initiatives, private practices, socioeconomic and ecological variables, and other factors account for various outcomes. At the same time, these find-ings suggest that the CRA might be part of a broader toolkit for ame-liorating those disparities (Gottdiener and Feagin 1988).

Our findings suggest the need to modify current theoretical explanations of racial/ethnic segregation, mobility, and inequality generally, particularly in terms of the processes for breaking down traditional barriers. Previous research has addressed the role of policy in creating segregated living patterns and ghetto neighborhoods (e.g., exclusionary zoning ordinances, urban renewal, concentration of public housing) (Gotham 2002; Jackson 1985; Massey and Denton 1993). Much of this research, however, while acknowledging the role of policy, does not adequately quantify the effect of policy in perpetuating segregation, relative to other factors such as residential preferences. Without an explicit focus on policy, it is hard to understand patterns of racial/ethnic segregation and mobility. In addition, far less is known about the role of policy in dismantling dual housing markets and opening up minority access to traditionally inaccessible neighborhoods.

As the two dominant theoretical traditions suggest, a combination of economic forces, demographic characteristics, and power relations have framed the opportunity structure facing racial and ethnic minorities in metropolitan areas. Fair housing advocates have long promoted a range of policies, but there has been little formal testing of the impact of those initiatives (Sidney 2003). Our results indicate the independent effect of at least one policy, CRA, in accounting for residential mobility. Further understanding of these processes and patterns requires bringing the role of agency and the impact of specific policy initiatives (e.g., legislation, regulations, court decisions) into the center of the debate and future research.

In bringing policy in, it is critical to be cognizant of the milieu in which such concerns are introduced. CRA and other fair lending and fair housing policies generally do not play out in a neutral world. Rather, it is a world characterized by interests, power relations, conflicts (racial, ethnic, and others), and other dimensions of uneven metropolitan development. Policies are often introduced in an effort to ameliorate inequalities and level the proverbial playing field. The CRA provides a tool that can enable less powerful groups to win out, at least on some occasions, over more powerful institutions. Armed with the law, neighborhood activists are sometimes able to encourage private businesses (e.g., lenders) and public institutions (e.g., lending regulators) to behave differently. Such community organizations are more successful when they ally with church groups, labor organizations, supportive public officials, friendly reporters, and other groups, as we discuss further in the concluding chapter (Dreier 2003; Squires 2003). This does not necessarily argue for a pluralist conception of community power or social change, however. In fact, lenders and other financial service providers often shape the policymaking process in ways that favor their interests, undercutting progressive community actors, as was the case with the 1999 bank reform law and subsequent CRA regulatory changes discussed earlier. Business still has a privileged position in urban economies (Lindblom 1977; Logan and Molotch 1987). Policy, including civil rights and fair lending policy, constitutes highly contested terrain (Branch 1988, 1998; Goering and Wienk 1996; Katznelson 1981; Squires 2003). Understanding the struggles that have shaped urban development, the structure of housing markets, and efforts to overcome traditional barriers requires exploring the central role of policy.

Policy Implications

Our findings have implications for current policy debates over lending and community reinvestment generally and the role of CRA in particular. One critical reform would be to expand the scope of CRA-covered lenders. Currently, as indicated earlier, only depository institutions are covered. Mortgage banking affiliates, independent mortgage bankers and brokers, insurers, and other financial institutions that are making an increasing share of mortgage loans are not covered. The CRA Modernization Act (H.R. 4893, 106th Congress, 2nd Session) would apply this act to the affiliates of all depositories and their holding companies and to mortgage lenders not currently affiliated with a depository institution or bank holding company.

One critical area being scrutinized by regulators is how to evaluate the lending activities of CRA-covered financial institutions. Currently, lending activity is assessed on the basis of the amount of lending conducted by an institution, the geographic distribution of loans (as measured primarily by income levels of communities), borrower characteristics (again, primarily measured in terms of income and economic status), the extent of community development lending, and the extent of innovative and flexible lending practices (Code of Federal Regulations, Title 12, Part 228, July 1, 1997). Innovative and flexible lending practices are defined, in part, as those that "augment the success and effectiveness of the institution's lending under its community development loan programs or, more generally, its lending under its loan programs that address the credit needs of low- and moderate-income geographies or individuals" (Federal Financial Institutions Examination Council 2003). No reference is made to the race of applicants or racial composition of neighborhoods.

The lending test should be revised to explicitly include lending to racial minorities and minority communities as part of the CRA exam and as a criterion on which the final CRA rating will be based. Several community organizations have long advocated that race be part of the exam process (National Training and Information Center 2002; Silver 2001), and the CRA Modernization Act would mandate service to minority areas as well as low- and moderate-income communities.

In addition to taking into consideration the distribution of loans to racial minorities and minority communities, the CRA regulations should be revised to reward lending that facilitates access to traditionally inaccessible neighborhoods. That is, loans to racial minorities for the purchase of homes in predominantly white neighborhoods should be viewed as a "plus" in the CRA exam. Perhaps the definition of "innovative" lending could be modified to provide additional incentives for such loans.

No Permanent Victories

Residential racial segregation and its many costs are, obviously, long-standing and complex social problems that contribute to the uneven development of metropolitan areas and the unequal distribution of privilege. Creating access for racial/ethnic minorities in neighborhoods that have traditionally been inaccessible remains a challenge. It is often said that the devil is in the details. One of the devilish details shaping the racial demography of metropolitan areas is the set of regulations governing the behavior of financial institutions. They matter, and they are changing. Social science research is beginning to understand the role of policy, politics, and power and how they shape the opportunity structure facing diverse segments of the nation's population. How the rules implementing the Community Reinvestment Act are altered, for example, will influence housing opportunities for racial minorities in US urban areas. The empirical findings of this chapter reveal that aggressive implementation of the CRA can increase minority access to predominantly white communities, thus increasing their access to a wide range of public and private goods and reducing urban inequality.

If significant progress has been made in increasing minority access to mortgage loans and other traditionally inaccessible amenities, questions have arisen regarding the terms and conditions of those loans. To some extent, mortgage lending gaps in terms of access to credit have been met by so-called subprime lenders, many of which provide exploitative loan products that often result in foreclosure, the loss of a home, and the loss of a family's life savings.

Many traditional victims of redlining and discriminatory practices now find they can obtain a loan, but only at exorbitant costs that exceed the risk they actually pose to their lenders. For some households and communities, therefore, a problem of limited access to loan products has turned into an "oversupply" of harmful services. The controversy over predatory lending is the subject of the next chapter.

Notes

A previous version of this chapter appeared as Samantha Friedman and Gregory D. Squires. (2005). "Does the Community Reinvestment Act Help Minorities Access Traditionally Inaccessible Neighborhoods?" *Social Problems* 52 (2): 209–231. © 2005 by Society for the Study of Social Problems, Inc. Reprinted by permission of the University of California Press.

1. For more detailed information on CRA, see the website of the Federal Financial Institutions Examination Council, http://www.ffiec.gov/.

2. The federal Fair Housing Act (42 U.S.C. §§ 3601-19 (1994)) prohibits discrimination on the basis of race, color, religion, sex, familial status, national origin, or disability in the provision of housing and housing-related services, including housing finance. The Department of Housing and Urban Development is the primary enforcement agency, though plaintiffs can file lawsuits in the courts or complaints with the US Department of Justice. If found in violation of the law, defendants can be fined or issued cease-and-desist orders. For more detailed information on the Fair Housing Act, see the website of the US Department of Housing and Urban Development, http://www.hud.gov/.

3. We focus on conventional home purchase loans and do not include FHA and other government-insured loans. Although government-insured loans are an appropriate product for some borrowers, these programs have also long been implemented in a manner that promotes segregation (Bradford 1979). Excluding these loans, which today go disproportionately to minority borrowers, may result in a data set that weakens the actual connection between CRA and minority access to white neighborhoods. Consequently, our results are likely to understate the connection that may exist between CRA and minority access to traditionally inaccessible neighborhoods.

4. HMDA data are categorized as either one- to four-family or multifamily dwellings. Although the former comprises loans and applications made for the purpose of purchasing a residential dwelling for one to four families, we cannot disaggregate those loans and applications made for the purpose of purchasing just single-family homes. Therefore, consistent with previous research (see the Joint Center for Housing Studies 2002b), we use the one- to four-family homes and not loans or applications made for multifamily dwellings (five or more families) for our analysis.

5. We focus on metropolitan areas as defined by the Office of Management and Budget in 1999, the same definitions used in tabulations of Census 2000 on American FactFinder. Specifically, we focus on primary metropolitan statistical areas, metropolitan statistical areas, and New England county equivalent metropolitan areas. Because we merge census and HMDA data, we must aggregate the HMDA data first to the counties that form the basis of these metropolitan areas and then up to the metropolitan-area level.

6. Predominantly white tracts are those in which non-Hispanic whites comprised at least 90 percent of the population in 2000. Racially integrated neighborhoods are those in which: (1) non-Hispanic whites comprised more than 50 percent but less than 90 percent of the population in *both* 1990 and 2000 *and* there was no more than a 10 percentage point decrease in the percent white over the decade; and (2) non-Hispanic whites comprised more than 90 percent of the population in 1990 and between 50 and 90 percent of the population in 2000 *and* there was no more than a 10 percentage point decrease in the percent white over the decade. By using data from both censuses, our definition of racial integration reflects integration that is more stable. Moreover, recent research has used both the aggregate racial/ethnic mix and level of change over time to identify stable integration (Nyden et al. 1998). Predominantly minority neighborhoods are tracts in which non-Hispanic whites comprised 50 percent or less of the population in 2000.

7. Because this is the entire population of cases—and not a sample—the use of inferential statistics for our analysis will be unnecessary.

8. We log this variable to correct for skewness.

9. As with income, we log this variable to correct for skewness.

10. We adopted the methodology used by the Lewis Mumford Center (2001a). Blacks here refer to all blacks; whites refer to non-Hispanic whites. For a complete discussion of the dissimilarity index and other measures of segregation, see White (1986) and Massey and Denton (1988).

11. We do not use statistical significance tests here because we are dealing with total population rather than sample data for all conventional home purchase loans originated to these groups.

12. Because we do not know the racial/ethnic composition of the neighborhoods in which blacks and Latinos lived before they acquired their home mortgage loan, we cannot necessarily say that this is the first access they have had to predominantly white neighborhoods. Nevertheless, the finding that minorities have more access to such neighborhoods in metropolitan areas with relatively more CRA-covered lending is substantively significant because it suggests a force potentially contributing to the wealth potential of these households.

13. It should be noted that in other analyses not shown here, we found that CRA coverage is *positively* related to the proportion of loans made to Latinos and blacks in minority neighborhoods. Therefore, in addition to opening up minority access to predominantly white neighborhoods, the CRA is having its intended impact.

3

Predatory Lending: The New Redlining

It is clear that we need to focus a spotlight on predatory lenders whose sole purpose is to hijack the American dream from unsuspecting borrowers. We should leave no stone unturned to find and crack down on predatory lenders and Congress must pass the strongest legislation possible to end this pernicious practice.
—Senator Charles Schumer (D-NY)
(quoted in National Community Reinvestment Coalition 2002a: 5)

The proverbial American dream of owning a home has become an all-too-real nightmare for a growing number of families. Take the case of Florence McKnight, an eighty-four-year-old Rochester widow who, while heavily sedated in a hospital bed, signed a $50,000 loan secured by her home for only $10,000 in new windows and other home repairs. The terms of the loan called for $72,000 in payments over fifteen years, at which point she would still owe a $40,000 balloon payment. Her home is now in foreclosure.

And there is the case of Mason and Josie, an elderly African American couple with excellent credit and a primary source of income from Mason's veteran benefits. A broker convinced them to consolidate their 7 percent mortgage with some credit card debt. The first mortgage for $99,000 was at 8.4 percent, but the broker added a second mortgage for $17,000 at 13 percent. The initial loan financed almost $6,000 in broker and third-party fees, and both loans contained prepayment penalties for three and five years, respectively. In addition, after fifteen years, both loans had balloon payments, which require borrowers to pay off the entire balance of the loan by making a substantial payment after a period of time during which they have been making regular monthly payments. After making monthly payments of almost $950 for fifteen years, they will face a payment of $93,000.

Other examples include a West Virginia widow who refinanced her mortgage seven times in fifteen months, only to lose it in foreclosure. A disabled Portland, Oregon, woman was charged more than 30 percent of the amount of her home loan to cover credit life insurance and other financing fees. A sixty-eight-year-old Chicago woman refinanced her loan three times in five years and found her monthly payments exceeded her income (ACORN 2002: 3, 4; LaFalce 2000: 4).

Unfortunately, these are not isolated incidents. Predatory lending has emerged as the most salient public policy issue in financial services today. In this chapter we examine the rise of predatory lending practices and what is being done to combat them. If, as indicated in the previous chapter, progress has been made to sever the ties of residence and race by increasing access to capital, including home mortgage loans, for racial minorities, low-income families and economically distressed communities, that progress has come with great struggle. And it appears there are few, if any, permanent victories. The emergence of predatory lending practices demonstrates that the struggle against redlining has not been won but simply has taken some new turns and that the link between place and race persists.

After decades of redlining that starved many urban communities of credit and denied loans to racial minorities throughout metropolitan areas (Bradbury et al. 1989; Dedman 1988, 1989; Munnell et al. 1996; Squires 2004; Squires and O'Connor 2001; Turner and Skidmore 1999), today a growing number of financial institutions are flooding these same markets with exploitative loan products that drain residents of their wealth. Such "reverse redlining" may be as problematic for minority families and older urban neighborhoods as was the withdrawal of conventional financial services. Instead of contributing to homeownership and community development, predatory lending practices strip the equity homeowners have struggled to build up and deplete the wealth of those communities for the enrichment of distant financial services firms.

Researchers debate the extent to which subprime lending increases access to credit for borrowers with some blemishes on their record, albeit on more expensive terms, or simply exploits vulnerable borrowers. The distinction between subprime and predatory lending, in fact, can be fuzzy. The National Community Reinvestment Coalition

(NCRC) recently offered the following definitions to help clarify the differences. NCRC defined subprime lending in the following terms:

> A subprime loan is a loan to a borrower with less than perfect credit. In order to compensate for the added risk associated with subprime loans, lending institutions charge higher interest rates. In contrast, a prime loan is a loan made to a creditworthy borrower at prevailing interest rates. Loans are classified as A, A-, B, C, and D loans. "A" loans are prime loans that are made at the going rate while A- loans are loans made at slightly higher interest rates to borrowers with only a few blemishes on their credit report. So-called B, C, and D loans are made to borrowers with significant imperfections in their credit history. "D" loans carry the highest interest rate because they are made to borrowers with the worst credit histories that include bankruptcy. (National Community Reinvestment Coalition 2002a: 4)

Predatory loans are defined in the following terms:

> A predatory loan is an unsuitable loan designed to exploit vulnerable and unsophisticated borrowers. Predatory loans are a subset of subprime loans. (Not all subprime loans are predatory, but virtually all predatory loans are subprime.) A predatory loan has one or more of the following features: 1) charges more in interest and fees than is required to cover the added risk of lending to borrowers with credit imperfections, 2) contains abusive terms and conditions that trap borrowers and lead to increased indebtedness, 3) does not take into account the borrower's ability to repay the loan, and 4) often violates fair lending laws by targeting women, minorities and communities of color. (National Community Reinvestment Coalition 2002a: 4)

A variety of predatory practices have been identified. They include the following:

- higher interest rates and fees than can be justified by the risk posed by the borrower,
- balloon payments,
- required single premium credit life insurance, where the borrower must pay the entire annual premium at the beginning of the policy period rather than in monthly or quarterly payments and with this cost folded into the loan, the total cost, including interest payments, is higher throughout the life of the loan,
- forced placed homeowners insurance where the lender

requires the borrower to pay for a policy selected by the
lender,

- high pre-payment penalties which trap borrowers in the loans,
- fees for services that may or may not actually be provided,
- loans based on the value of the property with no regard for the
borrower's ability to make payments,
- loan flipping, whereby lenders use deceptive and high-pressure
tactics resulting in the frequent refinancing of loans with additional fees added each time,
- negatively amortized loans and loans for more than the value
of the home which result in the borrower owing more money
at the end of the loan period than when they started making
payments. (ACORN 2002: 31)

There are no precise quantitative estimates of the extent of predatory lending, but the growth of subprime lending in recent years, coupled with growing law enforcement activity in this area, clearly indicates a surge if not resurgence, of a range of exploitative practices
with economically most vulnerable populations the most likely to be
victimized. The Joint Center for Housing Studies (2002a: 14) at
Harvard University reported that mortgage companies specializing in
subprime loans increased their share of home purchase mortgage
loans from 1 percent to 13 percent between 1993 and 2000. One
industry source reported that the volume of subprime home loans
grew from \$35 billion to over \$530 billion between 1994 and 2004
(Inside Mortgage Finance Publications 2005, cited in Avery et al.
2005b: 349). Subprime loans are concentrated in neighborhoods with
high unemployment rates and declining housing values (Pennington-
Cross 2002). Almost 20 percent of refinance loans to low-income
borrowers were made by subprime lenders in 2002, compared to just
over 7 percent for upper-income borrowers (ACORN 2004: 1).

The Center for Community Change (Bradford 2002: vii) reported
that African Americans are three times as likely as whites to finance
their homes with subprime loans, and the racial disparity is larger at
higher income levels. The US Department of Housing and Urban
Development (2000) found that residents of predominantly African
American neighborhoods are five times as likely as those in white
neighborhoods to receive subprime refinancing loans. When the 2004
HMDA data were released, the first year in which pricing information
was available, researchers with the Federal Reserve Board found that
32.4 percent of blacks, 20.3 percent of Hispanics, and 8.7 percent of

whites received high-priced home purchase loans. (High-priced loans are those with annual percentage rates that were 3 percentage points higher than yields on comparable US Treasury securities for first lien loans and 5 percentage points higher for subordinate liens.) After controlling for borrower income, loan amount, location of property, presence of co-applicant, and sex of applicant, blacks were still three times as likely as whites, and Hispanics twice as likely, to receive high cost loans (Avery et al. 2005b: 376–382). The National Community Reinvestment Coalition reported that even after researchers controlled for credit scores and housing market measures, they found that borrowers from minority neighborhoods and neighborhoods with many elderly households were more likely to purchase or refinance homes with subprime loans. After controlling for housing affordability, they also found subprime lending concentrated among women, minority, and low-income borrowers as well as borrowers from minority and low-income neighborhoods (National Community Reinvestment Coalition 2003; 2005b). Other econometric research has also revealed that race continues to be a factor in the distribution of subprime loans, after other individual and neighborhood factors are taken into consideration (Immergluck 2004; Joint Center for Housing Studies 2004).

The National Training and Information Center traced a surge in foreclosures in the Chicago metropolitan area to an increase in subprime lending. Between 1993 and 1998, home loan foreclosures doubled, while subprime loans grew from just over 3,000 to almost 51,000 nationwide. Subprime lenders were responsible for 1.4 percent of foreclosures in 1993 and 35.7 percent in 1998 (National Training and Information Center 1999: 4). Subsequent research on Chicago found that the rise in subprime lending between 1996 and 2001 was associated with a significant increase in the foreclosure rate in 2002, controlling for family income, unemployment rates, racial composition, owner-occupancy rate, median property value, and other neighborhood characteristics (Immergluck and Smith 2004a, 2004b). The 3,750 foreclosures that occurred in Chicago in 1997 and 1998 reduced area property values by more than $598 million, for an average of $159,000 per foreclosure (Immergluck and Smith 2004a, 2004b). According to William Apgar at Harvard's Joint Center for Housing Studies, borrowers with subprime loans are eight times more likely to default than those with prime conventional loans (Kilborn 2002: sec. 1, p. 30).

Even if most subprime loans serve the useful purpose of enabling high-risk borrowers to access credit for home purchase and refinance

(Gramlich 2002), many of these loans do not serve the best interests of the borrowers. Fannie Mae and Freddie Mac have estimated that between 30 and 50 percent of those receiving subprime loans would, in fact, qualify for prime loans (Engel and McCoy 2002a: 1578). These borrowers are paying more than they should, given the level of risk they actually represent. A case study of Newark, New Jersey, found that the rise in subprime lending could not be explained in terms of borrower characteristics. In fact, among identically qualified borrowers, those taking out home improvement or refinancing loans in 1999 were forty times more likely to be offered subprime loans than in 1993 (Newman and Wyly 2004). Research also has shown that minority borrowers are more likely to receive loans with prepayment penalties (with no interest rate benefit) and that prepayment penalties and balloon payments increased foreclosure rates by 20 to 50 percent, after controlling for income, credit rating, and other risk factors (Quercia et al. 2005; Bocian and Zhai 2005; Ernst 2005). If subprime loans do benefit some consumers, those subjected to predatory practices are clearly not being served.

In sum, targets of predatory lending frequently are older residents who have paid off their homes, particularly those who live in older urban neighborhoods with large minority populations. In other words, many of those families and neighborhoods that have long been underserved by traditional lenders find themselves victimized by what could be considered a form of reverse redlining. They are offered far more in the way of financial "services" than is in the financial interests of such households or communities. These practices perpetuate long-standing disinvestment of and discrimination against such communities and contribute to the uneven development of the nation's metropolitan areas.

Surging Inequality

When Lester Thurow (1987) characterized the 1970s and 1980s as a time of surging inequality, he also, perhaps unwittingly, accurately forecast economic trends into the new millennium. Income, wealth, and other key economic resources have been distributed in increasingly unequal ways, with one outcome being heightened economic segregation of the nation's metropolitan areas. These developments have fueled unequal access to financial services and have prepared the ground for predatory lenders.

A variety of measures point in the same direction. Between 1967 and 2003, the share of income going to the top 5 percent of households grew from 17.5 to 21.7 percent. The share going to the lowest fifth dropped from 4.0 to 3.4 percent. In 1967 households in the top quintile received 10.9 times as much as those in the bottom quintile. This ratio grew to 14.6 in 2001 (DeNavas-Walt 2004; DeNavas-Walt et al. 2004). Since the mid-1970s, compensation for the highest paid 100 chief executive officers went from $1.3 million, or 39 times the pay of an average worker, to $37.5 million, or more than 1,000 times the pay of the typical worker (Krugman 2002: 64). Wealth has long been and continues to be even more unequally distributed than income. The share of wealth held by the top 5 percent increased from 56.1 percent in 1983 to 59.4 percent in 1998. These wealth disparities are the highest in the industrial world (Wolff 2001: 40).

As discussed in Chapter 1, poverty and concentrated poverty, particularly in minority communities, persist at high levels. Suburbs have fared better than cities generally, though many inner-ring suburbs are now experiencing the ills long associated primarily with inner-city neighborhoods. Segregation has declined in some communities, but it remains a central, defining feature of most metropolitan areas. And these patterns reflect disparities that prevailed before subprime and predatory lending took off in the mid-1990s.

These trends translate into very real quality of life barriers for a growing number of people, particularly in the nation's cities. Access to jobs is adversely affected for residents of communities most in need of employment. Health care is more difficult to obtain. The physical environment is more polluted. Food and other consumer goods cost more. And financial services are less readily available (Dreier et al. 2001).

Inequality and the Restructuring of Financial Services

In a climate of surging inequality, bank deregulation has fueled the emergence of a two-tiered banking system featuring predatory lending in a variety of markets (Joint Center for Housing Studies 2004). In central city neighborhoods, the number of mainstream financial institutions has declined while the number of fringe bankers (e.g., check cashers, pawn shops, payday lenders) has grown, particularly where minority households are concentrated.

Another cause and consequence of these developments is the large number of households with no bank accounts. Approximately 10 million households—disproportionately low-income, African American and Hispanic, young adults, and renters—do not have a bank account (Caskey 2002: 1). The primary reasons for not having such banking relationships are economic. The unbanked report that they have virtually no month-to-month financial savings to keep in an account. They also report that bank fees and minimum balances are too high, and some are uncomfortable dealing with banks (Caskey 2002: 2).

But not having a conventional bank account is costly. Such households often use check-cashing businesses to pay bills or cash paychecks, for which they are often charged 2–3 percent of the face value. That adds up to hundreds of dollars annually, precisely for those who can least afford the cost. Some households take out so-called payday loans, which are basically short-term (often two-week) cash advances on paychecks that frequently involve annual interest rates of 1,000 percent (Hudson 1996). And these are not just one-time or occasional transactions. More than half of those who take out payday loans engage in seven or more transactions at one lender in a given year (Community Reinvestment Association–North Carolina et al. 2002). A typical user of check-cashing businesses and payday lenders spends $1,000 more each year than he or she would for comparable services at a mainstream bank (Fisher 2005: 2). Those with regular bank accounts, however, are often offered a range of financial services such as credit counseling and lines of credit for various purposes, including prime home mortgage loans from their banks. Without that banking relationship, households cannot gain access to these services (ACORN 2002: 30).

In some cases, however, conventional lenders have not left the central city. They may have closed their offices, but then they invest in or form partnerships with check cashers, payday lenders, and other fringe bankers. For example, Wells Fargo, the nation's seventh-largest lender at the time, arranged more than $700 million in loans between 1998 and 2002 to three large check-cashing chains: Ace Cash Express, EZ Corporation, and Cash America. In California more than 60 percent of check cashers and payday lenders are supported by major financial institutions, including Wells Fargo, Bank of America, J. P. Morgan Chase, and other household names. Chase Manhattan Bank, Citibank, Fleet Financial, Hong Kong and Shanghai Banking Corporation (HSBC), and other banks have partnered with check cashers in the New York metropolitan area, including parts of Connecticut, New Jersey, and New York (Fisher 2005). Mainstream financial institutions have created the opportunity for fringe institutions to enter the marketplace, ironically often after the former have closed their own offices in the very same neighborhoods.

Even more ironically, some of the steps taken to increase access to credit for traditionally underserved communities have inadvertently created incentives for predatory lending. The Community Reinvestment Act and the Fair Housing Act provided incentives for lenders to serve minority and low-income areas. FHA insurance and securitization of loans (whereby lenders sell loans to the secondary mortgage market, which, in turn, packages them into securities sold to investors) reduce the risk to lenders and increase capital available for mortgage lending. In turn, the federal government established affordable housing goals for the two major secondary mortgage market actors—Fannie Mae and Freddie Mac—whereby 50 percent of the mortgages they purchase must be for low- and moderate-income households (Engel and McCoy 2002b: 1267–1273). Such acts have increased access to capital, but sometimes by predatory lenders.

It is precisely this environment—growing inequality and the restructuring of financial institutions—that has nurtured predatory lending, particularly in minority neighborhoods, reinforcing the linkage between race and place in urban communities. And bank deregulation, discussed below, portends more of the same in the near future. Again, it is not just marginal institutions that are involved. Wall Street has been a major player by securitizing subprime loans. Such involvement of investment banks in subprime lending grew from $18.5 billion in 1997 to $56 billion in 2000 (ACORN 2002: 29, 30).

With passage of the Financial Services Modernization Act of 1999, the consolidation and concentration among financial services that had been occurring for decades—often at the expense of already distressed neighborhoods—received the blessing of the federal government (Leadership Conference on Civil Rights 2002: 43–47). Between 1970 and 1997, the number of banks in the United States dropped from just under 20,000 to 9,100, primarily as a result of mergers among healthy institutions (Bradford and Cincotta 1992: 192; Meyer 1998). The 1999 act removed many post-Depression laws that had provided for greater separation of the worlds of banking, insurance, and securities than now exists. Subsequent to this "reform," it became far easier for financial service providers to enter into each of these lines of business. One consequence is that commercial banks and savings institutions, which formerly made the vast majority of mortgage loans, now make approximately one-third of all home loans (Insurance Information Institute 2002: 29).

A critical implication of deregulation is the declining influence of the Community Reinvestment Act. Concentration and consolidation among financial institutions that have taken place for years reduced the impact of CRA by facilitating the entry into the mortgage market of many financial institutions that are not covered by that 1977 law. The share of mortgage loans subject to intensive review under the CRA dropped from 36.1 percent to 29.5 percent between 1993 and 2000 (Joint Center for Housing Studies 2002b: iii, v). But the 1999 law is not the last word on this debate. In many ways, community-based organizations, fair housing groups, and some elected officials are responding to these developments and the predatory practices that have proliferated.

Reactions to Predatory Lending

Public officials, community organizations, and lenders have begun to respond. Public officials, prodded by aggressive community organizing, have proposed many regulatory and legislative changes. During the 2001–2002 legislative year, five bills were introduced in Congress, thirty-three states considered new legislation, and fourteen cities and counties debated local ordinances. One year later, at least six states (North Carolina, New York, California, New Jersey, New Mexico, and Georgia) and three cities (New York, Los Angeles, and Oakland) enacted anti–predatory lending legislation (Kest 2003). As of the end of 2004, at least thirty-six states, the District of Columbia, three counties, and nine municipalities had passed laws addressing predatory lending (Engel and McCoy 2004). These proposals call for limits on fees, prepayment penalties, and balloon payments; restrictions on practices leading to loan flipping; and prohibitions against loans that do not take into consideration borrowers' ability to repay. They provide for additional disclosures to consumers in the case of high-cost loans, credit counseling, and other consumer protections (National Community Reinvestment Coalition 2002a). The Prohibit Predatory Lending Act (H.R. 1182), introduced in 2005, would have provided similar protections nationwide but would not have preempted stronger protections provided at the state or local levels (Center for Responsible Lending 2005).

In response to information provided and pressure exerted by

Association of Communities Organized for Reform Now (ACORN) and other consumer groups, the Federal Trade Commission (FTC) has taken enforcement actions against nineteen lenders and brokers for predatory practices and negotiated the largest consumer protection settlement in FTC history with Citigroup in 2002 (General Accounting Office 2004: 30–57; Kest and Hurd 2003). Citigroup agreed to pay $215 million to resolve charges against its subsidiary, the Associates, for various deceptive and abusive practices. The suit was aimed primarily at unnecessary credit insurance products the Associates packed into many of its subprime loans (Federal Trade Commission 2002). The Office of the Comptroller of the Currency reached a $300 million settlement with Providian National Bank in California to compensate consumers hurt by its unfair and deceptive lending practices (Gramlich 2003). Despite the scope of the refunds and reductions in loan balances for the victims, some consumer groups maintained the settlement was inadequate, given the resources and extent of abusive practices on the part of the lender (Reddy 2002). A month later, Household International reached a $484 million agreement with a group of states attorneys general in which it agreed to many changes in its consumer loan practices. Household agreed to cap its fees and points, to provide more comprehensive disclosure of loan terms, to provide for an independent monitor to assure compliance with the agreement, and many other changes (Household International 2002). In addition, Household International negotiated a $72 million foreclosure avoidance program with ACORN in which the company agreed to interest rate reductions, waivers of unpaid late charges, loan principal reductions, and other initiatives to help families remain in their homes (ACORN 2003a).

The National Community Reinvestment Coalition, more than thirty of its member organizations, and other nonprofit organizations have developed loan rescue programs to help victims of predatory lending to refinance those loans on terms that do serve the financial interests of the borrowers. Such programs have been initiated in cities in every region of the country, including Atlanta, Baltimore, Cincinnati, Las Vegas, Milwaukee, and Omaha, among others. Many lenders participate in these rescue programs and in related financial literacy programs to educate borrowers about financial services (Gramlich 2003; National Community Reinvestment Coalition 2002a; Wertheim 2002).

Many lenders, often in partnership with community-based organizations, have launched educational and counseling programs to steer consumers away from predatory loans. One example is BorrowSmart in Richmond, Virginia. Financial service providers Wachovia Corporation and Saxon Capital joined with the fair housing group Housing Opportunities Made Equal (HOME) to launch this counseling effort with several lenders and counseling agencies in that community. To make them more knowledgeable borrowers, consumers will be advised on the types of information they should obtain, as well as what kinds of practices to be wary of (Lewis 2002).

But progress cannot be assumed. Three federal financial regulatory agencies (Comptroller of the Currency, National Credit Union Administration, and Office of Thrift Supervision) have issued opinions that federal laws preempt some state predatory lending laws for the lenders they regulate (General Accounting Office 2004: 68–71). In communities where anti–predatory lending laws have been proposed, lobbyists for financial institutions have introduced state-level bills to preempt or nullify local ordinances or to weaken consumer protections. Legislation also has been introduced in Congress to preempt state efforts to combat predatory lending (ACORN 2003b). The 2005 Responsible Lending Act (H.R. 1295), although described as combating predatory lending, would fail to prevent many exploitative practices and, perhaps most importantly, preempt all state and local initiatives (Center for Responsible Lending 2005a, 2005b).

Preliminary research on the North Carolina anti–predatory lending law—the first statewide ban—suggested that restrictions provided by this statute reduced the supply and increased the cost of credit to low-income borrowers (Elliehausen and Staten 2002, 2003). Subsequent research, however, found that the law had the intended impact; there was a reduction in predatory loans but no change in access to or the cost of credit for high-risk borrowers (Quercia et al. 2003). A more recent study of anti–predatory lending laws in twenty-four states found that many consumers get stronger protections and lower costs in states with laws that exceed protections provided by federal rules. Researchers found that borrowers in those states have abundant access to subprime loans, they pay the same or less for such loans as do borrowers in states without such laws, and the loans they receive have fewer abusive terms (Li and Ernst 2006). Debate continues over the impact of such legislative initiatives (Comptroller of the Currency 2003, 2004), and the fight against redlining, in its traditional or "reverse" forms, remains an ongoing struggle.

The tools that have been used to combat redlining have always emerged from conflict. The Fair Housing Act of 1968 was the product of a long civil rights movement and probably would not have been passed until several years later if it were not for the assassination of

Martin Luther King Jr. that year (Massey and Denton 1993: 186–194). Passage of the CRA followed years of demonstrations at bank offices, the homes of bank presidents, and elsewhere (Bradford and Cincotta 1992; Trapp 2004). And recent fights against predatory lending reflect the maturation of several national coalitions of community advocacy and fair housing groups, including ACORN, the National Community Reinvestment Coalition, the National Training and Information Center, the National Fair Housing Alliance, and others (Squires 2003). As Frederick Douglass famously stated in 1857:

> If there is no struggle, there is no progress.
> Those who profess to favor freedom and yet deprecate agitation
> Are men who want crops without plowing the ground.
> They want rain without thunder and lightning.
> They want the ocean without the awful roar of its waters.
> Power concedes nothing without a demand.
> It never did, and it never will. (Blassingame 1985: 204)

Homeownership remains the American dream, though for all too many it is a dream deferred. The predatory practices highlighted in this chapter constitute a major impediment, particularly for residents living in low-income minority neighborhoods. Access to mortgage loans and capital generally is essential for more balanced development, but it must be access on equitable terms. The exploitative practices documented in this chapter simply reinforce traditional patterns of uneven development and racial inequality and undermine the progress that has been made by the community reinvestment movement generally. Progress in responding to predatory practices is critical if progress is to continue.

Before a potential homeowner can even begin shopping for a loan, however, a property insurance policy must be obtained to protect both the borrower and the lender. The policies and practices of the property insurance industry have long constituted another arena of conflict. As the following chapter documents, place and race have been central to long-standing policy debates over the issue of insurance redlining.

Notes

A previous version of this chapter appeared as Gregory D. Squires, "The New Redlining: Predatory Lending in an Age of Financial Service Modernization," *Sage Race Relations Abstracts* 28, nos. 3–4 (2003): 5–18.

4

Racial Profiling, Insurance Style

*Very honestly, I think you write too many blacks. ... You got to sell
good, solid premium paying white people. ...The white works.*
—Sales manager for American Family Mutual Insurance Company,
1988 (from case files in *NAACP v. American Family
Mutual Insurance Company,* 1992)

It is unclear whether the mortgage lending or property insurance
industry "pioneered" the use of the neighborhood, and particularly
the racial composition of the neighborhood, in evaluating applicants
for housing-related financial services. But such redlining practices
have a long history. And if racial profiling is most closely associated
with the behavior of certain police officers and other security officials, it has a "rich" tradition in insurance.

Racial profiling has emerged as a leading civil rights issue in
social science research and policy circles today. Profiling refers to
practices through which individuals are classified, at least in part, on
the basis of their race or the racial composition of their neighborhoods
and treated differently as a result. Although the debate over racial profiling most frequently focuses on policing and administration of justice issues, a topic explored in Chapter 6, such practices are not
restricted to this arena. In fact, at least financially and economically,
racial profiling does far more damage in other areas of public and private life. One of those is the property insurance industry. The costs
include not just diminished opportunities for racial minorities but also
the exacerbation of uneven development of metropolitan areas and the
many costs associated with that pattern. In this chapter we examine
historical and ongoing practices of racial profiling and related discrim-

inatory actions on the part of the property insurance industry in the United States—actions that helped to create and reinforce the linkages among place, race, and privilege. These practices are hardly unique to any particular industry. In fact, they reflect long-standing racial stereotypes that have stigmatized racial minorities throughout much of American society and continue to do so at great expense to minority communities and metropolitan areas generally. Remedies are available, and directions for future policy initiatives are explored.

Insurance, Homeownership, and Urban Development

The property insurance industry has a long and continuing tradition of racial profiling. If such practices were once considered sound professional business practices and explicitly endorsed by the industry, few publicly defend them today. Yet they persist. Redlining and racial discrimination by mortgage lenders and banking institutions have long been subject to research and public policy initiatives (Goering and Wienk 1996; Haag 2000; Munnell et al. 1996; Ross and Yinger 2002; Stuart 2003), but the behavior of the property insurance industry, although equally pernicious, has been less scrutinized (Badain 1980; Galster et. al. 2001; Squires 1997). Yet insurance is critical, or, in the industry's term, "essential." If a potential homebuyer cannot obtain a property insurance policy, no lender can provide a mortgage. The risk of financial loss to the mortgage lender would simply be too great if the property was not insured. Should the home be damaged, the lender needs to know that its investment is secured and that the loan will be repaid. Property insurance on the home, along with the value of the land that could be sold in case the home were totally destroyed, provides that security. Without a mortgage, the vast majority of homeowners would not have been able to purchase their homes. In light of the essential nature of home insurance, lenders often refer their customers to local insurance agents or increasingly now offer insurance services themselves. So, as the Seventh Circuit Court of Appeals stated in the 1992 case *NAACP v. American Family Mutual Insurance Co.*, "No insurance, no loan; no loan, no house; lack of insurance thus makes housing unavailable."

Households experiencing what the industry refers to as a problem of "insurance availability" are not randomly scattered throughout metropolitan areas. They tend to be located within central city neighborhoods, usually with high concentrations of nonwhite residents. Although some rural communities experience availability problems due primarily to limited fire protection, for a variety of reasons this has been a particularly urban problem. For example, in Milwaukee, 72.4 percent of homes in white areas, compared to 61.6 percent of homes in black areas, were covered by insurers required to comply with that state's disclosure rules in 1999. (Very few states have such requirements, as will be discussed below.) Remaining homes either have no coverage or are protected by smaller insurers or so-called surplus lines or offshore or nonadmitted insurers. These insurers are not regulated by the states and, therefore, are not included in state guaranty funds, which means consumers are not protected if the companies should go bankrupt (Squires et al. 2001).

Urban communities tend to have older homes with electrical, heating, and other major systems that have not been updated in recent years. Older wood frame homes, generally concentrated in cities, pose a greater fire risk than newer suburban brick homes. The dense nature of housing patterns means that a fire on one property may damage a nearby property, leading insurers to avoid high concentrations of policies in a particular neighborhood. Theft rates are higher in many urban neighborhoods than in most suburban communities. Relatively lower valued dwellings in cities also make urban properties less profitable to insure. A recent insurance industry study of loss costs in eight major metropolitan areas between 1989 and 1994 found that the frequency of claims was 18 percent higher in cities than in the neighboring communities within 5 miles of the city boundaries; there were 124 claims per 1,000 insured homes in the cities, compared to 105 claims in the surrounding communities. And the average claim was 20 percent higher in cities. Consequently, industry costs per insured home were 42 percent greater for urban than suburban policyholders (Insurance Research Council 1997).

But in addition to risk factors that may differ between some cities and suburbs in general, a host of other practices that are not based on risk adversely affect urban communities. Redlining of older urban neighborhoods, including practices of racial profiling and discrimination, exacerbates urban insurance availability and affordability problems. Compounding the racial effect is the fact that racial minorities tend to have lower incomes, live in lower-valued homes, and reside in cities (U.S. Census Bureau 2002a). The connection between property insurance practices and the fate of cities was captured by a federal advisory committee in 1968, which observed:

Insurance is essential to revitalize our cities. It is a cornerstone of credit. Without insurance, banks and other financial institutions will not—and cannot—make loans. New housing cannot be constructed, and existing housing cannot be repaired. New businesses cannot expand, or even survive.

Without insurance, buildings are left to deteriorate; services, goods and jobs diminish. Efforts to rebuild our nation's inner cities cannot move forward. Communities without insurance are communities without hope. (President's National Advisory Panel 1968: 1)

There is a direct connection between the actions of the property insurance industry and the critical problems facing the nation's most distressed urban communities that was captured in the title of one law review article, "Property Insurance and the American Ghetto: A Study in Social Irresponsibility" (Yaspan 1970). If progress has been made since the federal advisory report in 1968, the problems of urban insurance availability and affordability, including their racial dimensions, retain their largely urban character. As another legal scholar concluded: "Hardest hit by unavailability and unaffordability difficulties are transitional neighborhoods in older cities and members of minority groups. So long as unavailability and unaffordability problems remain, communities without affordable insurance become communities with diminishing hope" (Badain 1980: 76).

A related reason for the significance of property insurance for cities and the economy in general is the sheer size of the industry. In 2001 the total assets of the insurance industry reached $4.2 trillion, with the assets of those other than life insurers totaling $881 billion. For all financial services sectors, including banks and securities, total assets were $37.6 trillion. So insurers accounted for just over 11 percent and non–life insurers accounted for just over 2 percent of total assets in financial services sectors (Insurance Information Institute 2003: 4). In 2000 the property insurance industry (which includes automobile, commercial, marine, and homeowners insurance) received $299.6 billion in premiums. (Premiums are the dollars collected for policies that are sold.) Homeowner premiums accounted for $32.4 billion of that amount. In 1999 the property insurance industry's net income was $20.6 billion. And the insurance industry generally, including life and health insurers as well as property insurers, employed 2.3 million people in the United States (Insurance Information Institute 2002: vii, 60).

Not surprisingly, in 1999 the states that generated the most premiums were primarily large urban states: California ranked first, followed by New York, Texas, Florida, and Illinois. Average premiums ranged from a low of $266 in Wisconsin to a high of $861 in Texas. Insurers generally pay out more in losses and loss cost expenses than they collect in premiums. In 2000 property insurers paid out approximately 10 percent more than they received from their underwriting activities. But in most years, earnings from invested funds, along with money set aside as loss reserves, compensate for underwriting losses and enable insurers to generate a profit (Insurance Information Institute 2002: 14, 64).

The property insurance industry, therefore, constitutes an important actor, economic and otherwise, in urban and metropolitan areas. It is also an integral piece of the institutional infrastructure of inequality in urban and metropolitan areas. The industry reflects and reinforces the role of race and place in framing opportunities confronting residents of the nation's cities and surrounding communities. The restructuring of US cities in the post–World War II decades has been accompanied by growing inequality and concentration of poverty, along with a range of social problems associated with those developments (Goldsmith 2002; Harrison and Bluestone 1988; Jargowsky 1996, 2003; Massey and Denton 1993; Wilson 1996; Wolff 1995). If the overt expression of racist sentiments has been subdued, the continuing reality of racial profiling, grounded in long-standing and persistent racial stereotypes, reveals the ongoing centrality of racism in the political economy of urban communities.

Using documents describing industry underwriting guidelines and marketing strategies, court documents, and research by government agencies, industry and community groups, and academics, we examine historical and contemporary practices of racial profiling and related forms of redlining and racial discrimination on the part of the property insurance industry. Such practices incorporate elements of both disparate treatment and disparate impact discrimination that are unlawful under the federal Fair Housing Act and many state statutes. Under the disparate treatment standard, plaintiffs must establish that the respondent intentionally discriminated on the basis of a protected class membership (e.g., race, ethnicity, gender). Under the disparate impact standard, intent is not necessary. The universal application of an apparently neutral policy or practice that excludes a disproportionate share of protected class members (e.g., racial minorities) would violate the act, unless the respondent could establish that there was a legitimate business purpose for that policy or practice and that no lesser discriminatory alternative was available to accomplish that objective (Crowell et al. 1994: 158–162). No parallel legal definition of racial profiling has emerged from the legislative debates and court cases in the fair housing area, but given the legal standards that have emerged, profiling clearly incorporates many of the elements of unlawful practices that have been identified.

Following the discussion of past and present profiling and discrimination, we explore successful efforts to combat these practices and offer policy recommendations to further reduce the role of race in the delivery of property insurance products and services. Racial profiling may not be as visible within the property insurance industry as it is in law enforcement, but insurers are equally proficient, perhaps because they have had so much practice.

The Insurance Industry's Character Problem: Moral, Morale, and Other Hazards

Insurers generate their revenue from the sale of insurance policies. In so doing, they incur a range of costs. In 2000 for each dollar collected in premiums, insurers paid 79.6 cents for claims, 25 cents for sales and administrative expenses, 2.5 cents in taxes and 1.3 cents in dividends. As noted above, these costs come to more than 100 percent, which is normal for most insurers' underwriting activities. Investment income compensates for these losses and permits insurers to generate a profit and continue making insurance available (Insurance Information Institute 2002: 14). But in order to stay competitive and maximize their returns, insurers need to determine whether a given applicant is eligible for a policy and, if so, how much to charge.

The insurance industry has one major problem. It does not know the actual cost of its product (an insurance policy) when the product is sold. That makes the decision to sell a policy, the price at which it should be sold, and other terms and conditions most problematic. Property insurance policies that cover homes are generally sold on an annual basis. A premium or price is charged and is often paid in full at the beginning of the policy period. But the cost to the insurer will not be known until the end of that time period. In most cases, no measurable damage to the home occurs, no claims are filed, and the insurer incurs few expenses other than transaction costs involved in processing the application and premium payments. In other cases, the property that is insured is damaged and, on occasion, totally destroyed. These costs generally far exceed the annual premium.

So the industry tries to determine in advance who is likely to experience a loss and how large those losses will be, and because it is too expensive to collect information on the unique characteristics of each applicant, the industry categorizes applicants into groups based on expected losses. Insurers attempt to identify those attributes that account for losses and which people share those attributes. Actuaries develop risk classifications, and underwriters determine in which class a given applicant belongs. Two sets of considerations generally enter into this process: (1) the characteristics of the property to be insured and the neighborhood in which it is located and (2) the characteristics of the people to be insured. Compounding the complexities is the fact that decisions by insurers can affect the behavior of those insured. Once a homeowner is insured against a particular risk or event that could cause a loss, the household has less of an incentive to avoid such situations and may take fewer precautions to reduce the chances of such an event occurring.

Several property-related factors affect whether or not an applicant is eligible and, if so, under what terms. They include the construction of the dwelling, which involves the type and age of materials, condition of the building, and adequacy of maintenance. For example, a wood frame building is more susceptible to fire than a brick structure, so all else being equal, a wooden home is more expensive to insure. Occupancy, or the purpose for which the home is used, is another factor. If the home is also used for certain types of businesses, it might be ineligible for home insurance, forcing the owner to seek out a commercial policy. Protection is a third consideration. The presence (or absence) of smoke alarms, security systems, and other protective devices can affect eligibility for coverage. Proximity to fire hydrants and the quality of local fire protection services are additional factors. Exposure is another property-related consideration. That term refers to hazards or risks in neighboring properties, such as certain types of industrial concerns, abandoned lots, or other environmental hazards (Wissoker et al. 1998).

Characteristics of the people living in the home also matter. The industry identifies two general types of hazards that relate to the character and behavior of applicants and insureds: "moral hazards" and "morale hazards." The former refers to any condition that increases the likelihood of fraud. Someone who is intent on fraud can pose challenges to an insurer. The industry argues, for example, that someone in financial trouble may be more likely to submit fraudulent claims. Requiring credit reports as part of the underwriting process is justified as part of an effort to learn if the applicant poses such a risk. Some companies will not provide a full replacement cost policy (i.e., a policy that will pay the full cost for repairing or replacing damage resulting from a loss) if the market value of the home is substantially less than its replacement cost. A market value policy might be offered, but such a policy covers only the current market value (purchase price less depreciation) of items, which is often insufficient to replace them. The fear is that such an insured has an incentive to burn the house down for the insurance money.

A morale hazard refers to a situation where an insured simply becomes less careful once their property is covered. Though no fraud is intended, knowing that an insurance policy is in force may cause some to be less careful in preventing loss than would otherwise be the case. This problem can be dealt with, at least in part, by offering incentives to take preventive action. For example, discounts can be offered for the installation of smoke alarms or security systems. Deductibles are often included, whereby the insured is responsible for at least the first few hundred or thousand dollars of any loss (Heimer 1982, 1985).

The challenge for the insurance industry is to identify those characteristics of individual properties and people that are conducive to loss and either avoid them or charge higher premiums. The overriding problem confronting insurers remains the fact that they still do not know the cost of its product when it is sold to the consumer. Race has been used as part of the effort to solve that problem. That is, in addition to the tools noted above, a long-standing practice of the industry has been to use race—both the race of individual applicants and the racial composition of neighborhoods—to classify and price risks. Where race is associated with loss, insurers may have a financial incentive to engage in "statistical discrimination," but these practices are illegal nevertheless. It is unlawful to use average characteristics of a racial group to determine whether housing-related services will be provided to any particular individual (Yinger 1995: 67–69). Where race is used but is demonstrably not predictive of loss, there is virtually no justification for such practices. Yet drawing on traditional stereotypes that persist throughout the United States (e.g., racial minorities and particularly blacks are still viewed as less motivated to work, more likely to be engaged in crime; see Feagin 2000; Bobo and Massagli 2001; Schuman et al. 1997), racial profiling in the insurance industry has been a fact of life that undercuts economic development opportunities for stigmatized groups and hinders urban redevelopment in general (Badain 1980; Metzger 2001; Powers 1997; Smith and Cloud 1997; Yaspan 1970). Consequently, minorities, particularly those who live in distressed neighborhoods, face the double whammy of race and place.

The Role of Race in Evaluating Risk and Marketing Products

The property insurance industry has long asserted that risk drives underwriting and pricing activity and that race has virtually nothing to do with these practices. Urban insurance availability and affordability, from this perspective, simply reflect the higher losses in those neighborhoods. As indicated above, one study of loss costs in eight major metropolitan areas found that as a result of greater frequency and higher costs of claims in urban communities than in surrounding neighborhoods, urban policyholders cost insurers 42 percent more per policy than did policyholders in nearby neighborhoods (American Insurance Association 1993; Insurance Research Council 1997; National Association of Independent Insurers 1994). Yet race has long been explicitly taken into consideration in evaluating risk (Heimer 1982; Yaspan 1970). Even if that were not the case, many industry practices have an adverse, disparate impact on minority communities, resulting in a higher share of residents in these communities being denied policies, charged higher prices, or otherwise offered less advantageous terms and conditions (Kincaid 1994; Powers 1997).

The following statement by one marketing consultant illustrates the importance of race, and the link between character and race that was widely and openly expressed, at least through the 1950s:

> It is difficult to draw a definite line between the acceptable and the undesirable colored or cheap mixed white areas; the near west side (Madison Street) and near north side (Clark Street) still attract the derelict or floating elements with "honky tonk," mercantiles and flop houses. Any liability in the areas described should be carefully scrutinized and, in case of Negro dwellings, usually only the better maintained, owner occupied risks are considered acceptable for profitable underwriting. (National Inspection Company 1958)

This statement makes it clear that one of the keys to profitable underwriting was racial discrimination. Apparently, where there were colored or mixed areas it was difficult to determine acceptable from unacceptable areas. And it was the racial composition of such neighborhoods that raised the initial question about acceptability. What was it about race that matters? Apparently, it was the association with derelict behavior. If there was profitable business to be written for "Negroes" (but apparently not for whites), only well-maintained properties in which the owner resides were acceptable.

More recently, through the early 1990s, at least one major insurer used explicit racial stereotypes to identify neighborhoods in Richmond, Virginia, where it avoided writing insurance. Among the neighborhood descriptions found in that company's marketing guidelines were the following:

> Difficult Times—Black Urbanite households with many children. … they do watch situation comedies and read T.V. guide.
> Metro Minority Families … mostly black families with school children. … they enjoy listening to news/talk radio, and watching prime time soap operas. (Housing Opportunities Made Equal 1998)

In part because of such marketing practices, a jury ruled that Nationwide Insurance Company violated the Virginia fair housing act (*Housing Opportunities Made Equal, Inc. v. Nationwide Mutual Insurance Company et al. No. 2B-2704,* Circuit Court, Richmond, VA, 1999).

Other labels recently employed by various consultants to characterize different types of neighborhoods that have guided insurers and other financial service providers in their marketing include "Low Income Southern Blacks," "Middle Class Black Families," and "Urban Hispanics." At least one of these firms has dropped the race and ethnic labels, but in ways that reflect a downgrading of those neighborhood clusters. "Middle Class Black Families" was changed to "Working Class Families," and "Low Income Southern Blacks" was replaced with "Hard Times" (Metzger 2001). The primary result is that many residents of such areas are offered less attractive products than are available in other communities, in part for reasons that are unrelated to the actual risk they pose. The American Family sales manager quoted at the beginning of this chapter makes it clear that race is important and offers a stereotypical explanation: whites work.

In a 1995 survey of insurance agents in the Lehigh Valley in southeastern Pennsylvania, 3 percent stated that an applicant's race was a factor in their decision to insure a home. When asked to agree or disagree with the statement, "The race of a homeowner is never a factor when deciding whether or not to insure a home," 94 percent said they "completely agree." When asked about "the racial mix of a neighborhood," 88 percent "completely agree" it was never a factor. The vast majority, in other words, state that race or racial composition is never a factor (Community Action Committee of the Lehigh Valley 1995: 5, 7). Yet more than twenty-five years after the Fair Housing Act was passed, at least some agents continue to openly endorse the use of race in the underwriting of insurance policies. This finding may well understate the number of agents who explicitly take race into account. Survey respondents often give what they perceive to be socially acceptable responses to interviewers that may differ from their true beliefs. When questions concern race, people generally provide answers that reflect a more liberal or tolerant attitude than some respondents actually hold (Schuman et al. 1997: 92–98).

In a confidential conversation in 2002, an insurance broker said he was often asked by a company he represented the following two questions in what he referred to as "verbal underwriting" for multi-family dwellings: (1) Is there any Section 8 at these properties? and (2) Are the kids in this neighborhood more likely to play hockey or basketball? Both of these questions were understood by this broker and by others to be subtle code words to elicit information on the race of the tenants (Luquetta 2002).

Much of this evidence is anecdotal, but there is also quantitative evidence of the systematic use of race and of practices that have a disparate impact on racial minorities. The National Association of Insurance Commissioners (NAIC), an organization of state law enforcement officials who regulate the insurance industry, examined the distribution and costs of homeowners insurance policies across thirty-three metropolitan areas in twenty-five states in the mid-1990s. Researchers found a statistically significant connection between the racial composition of the neighborhood and the number and cost of policies, even after controlling on loss experience and other demographic factors (Klein 1995, 1997; for contradictory findings in Texas, where the effect of race was not significant, see Grace and Klein 1999).

Some of the reasons for these disparities have been uncovered by fair housing organizations in audit or paired-testing studies. In these experiments, white and nonwhite "mystery shoppers" (or shoppers from white and nonwhite neighborhoods) are assigned the same relevant individual, home, and neighborhood characteristics and then they contact various insurance agents in their communities, posing as householders interested in purchasing a policy for their homes. The only difference between each pair is their race or the racial composition of the neighborhood where the home they want to insure is situated. Because each pair is matched on the relevant criteria (e.g., income and occupation of householder, age and construction of home, fire protection ratings of residential neighborhoods), any differences in treatment are assumed to constitute racial discrimination.

Tests of major insurers conducted by several fair housing organizations around the country have routinely found disparities in the way white and nonwhite testers and neighborhoods have been treated. White testers and testers from predominantly white neighborhoods generally have been aggressively pursued as customers, but blacks and Hispanics, as well as testers from black and Hispanic neighborhoods, have confronted many barriers, including insurers:

- showing willingness to provide a policy for whites but denying or referring minority applicants elsewhere;
- not returning calls from minority testers while promptly responding to whites;
- offering policies with different terms and conditions (e.g., full replacement cost policies for whites, market value policies for nonwhites);
- charging different prices for the same policy;
- requiring inspections in nonwhite but not white areas;
- requiring nonwhites to supply Social Security numbers (so credit checks could be run) but not soliciting such information from whites.

Between 1992 and 1994, the National Fair Housing Alliance tested major insurers in nine cities and found evidence of unlawful discrimination in the following percentages of tests in the respective cities: Chicago, 83 percent; Atlanta, 67 percent; Toledo, 62 percent; Milwaukee, 58 percent; Louisville, 56 percent; Cincinnati, 44 percent; Los Angeles, 44 percent; Akron, 37 percent; and Memphis, 32 percent (Smith and Cloud 1997: 108–109).

Similar disparate treatment has been found in the late 1990s in approximately half the tests of major insurers conducted by several fair housing organizations (National Fair Housing Alliance 2000; Smith and Cloud 1997; Toledo Fair Housing Center 1999). The one study that attempted to assess the extent of racial discrimination marketwide (rather than among particular insurers, as has been the case with most insurance testing that has occurred) did not find differences in terms of access to insurance. Researchers with the Urban Institute examined the Phoenix and New York City markets and found that quotes were offered to the vast majority of white, black, and Hispanic testers. But in Phoenix, Hispanics were slightly less likely to be offered full replacement coverage on the contents of their homes than were whites (92 percent and 95 percent, respectively) and were more likely to be told the quote would not be guaranteed without an inspection of the home (3 percent of Hispanics, compared to 0.4 percent among white testers who contacted the same agents). Quotes were also 12 percent higher for Hispanics, though in line with rates filed with the state insurance commissioner for different rating territories, which raises questions about the validity of those state-approved delineations. And in New York, white testers were slightly more likely to receive both a written and verbal quote (18.1 percent), compared to 11.8 percent for blacks, who were more likely to receive just a verbal quote. Though not large, these differences were statistically significant (Galster et al. 2001; Wissoker et al. 1998: 3).

Many insurers market their products in ways that, by intent or effect, favor white neighborhoods. The location of agents is one key indicator of where an insurer intends to do business. A study of agent location and underwriting activity in the Milwaukee metropolitan area found that two-thirds of all policies sold by these agents covered homes within the zip code or one that bordered the zip code in which their office was located. Coupled with the fact that the proportion of insurance agents in metropolitan areas located in central cities has consistently declined as their numbers have increased in suburban communities, the location (and relocation) of agents has an adverse, disparate impact on the service available in minority communities. In Milwaukee, for example, the number of suburban agents increased from thirty-two to 297 between 1960 and 1980; the number in the city initially grew from 113 to 157 during the 1960s but then dropped to 125 by 1980. The ratio of agents per 1,000 owner-occupied dwellings remained virtually constant in the city (1.01 and 1.09) while increasing from 0.34 to 1.25 in the suburbs (Squires et al. 1991). A study of two major insurers within the city of Chicago also revealed a concentration of agents in predominantly white neighborhoods, and an avoidance of nonwhite neighborhoods, within the city limits (Illinois Public Action 1993). Housing values, loss experience, and other economic and demographic changes might account for some of this movement. But studies of agent location in the St. Louis

and Milwaukee metropolitan areas found that the racial composition
of the neighborhood was associated with the number of agents and
agencies even after controlling for various socioeconomic characteristics, including loss experience, income, housing value, and age of
housing (Schultz 1995, 1997; Squires et al. 1991).

Underwriting guidelines used by many insurers have an adverse
impact on nonwhite communities. Restrictions associated with credit
history, lifestyle (e.g., prohibitions against more than one family in a
dwelling; references to morality, stability), employment history, and
marital status are frequently utilized though no business necessity has
been demonstrated (Powers 1997). Two commonly employed underwriting guidelines are maximum age and minimum value requirements. For example, insurers often reject or limit coverage for homes
that were built prior to 1950 or are valued at less than $100,000. The
disparate impact of maximum age and minimum value guidelines is
most evident. In 1999, 23.6 percent of owner-occupied housing units
nationwide were built prior to 1950. But 30.6 percent of black owner-
occupied housing units and 41.7 percent of Hispanic units were built
before 1950. And although 46.0 percent of all owner-occupied housing units were valued at less than $100,000, for blacks the figure was
65.5 percent, and for Hispanics it was 50.8 percent. Clearly, these two
underwriting guidelines exclude a larger share of black and Hispanic
households than white ones (US Census Bureau 2002a). Practices
that exclude a disproportionate share of a protected group may constitute unlawful, disparate impact discrimination, even in the absence
of evidence of intent to discriminate. These underwriting guidelines
may fall into this category and, arguably, would not constitute racial
profiling. But the impact of these underwriting guidelines is foresee-
able and, therefore, perhaps the racial effect is not unintentional.
Consequently, they comprise part of the complex web of practices
that constitutes racial profiling in the property insurance industry.

A related problematic underwriting rule is the moral hazard,
noted above, that many insurers assume exists when a property's
replacement value (what it would cost to repair or rebuild a home)
exceeds the market value (what it would sell for). For example, if a
home would cost $100,000 to rebuild but would sell for only
$50,000, the fear is that a homeowner would intentionally burn the
home in order to collect the insurance proceeds. Others contend that,
despite the apparent incentive, owner-occupants have many social
and psychological, as well as financial, investments in their homes
and do not present such a risk. The industry itself is split on the ques-

tion of whether or not homeowners are engaged in any significant arson-for-profit schemes. Arson has long been a problem in urban communities, but it is primarily a problem with commercial rather than personal property. In 1998 arson was reported to be a cause of fires in 10.8 percent of residential and 20.4 percent of nonresidential fires. Property damage from arson grew from $1.5 billion in 1991 to $2.4 billion in 1992 and then declined to $1.3 billion in 2000 (Insurance Information Institute 2002: 92, 96). Arson occurs primarily where property owners have encountered financial difficulties. They may owe back taxes, payments on loans that are overdue, or other debts they are unable to meet. They may have encountered an immediate emergency such as a medical crisis for a family member. But no empirical evidence has been presented to establish that homeowners residing in properties where replacement value exceeds market value are indeed "selling their homes to the insurance industry" (Brady 1984). Given the neighborhoods where replacement value most often exceeds market value, such an underwriting rule excludes a substantially higher share of homes in nonwhite than in white neighborhoods (Powers 1997).

Though clearly an under-researched issue, the claims process is also affected by racial and ethnic stereotypes held by many adjustors. (Adjustors are insurance professionals who evaluate losses and settle claims filed by policyholders [Brenner 1993: 4]). According to one former adjustor for a major insurer, "black claimants routinely received smaller settlements than white claimants," and her company "routinely set lower reserve amounts for Hispanics than for any other type of claimant" (Saadi 1987: 55, 58). Her company questioned claims filed by blacks and Hispanics more than those filed by whites, in part because of beliefs that racial and ethnic minorities did not occupy the same occupational status and, therefore, might falsify a claim to get more money or could simply be fooled into accepting less. Lower claims settlements were also justified on the grounds that the medical profession would not provide the same level of care for minorities, and therefore such claimants could not utilize the funds to the same extent as whites (Saadi 1987: 55–62).

An examination of claims settled following Hurricane Andrew in southern Florida in 1992 concluded that Hispanic claimants were 60 percent less likely than whites to be paid within sixty days of filing, after controlling for income and education of claimants and level of damage to homes. A law professor and a sociologist at the University of Miami observed insurance claims mediations and interviewed claimants, adjustors, and mediators. They noted the strong subjective dimension of the claims settlement process and the types of indicators adjustors looked for to identify the likelihood of fraud. The type of neighborhoods people lived in, the cars they drove, their business or professional background, their immigrant status, and other social attributes were openly acknowledged by adjustors as factors they take into consideration. Stereotypes adjustors held about immigrants generally and Hispanics in particular led them to be more suspicious of claims from these groups. There was no difference in the dollar amount of claims ultimately paid, just the length of time in paying them, which reinforced the conclusion that untrustworthiness was a major factor underlying the claims adjustment process (Baker and McElrath 1996, 1997).

There is a contradictory element to these stereotypes. If racial minorities are easier to exploit in the claims process, arguably they would be more profitable (and desirable) customers. But there is no evidence that the industry favors minority applicants on any systematic basis, and it appears just the opposite is the case. Again, limitations in data availability hinder efforts to precisely quantify the role of race in the sale and service of insurance products.

The insurance industry is primarily concerned with risk exposure when it writes policies. But perceptions of race and the places that minorities occupy have long influenced the industry's methods for assessing and responding to the ambiguous liabilities it assumes when it issues a policy. Debates over redlining and racial discrimination in the property insurance industry have raged for decades, but in recent years more aggressive responses have been proposed and in some cases implemented by community organizations, law enforcement officials, and the industry itself.

From Redlining to Reinvestment?

Responses to urban insurance availability problems, or redlining and racial discrimination by property insurers, have taken several forms. The NAIC has issued model laws prohibiting what is referred to as "unfair discrimination," and several states have implemented those statutes. But there has been little enforcement. State insurance commissioners have been missing in action in the insurance redlining debate. Their activities focus on rate regulation, establishing licensing procedures, reviewing financial statements, and determining solvency standards. Their primary concern is to ensure that companies remain solvent (Brenner 1993: 90). Several insurers have launched a range of voluntary initiatives, including educational programs, mentoring initiatives, and related outreach efforts. The most effective responses have come from fair housing organizations that have filed a series of lawsuits and administrative complaints, resulting in substantial institutional changes on the part of the nation's largest insurers. But given the absence of publicly available data on underwriting and marketing activities, it remains unclear how much progress has been made in eradicating the role of race and ameliorating urban insurance availability problems.

Two problems have undercut the effectiveness of state insurance commissioners: the absence of political will and the lack of resources. Those who enforce the law are often closely connected to the industry they are charged with regulating. A study of state legislators who are members of insurance committees in ten large states found that almost one-fifth either own or are agents for an insurance business or are attorneys with law firms that have large insurance practices (Hunter and Sissons 1995). Many state insurance commissioners came from and went to the industry before and after their public service as their state's chief insurance law enforcement officer (Paltrow 1998). And the resources available at the state level to regulate what are increasingly global corporations are insufficient. To illustrate, as of 1998, thirteen state insurance commissioners offices employed no actuaries to examine the fairness of rates that companies charged and the states approved. Indiana received 5,278 consumer complaints in 1997, bringing the total for the previous four years to more than 21,000. Disciplinary action was taken against eleven insurers. With a limited staff, the Indiana Department of Insurance simply forwarded most complaints to the companies against whom the complaints were filed (Paltrow 1998: A1).

Some states are engaged in a range of educational and outreach activities, often in conjunction with insurers and trade associations. The Neighborhood Reinvestment Corporation created a National Insurance Task Force, consisting of several leading insurance companies, state insurance commissioners, and trade associations, to conduct a range of educational initiatives. Homeowners are advised on loss prevention programs, including fire safety, crime prevention, and home maintenance efforts in order to reduce their risk potential and increase their eligibility for insurance. Insurance companies and agents are educated on how to identify good business in urban areas and to market their products in previously underserved communities (Neighborhood Reinvestment Corporation 1995, 1997).

The Cincinnati-based National African American Insurance Association is working with Howard University and the District of Columbia insurance commissioner to train minority students for careers in insurance (Mazier 2001a). The Independent Insurers Association of America and several insurers, including Chubb, Safeco, and Travelers, have joined in an effort to provide additional support for and to mentor minority agents (Mazier 2001b; Thomas 1999). These same insurers, along with others, have also launched formal diversity training to assist their agents in serving and working with minority communities (Ruquet 2001). Some insurers are simply finding profitable business in neighborhoods they had ignored in the past (Bowers 1999).

Fair housing organizations have been the most effective vehicle for changing the way property insurers serve urban communities in general and minority markets in particular. Since 1995, evidence produced primarily from paired testing audits conducted by nonprofit fair housing organizations has led to settlements of administrative complaints and lawsuits and one jury verdict involving several leading insurers (Allstate, State Farm, Farmers, American Family, Nationwide, Liberty, and others). This group represents the four-largest, and six of the ten-largest, homeowners insurers, accounting for half the premiums written in the US market in 2000 (Insurance Information Institute 2002: 61). As a result of these actions, these insurers have provided financial compensation to plaintiffs, eliminated maximum age and minimum value underwriting guidelines, opened agencies in previously underserved urban neighborhoods, developed educational and marketing campaigns in these communities, and financed future testing as part of an effort to evaluate the effectiveness of these reinvestment efforts. In some cases, funds have been made available to assist homeownership in urban communities, and in one case an affirmative action plan was implemented to increase employment opportunities for minorities at all levels within the company. One example is a $17 million commitment by Nationwide for damages and various reinvestment efforts in Richmond, Virginia (*Housing Opportunities Made Equal, Inc. v. Nationwide Mutual Insurance Company et al. No. 2B-2704*, Circuit Court, Richmond, VA 1999; Millen and Chamberlain 2001). American Family negotiated a $14.5 million agreement that included $5 million for plaintiffs and $9.5 million to subsidize loans and grants for home purchase and repair (*United States v. American Family Mutual Insurance Company*, C.A. No. 95-C-0327, E.D. Wisc. 1995); *NAACP v. American Family Mutual Insurance Company*, 978 F.2d 287, 7th Cir. 1992). Discussions are currently under way with insurers in several cities, and more settlements are likely.

An emerging point of contention is the industry's use of mathematical formulas, in which credit scores are systematically used in determining eligibility for and the price of insurance policies. Credit information had been used by some insurers for selected applications in the past, but now approximately 90 percent of property insurers use credit scores systematically in their underwriting or pricing activities (Ford 2003). Insurers claim that people with better credit scores are less likely to file claims. It is argued that those who are more careful in the management of their financial assets also will be more careful in their handling of other assets, including their homes and automobiles. Because credit scoring leads to more accurate pricing of insurance policies, according to this perspective, the market is more competitive, with more companies offering policies, resulting in greater choices for consumers (American Insurance Association, n.d.; Snyder 2003; Texas Department of Insurance 2004). Critics contend that due to racial disparities in income, debt ratios, bankruptcies, inaccurate credit reports, and other financial matters, the use of credit reports exerts a negative impact on minority communities and therefore constitutes a new form of redlining. One problem is that the data the industry rely on in drawing its conclusions are not available for public scrutiny, making independent verification of its claims difficult (Birnbaum 2003, 2004; Willis 2003). One outcome of this debate was the introduction of the 2003 Insurance Credit Score Disclosure and Reporting Act in the 107th Congress by Rep. Luis Gutierrez (D-IL). This bill would require insurers to disclose the use of credit scoring to all applicants, along with the impact of the credit score on the price of all policies; prohibit insurers from taking any adverse action regarding insurance coverage based solely on credit history; require insurers to refund premiums calculated on the basis of inaccurate credit information; and provide for additional protections for consumers in the use of credit information.

Despite the wide range and large number of new initiatives, it remains unclear just how differently property insurers are serving older urban communities and racial minorities. A critical piece of a future agenda is the documentation of precisely how effectively various communities are being served.

Beyond Racial Profiling:
Future Research and Policy Implications

Thirty-five years ago, when financial institutions were widely accused of redlining and racial discrimination, Congress stepped in and enacted three critical pieces of legislation, as discussed in Chapter Two. The Civil Rights Act of 1968 (the federal Fair Housing Act) banned racial discrimination in mortgage lending. In 1975 the Home Mortgage Disclosure Act (HMDA) required most mortgage lenders to annually disclose the number, type, and dollar amount of loans they made by census tract in all metropolitan areas. The act has been modified several times and now requires lenders to report the race, gender, and income of all applicants; the disposition of applications (e.g., whether they were approved or denied); and pricing information on selected high-cost loans. In 1977 the Community Reinvestment Act (CRA) prohibited redlining at the federal level. It places on all federal depository institutions (e.g., banks and savings and loans) an affirmative obligation to ascertain and be responsive to the credit needs of the communities they serve, including low- and moderate-income neighborhoods.

These statutes are widely credited with increasing lending activity in low- and moderate-income communities and for racial minorities in particular, as noted previously (Avery et al. 2005a; Gramlich 1998, 2002; Joint Center for Housing Studies 2002b; Meyer 1998). Disclosure, coupled with federal prohibitions, appears to have had the intended effect. No comparable requirements exist for property insurers. The limited disclosure data available have had some salutary effects. A broader, nationwide proposal might do for insurance what HMDA has done for mortgage lending.

A recent survey of all state insurance commissioners solicited information on HMDA-like disclosure requirements that were currently in place. Just eight states had some geographic disclosure requirements, all at the zip code level. Data on individual insurance companies were available in just four of these states. Loss experience and cost information were available at the aggregate level in three states. No state made loss or cost data and pricing information available for individual insurers (Squires et al. 2001).

Despite the limitations of available data, they have proven useful in some instances. Plaintiffs in the American Family case noted above utilized the Wisconsin disclosure data in negotiations that resulted in the $14.5 million settlement, including commitments to write at least 1,200 new policies and open new offices in Milwaukee's black community, to eliminate maximum age and minimum value underwriting guidelines, to provide $9.5 million in subsidized loans to support homeownership, and to carry out other reinvestment initiatives (Lynch 1997; Ritter 1997).

In an analysis of 1999 Wisconsin data, researchers found that six insurers had a market share in white zip codes that was at least 50 percent larger than their share in black areas. In regressing the percentage of owner-occupied dwellings covered on racial composition, race was negatively and statistically significantly associated with coverage for each insurer. Controlling on income resulted in a statistically significant finding for two insurers, Prudential and Integrity Mutual (Squires et al. 2001). Data on loss experience were not available. Research reported above by Robert W. Klein (1997) and Jay D. Schultz (1995, 1997) did control on loss experience because in their capacity as employees of the National Association of Insurance Commissioners and the Missouri Department of Insurance, they had access to information not available to the general public. Independent investigation of Prudential by fair housing organizations found that this insurer used maximum age and minimum value underwriting rules that adversely affected minority neighborhoods, placed relatively few agents in minority communities, refused to provide African American and Hispanic callers with the same level of information provided to white callers, and took other actions that made insurance less available in minority neighborhoods in Milwaukee, Philadelphia, Richmond, and Washington, D.C. A formal fair housing complaint was filed and is currently pending (*National Fair Housing Alliance v. Prudential*, Case Number 1:01CV02199, US District Court for the District of Columbia 2001).

From a public policy perspective, the logical next step is to enact a federal disclosure requirement for property insurers modeled on HMDA. Such a requirement would call for insurers to annually report information on applicants, properties, and neighborhoods, including the race, gender, and income of applicants; type of policy and amount of coverage applied for; replacement value of home; disposition of those applications; price of policy; census tract in which the property is located; structure (e.g., brick or frame) and age of home; number of rooms and square feet of home; number and severity of claims; and distance to nearest fire hydrant.

Such disclosure would allow for far more comprehensive understanding of which, if any, markets were underserved and would facilitate understanding of the extent to which race remains a factor. This information could assist insurers in their marketing strategies. It would help state insurance commissioners target scarce enforcement resources. And it would help community organizations identify potential partners for reinvestment initiatives. As John Taylor, executive director of the National Community Reinvestment Coalition, observed regarding disclosure in mortgage lending, "The mere act of data disclosure motivated partnerships among lending institutions, community organizations, and government agencies for designing new loan products and embarking on aggressive marketing campaigns for reaching those left out of wealth building and homeownership opportunities" (National Community Reinvestment Coalition 2001b).

Many fair housing and community development advocates, along with some policymakers, have also endorsed CRA-like requirements for the insurance industry. The proposed Community Reinvestment Modernization Act of 2001 (H.R. 4893, 106th Congress, 2nd Session, which has been introduced in subsequent years but not enacted) would establish an affirmative obligation for insurers to provide insurance products and investment activity in low- and moderate-income neighborhoods, along with comprehensive disclosure of where such services were being offered. Massachusetts requires insurers to invest in low-income communities in exchange for tax relief by that state. California has created a voluntary program in which community groups bring investment opportunities to the insurance commissioner, who attempts to attract commitments from insurers in that state to finance those projects (Luquetta and Goldberg 2001).

These are baby steps, however, relative to what lenders have been doing for decades and what appear to be the needs of many low-income and particularly minority neighborhoods. Again, absent systematic disclosure, it is difficult to identify areas of greatest need or appropriate intervention strategies. State regulators currently have the necessary data or the authority to collect them, but few have demonstrated a desire to do so. Social reform frequently bubbles up from the local level to states and the federal government. In light of the history of racial profiling and redlining in the property insurance industry, the contentious nature of responses, and the questions that persist, the time appears ripe for a federal insurance disclosure requirement.

Despite the limitations of current data availability, there is substantial anecdotal and quantitative evidence that indicates the persistence of racial profiling, discrimination, and redlining on the part of property insurers. But the fundamental causes of these problems extend far beyond the insurance industry. The specific policies and practices that have been identified are firmly grounded in stereotypes that continue to permeate the United States. A number of regulatory, legislative, and voluntary industry initiatives could ameliorate racial profiling and discrimination within the property insurance industry. But more meaningful progress in combating these industry-related problems may await more progress in addressing the problems of stereotyping and discrimination in American society generally.

Research on racial attitudes demonstrates that white Americans continue to view blacks as being less intelligent, less hardworking, and more prone to criminal behavior than whites (Feagin 2000: 109–140). When asked to account for racial disparities, many whites agree with the argument that blacks lack of motivation. Blacks' problems would be largely solved if they worked harder, according to this dominant perspective. Whites exhibit little recognition of past or present discrimination as a factor blocking black progress (Schuman et al. 1997: 155–170). Such beliefs reflect and reinforce patterns of inequality, leading to structured or institutionalized racial inequalities that often appear to be inevitable, if not natural, outcomes of intrinsic cultural characteristics (Bobo and Massagli 2001). Concerns with work and morality on the part of insurance agents, underwriters, and others simply reflect stereotypical attitudes that transcend any one industry.

Once formed, stereotypes, and the structured inequalities they generate, change slowly. If there is a kernel of truth to stereotypes (e.g., black unemployment is higher than white unemployment), there is a tendency to paint everyone in the group with the same broad brush. People respond to labels and their stereotypical images of those to whom the label has been attached, rather than to individuals in those groups. This results in sweeping misjudgments that have critical racial and spatial consequences (Bobo and Massagli 2001). Racial segregation, the uneven development of metropolitan areas characterized by urban sprawl and concentrated poverty, and the associated social costs are just some of those consequences (Orfield 1997, 2002; Rusk 1999). For an industry like insurance that depends on risk classification and the categorization (influenced by stereotypes) that it entails, the negative consequences are magnified.

It may well be that some urban neighborhoods pose greater risks to insurers than other neighborhoods that are not underserved.

Insurers may be responding to signals of the marketplace in their underwriting and pricing decisions. But to the extent that objective measures of risk explain the industry's behavior, a key question is why various neighborhoods pose different risk levels. To the industry, such uneven development is largely a reflection of the culture, morality, and behavior of residents, with race being a major determinant. Rarely does the industry point to disinvestment by private industry, fiscal crises of municipalities, public policy decisions that have long favored suburban over urban communities (e.g., federal highway construction, exclusionary zoning laws, mortgage deductions, and other subsidies for homeownership), steering by real estate agents, subjective and discriminatory property appraisals, and related examples (Gotham 2002; Jackson 1985, 2000; Massey and Denton 1993). Given these structural realities and the subjective stereotypes of the industry, eventually the prophecy becomes self-fulfilling, and it becomes "rational" to avoid some minority communities. But this reflects the "crackpot realism" Mills wrote about more than forty years ago (Mills 1958: 185–186). Such behavior is rational only given the larger irrationality of private practices and public policies that have nurtured uneven development (Dreier et al. 2001). As the evidence cited earlier indicates, however, the industry is not responding just to risk. Race appears to have an independent and adverse impact, even after loss experience, risk, and other objective measures are taken into account (Klein 1997; Schultz 1995, 1997).

Racial profiling persists in the insurance industry. It leads to unlawful disparate treatment and disparate impact discrimination and exacerbates uneven development and racial inequality generally. This dynamic is grounded in unflattering racial stereotypes that reinforce these structural dimensions of inequality. Profiling and discrimination may be less pervasive today than in previous decades, or these practices may simply be more subtle. Progress appears to have been made in recent years in part from "universal" approaches like loss mitigation and other educational efforts directed at urban consumers and insurers generally. (The broader ongoing debate between universal and race-specific policies is discussed in Chapter 7.) But racial disparities resulting from both objective economic factors and subjective discriminatory practices continue, and proposed remedies, to be effective, should be mindful of both overt and subtle racial dynamics. The necessary data do not exist to draw precise conclusions regarding the extent to which objective and subjective considerations drive these decisions. Insurers will always face the problem of not knowing the actual costs of its product when that product is sold, but steps can be taken to maximize the extent to which such decisionmaking is predicated on actual risk and minimize the role of race.

Insurance unavailability, or the availability of insurance on unequal terms and conditions, can deny homeownership before a family even has applied for a mortgage loan to buy a home. Insurance redlining denies homeownership, particularly in better neighborhoods, forcing families to seek housing in less desirable communities characterized by inferior education, limited opportunities for employment, exposure to crime, and other indicators of distress. These patterns reinforce the links among race, place, and privilege. In this chapter we have shown that insurance plays a critical gatekeeping function in the distribution of privilege.

The fact that racial discrimination persists in the insurance industry does not deny the fact that compensable losses do occur or suggest that they are randomly distributed throughout metropolitan areas. A major cause of loss is crime, a problem concentrated in particular neighborhoods. Insurers have long worked with law enforcement authorities and others to mitigate criminal activity. But most of their attention has been on what innocent individuals and households can do to reduce their chances of being a victim or increase opportunities for former offenders to find more productive outlets for their activities. Lost in virtually all debates over what to do about crime are actions that institutional actors can take to reduce crime. The following chapter examines the role that financial institutions, which have long provided the underpinnings for homeownership and business development, can take to reduce crime through community reinvestment initiatives.

Notes

A previous version of this chapter appeared as Gregory D. Squires, "Racial Profiling, Insurance Style: Insurance Redlining and the Uneven Development of Metropolitan America," *Journal of Urban Affairs* 25, no. 4 (2003): 391–410. Reprinted by permission of Blackwell Publishing.

5

How Home Mortgage Money Reduces Crime

You can't incarcerate your way out of this problem.
—Dan Satterberg (quoted in Butterfield 2003, A1)

In 2000 mortgage loan dollars were far more readily available than ever before to low-income borrowers, racial minorities, and residents of low-income and minority communities. Cities were also safer, and perceived to be safer by their residents, than had been the case in years (Federal Financial Institutions Examination Council 2003c; Grogan and Proscio 2000). A question that arises is whether neighborhood crime rates are lower where mortgage money is more available. If so, does public policy affect this equation? In the following pages, we find that the answer to both questions is yes. Therefore, if lower crime rates are critical for achieving the "good life" as discussed in Chapter 1, these findings suggest yet another path toward that end.

Access to credit reflects, at least in part, important public policy initiatives including enforcement of the Federal Fair Housing Act and the Community Reinvestment Act (Gramlich 1998; Joint Center for Housing Studies 2002b; National Community Reinvestment Coalition 2001a; Schwartz 1998a). Although racial discrimination persists in mortgage markets today (Turner et al. 2002), it appears that fair lending policy has had a positive influence. Housing opportunities are far more readily available to minority households and, as we demonstrated in Chapter 2, passage of the CRA has helped them access traditionally inaccessible predominantly white neighborhoods.

The perception and reality of safer streets also reflects, again at least in part, the contribution of public policy. As Paul S. Grogan and Tony Proscio (2000: 23, 29) observed in reference to the South Bronx—the site of Paul Newman's 1981 movie, *Fort Apache, the Bronx*—"it is a place where lower-income people can live affordably in tranquility and safety. ... Government was, throughout, an indispensable part of the solution."

Is the association between lending and crime coincidental? What is the relationship between access to capital and community crime rates? In this chapter we begin to address these questions by examining the relationship between one critical form of capital, home mortgage lending, and violent and property crime rates across neighborhoods in a US city in 2000.

Community development practitioners, city officials, and residents of many communities have long contended that both access to capital and safe streets are essential for healthy neighborhoods. Both are critical to the comeback many cities have experienced in recent years (Grogan and Proscio 2000). It is plausible that where home mortgage money is readily available, crime rates will be relatively low. If economic resources are plentiful, there is less incentive to resort to crime. But to date, no study has confirmed such a relationship.

What has been confirmed is that a range of neighborhood characteristics, independent of the traits of individual residents, are linked to crime. They include economic factors such as poverty, unemployment, public assistance, and homeownership, along with demographic characteristics such as population turnover, the number of young males, and the number of single-parent families. Access to capital and particularly home mortgages may affect several of these neighborhood characteristics. More lending obviously means more home-ownership. Homeownership is associated with lower levels of poverty and population instability (Long 1988; South and Crowder 1998a, 1998b). More importantly, however, mortgage lending may have an independent effect on neighborhood crime by providing capital for communities and their residents.

The link between mortgage lending and crime, however, has yet to be established, but doing so is critical. Anticrime policy in the past decade has focused heavily on tougher law enforcement and longer prison terms, a topic considered at length in Chapter 6. Many researchers reject this approach and call for investing in human capital and communities as a more effective strategy (Hagan 1994; Miller 2000; Sampson 2001). As budget deficits have skyrocketed, some governors and other elected officials are looking for alternatives to incarceration (von Zielbauer 2003). Such approaches are attractive for a variety of reasons. They can be more humane. They may save tax dollars. But until these approaches are demonstrated to be associated with lower crime rates, they are unlikely to become mainstream policy.

Social Disorganization and Urban Crime

Social disorganization theory has emerged as the critical framework for understanding the relationship between community characteristics and crime in urban areas. According to the theory, certain neighborhood factors can lead to social disorganization, defined as the inability of a community to realize the common values of its residents and maintain effective social controls (Kornhauser 1978: 120). Social disorganization, in turn, can cause crime.

Residential (in)stability is one community characteristic believed to be associated with social (dis)organization. Residential stability in communities lowers crime rates by promoting social organization and heightened levels of supervision or social control; stable neighborhoods are more likely to have thriving businesses and effective neighborhood organizations as well as residents that know one another, interact on a regular basis, and look out for and protect each other's property. Communities with high turnover rates, however, tend to have lower levels of social organization, lower levels of supervision and social control, and therefore higher crime rates (Sampson and Groves 1989; Warner and Rountree 1997).

An important correlate of residential stability is homeownership. In addition to the many individual- and community-level benefits described in previous chapters, homeownership is critical in promoting stability and organization in communities. After controlling for poverty, racial composition, and other factors, studies show that neighborhoods where residents own their own homes have lower crime rates than neighborhoods where most residents are renters. Richard D. Alba, John R. Logan, and Paul E. Bellair (1994: 412) find that owning a home enables residents to live in safer communities. According to their study, homeowners reside in communities where violent crime rates are significantly lower than in communities where comparable renters reside.

Because of greater access to mortgage dollars for minority and economically disadvantaged households, homeownership rates for these groups are at an all-time high. In 2000, African American homeownership was nearly 48 percent and the Hispanic homeownership rate was 46 percent—both record highs. White homeownership also was at an all time high at 74 percent (US Department of Housing and Urban Development 2000a). There is a clear link between mortgage lending, homeownership, and residential instability: mortgage loans promote homeownership (without a mortgage, homeownership would be financially impossible for the vast majority of families) and reduce residential instability in the long run—all of which contribute to lower crime rates. Access to capital—particularly home mortgages—would likely affect poverty, income, and wealth inequalities, in addition to homeownership and residential instability.

Most importantly, however, access to home loans may have a direct effect on crime by providing capital and its related expectations for communities. That is, lending may have an independent effect on crime, above and beyond its contribution to homeownership and other neighborhood factors. A simple cost-benefit analysis may account for such a relationship. As Robert K. Merton observed in his classic 1968 work *Social Theory and Social Structure*, when individuals have conventional goals (e.g., accumulation of wealth), but conventional means to their attainment are blocked, they often resort to unconventional or deviant, and sometimes criminal, means to obtain those goals. If access to capital is denied, and particularly if it is denied for what are perceived to be unfair or even illegal reasons, at the margin some individuals might resort to criminal means to obtain material wealth. Where loans, and therefore conventional means for achieving these goals, are available, there is less of an incentive to resort to criminal behavior.

Moreover, access to, or the absence of, mortgage lending sends a signal to residents, business owners, and others in a community that their neighborhood is prospering or is in distress. The level of mortgage lending activity has a symbolic value that translates into very real material differences in attitudes toward and the quality of life in a community. When residents learn that their neighbors cannot secure loans or can only secure government-insured loans, or when they see fewer banks and more check cashers, such patterns indicate to many that the area is in trouble. Alternatively, when conventional financial service providers actively market their products and residents are able to secure loans, it signals that the neighborhood is prospering. Residents of local communities and others in the metropolitan region are often quite sensitive to these signals. Many are visible from just living in and traveling through the community. Families talk to each other. Small business owners meet with their bankers. Residents read local newspapers. Observing these patterns of urban development and experiencing their consequences affects the cost-benefit analysis of at least some residents in their decisions to utilize conventional or unconventional means in pursuit of their goals. Consequently, the level of criminal activity is one correlate of neighborhood economic well-being (National Commission on Neighborhoods 1979; von Hoffman 2003).

Previous research has investigated the relationship between crime and residential mobility, poverty, unemployment, and other factors. To date, however, no study has systematically examined the relationship between mortgage lending and crime, in part because most studies focus exclusively on intra-neighborhood influences on crime. Social disorganization theory as traditionally conceptualized is hampered by a restricted view of community that fails to account for the larger political and structural forces that shape communities— forces that have been detailed in preceding chapters (Bursik and Grasmick 1993: 52; Dreier et al. 2001; Kubrin and Weitzer 2003; Orfield 2002; Sampson and Wilson 1995: 48; Squires 2002). As Robert J. Sampson (2001: 102) asserts, "neglecting the vertical connections (or lack thereof) that residents have to extra-communal resources and sources of power obscures the structural backdrop to community social organization." A more complete framework would incorporate the role of extra-community institutions (such as mortgage lenders and other financial institutions) and the wider political environment in which local communities are embedded. Neighborhoods differ greatly in their ties to external decisionmakers (Guest 2000) and hence in their capacity to lobby city government and businesses to invest in the community.

Moreover, many community characteristics hypothesized to underlie crime rates, such as residential instability, concentration of the poor, family disruption, and weak social networks and social control, appear to stem directly from planned governmental policies at local, state, and federal levels, as well as decisions by private investors. Redlining and disinvestment by banks, fueled by regulatory initiatives (or the lack thereof) may contribute to crime by encouraging neighborhood deterioration, forced migration via gentrification, and instability. Alternatively, access to mortgage loan dollars and effective regulation (e.g., enforcement of fair lending and community reinvestment requirements) may reduce crime directly by introducing capital into communities or indirectly by promoting homeownership and reducing residential instability in the long run.

Such a claim is not farfetched. Metropolitan statistical areas (MSAs) with relatively high levels of mortgage lending have relatively low crime rates. Among MSAs with populations greater than 500,000, the bivariate correlation between average home loan amount and crime is statistically significant and negative ($r = -.265$, p < .05).[1] Although this correlation at the national level is suggestive, a more appropriate analysis of the lending-crime relationship would be at the neighborhood level within cities. Crime is a local phenomenon and social disorganization theory is couched at the neighborhood level, as the main processes linking social environments and crime depend, at least to some extent, on interaction with others who live nearby (Sampson 1986). For this reason, we examined patterns of lending and crime across neighborhoods in one city: Seattle, Washington. With a population of over 550,000, of which nonwhites account for 30 percent, Seattle is fairly representative of cities in the United States and has been the focus of numerous studies of community crime rates (Crutchfield 1989; Kubrin 2000; Miethe and McDowall 1993; Warner and Rountree 1997). This study builds on that literature. In this chapter, we examine the direct effects of lending on crime, controlling for a range of variables traditionally associated with neighborhood crime rates.

Robert J. Sampson and William Julius Wilson (1995: 54) emphasize the importance of analyzing crime at the neighborhood level and the policy context in which crime occurs when they contend: "On the basis of our theoretical framework, we conclude that community-level factors ... are fruitful areas of future inquiry, especially as they are affected by macrolevel public policies regarding housing, municipal services, and employment." We agree wholeheartedly. To date no research has examined the effects of home mortgage lending practices on urban crime rates. In fact, there is very little overlap in the lending and crime literatures and policy debates, despite the widespread assumptions by many advocates about such a relationship. Thus, this chapter provides the first documentation of the relationship between capital and neighborhood crime.

The Research Strategy

To examine the relationship between lending and crime, we performed regression analyses using data on home mortgage loans in conjunction with census and crime data for census tracts in Seattle. Census tracts approximate neighborhoods and are the smallest geographic level for which the home mortgage lending and crime data are available.[2]

Data on lending come from the same 2000 Home Mortgage Disclosure Act (HMDA) reports that we used in Chapter 2. As before, we examine single-family-home purchase loans. Our focus is on the amount of loan dollars given to homebuyers, rather than the simple number of loans originated, because the former is a better measure of the aggregate investment in various neighborhoods. Loan amount is an explicit indicator of the dollars invested in the community. For example, two neighborhoods each could have received thirty new mortgage loans in a given year, but in one community the average loan amount might be twice as large as in the other community. As such, the number of loans would be a misleading indicator of the relative investment in those two neighborhoods. Also, given the multiplier effect of any investment including mortgage loans (Williamson et al. 2002), average dollar amount is a better indicator of the level of neighborhood investment. Thus, our lending measure of interest is the average HMDA loan dollar amount per homebuyer (created by dividing the total dollar amount of loans in a census tract by the total number of loans originated). Again, because CRA-covered institutions have an explicit legal mandate to serve low- and moderate-income neighborhoods and thus may have a greater impact on crime than mortgage lenders generally, we use another measure that reflects the average loan amount for CRA lenders (per homebuyer). The first measure captures the effect of lending practices on crime, and the second measure reflects the impact of public policy.

Eleven variables were constructed from the 2000 census to reflect critical neighborhood differences:

1. poverty rate, defined as the percentage of persons living below the poverty level;
2. percent on public assistance, defined as the percentage of households receiving public assistance, including (a) supplementary security income payments made by federal or state welfare agencies to low-income persons aged sixty-five years old or over, blind or disabled, (b) aid to families with dependent children, and (c) general assistance;
3. median household income;
4. unemployment rate, defined as the percentage of unemployed persons ages sixteen and over;

5. percent black, defined as the percentage of non-Hispanic blacks in the population;

6. percent young males, defined as the percentage of young males ages fourteen to twenty-four;

7. percent female-headed households, defined as the percentage of family households headed by females with no husband present and with children seventeen and under;

8. divorce rate, defined as the percentage of divorced persons ages fifteen and over;

9. residential mobility rate, defined as the percentage of persons ages five and over who have changed residences in the past five years;

10. renters rate, defined as the percentage of occupied housing units that are occupied by renters (as opposed to homeowners); and

11. median housing value, defined as the median housing value for owner-occupied housing units.

The social disorganization literature has demonstrated that these characteristics are related to community crime rates (Krivo and Peterson 1996; Kubrin 2000; Morenoff et al. 2001; Warner and Rountree 1997).

An important variable that classifies tracts as within or not within the Seattle central business district (CBD) is included in the analyses because few and atypical persons live in CBD tracts. In Seattle today, CBD residents tend to be urban professionals with high incomes or people who are poor and homeless. Controlling for whether tracts are inside or outside the CBD minimizes the likelihood that the unique characteristics of this area will distort the results (Crutchfield 1989; Kubrin 2000).[3]

Data to compute total, violent, and property crime rates at the census tract level came from Seattle Police Department annual reports. Following common practice, three-year (1999–2001) average crime rates (per 1,000 population) were calculated to minimize the impact of annual fluctuations. The violent crime rate sums murder, rape, robbery, and assault rates, whereas the property crime rate is calculated as a sum of the burglary, larceny, and auto-theft rates.[4]

One critical issue is the causal ordering of the lending-crime relationship. We argue that lending affects crime. However, a case could be made for reverse causal effects—that is, crime could affect lending. In other words, the relationship between lending and crime could be bidirectional. If that is true, standard linear regression models are problematic; these models assume that errors in the dependent variable are uncorrelated with the independent variables. When that is not the case, such as when relationships between variables are bidirectional, linear regression using OLS (ordinary least squares) no longer provides optimal model estimates. For this reason, we test the relationship between lending and crime using two-stage least-squares regression (2SLS), a common practice in neighborhood research (Bellair 2000; Markowitz et al. 2001).[5] One challenge with 2SLS is identifying instrumental variables—those that influence the independent but not the dependent variables (see discussion in Bellair 2000). However, we identified an effective instrumental variable: age of the housing stock (defined in the census as the average median year in which the homes were built for each census tract). The age of the housing stock is associated with lending practices, as older homes generally have lower market value, but not with crime rates. The 2SLS regression models are run in SPSS and the results reported below are adjusted to account for the effect of crime on lending. Consequently, we are able to take into consideration the bidirectional nature of the relationship between lending and crime.[6]

The Research Findings

The main finding is that lending is associated with crime. As will be shown below, this relationship holds after controlling for a range of neighborhood socioeconomic variables—most importantly, after accounting for homeownership and residential mobility—and after adjusting for the reciprocal effects of crime on lending. The relationship is strongest where CRA lending is involved.

Means, standard deviations, and bivariate correlations for all variables are presented in Table 5.1. The average mortgage loan amount per homebuyer across Seattle neighborhoods was $212,000, whereas the average CRA mortgage loan amount per homebuyer was slightly higher at $215,000. Consistent with crime patterns throughout the United States, property offenses comprised the majority of reported crimes in Seattle in 2000. The average rates for property and violent crime, respectively, were 83.85 and 8.36 per 1,000 population. As expected, the explanatory variables, and particularly disadvantage, have positive relationships with violent and property crime, excluding the percentage of female-headed households. More importantly, similar to the relationship found at the MSA level, mortgage lending is significantly negatively associated with crime. As the aver-

Table 5.1 Correlations and Descriptives for All Variables

	1	2	3	4	5	6	7	8	9	10	11	12	13	14	15	16	17	18	19
1. Total crime rate	1.00	.85[a]	.99[a]	.69[a]	.42[a]	-.65[a]	.52[a]	.46[a]	.63[a]	.63[a]	.69[a]	.27[a]	.58[a]	-.17	.47[a]	.61[a]	-.28[a]	-.28[a]	-.33[a]
2. Violent crime rate		1.00	.81[a]	.78[a]	.61[a]	-.73[a]	.61[a]	.66[a]	.80[a]	.51[a]	.64[a]	.38[a]	.54[a]	.10	.42[a]	.46[a]	-.44[a]	-.43[a]	-.47[a]
3. Property crime rate			1.00	.66[a]	.38[a]	-.62[a]	.49[a]	.42[a]	.59[a]	.63[a]	.69[a]	.25[a]	.57[a]	-.20[a]	.47[a]	.62[a]	-.26[a]	-.25[a]	-.30[a]
4. Poverty rate				1.00	.58[a]	-.84[a]	.65[a]	.60[a]	.89[a]	.65[a]	.73[a]	.58[a]	.71[a]	.07	.23[a]	.34[a]	-.47[a]	-.42[a]	-.44[a]
5. Percent public assistance					1.00	-.50[a]	.33[a]	.51[a]	.67[a]	.12	.27[a]	.22[a]	.17	.47[a]	.28[a]	.18	-.40[a]	-.45[a]	-.47[a]
6. Median household income						1.00	-.57[a]	-.52[a]	-.82[a]	-.67[a]	-.80[a]	-.52[a]	-.73[a]	.01	-.34[a]	-.33[a]	.65[a]	.60	.62[a]
7. Unemployment rate							1.00	.51[a]	.76[a]	.46[a]	.49[a]	.34[a]	.49[a]	-.04	.20[a]	.40[a]	-.38[a]	-.29[a]	-.30[a]
8. Percent black								1.00	.71[a]	.24[a]	.34[a]	.29[a]	.27[a]	.38[a]	.25[a]	.15	-.39[a]	-.36[a]	-.36[a]
9. Disadvantage factor									1.00	.48[a]	.62[a]	.43[a]	.55[a]	.20[a]	.29[a]	.35[a]	-.51[a]	-.45[a]	-.46[a]
10. Residential mobility rate										1.00	.90[a]	.57[a]	.95[a]	-.45[a]	.20[a]	.40[a]	-.28[a]	-.18[a]	-.19[a]
11. Renters rate											1.00	.51[a]	.93[a]	-.34[a]	.31[a]	.39[a]	-.33[a]	-.26[a]	-.28[a]
12. Percent young males												1.00	.73[a]	-.07	-.25[a]	-.01	-.48[a]	-.44[a]	-.45[a]

continues

Table 5.1 continued

	1	2	3	4	5	6	7	8	9	10	11	12	13	14	15	16	17	18	19
13. Residential mobility factor													1.00	−.40[a]	.09	.32[a]	−.37[a]	−.27[a]	−.28[a]
14. Percent female-headed households														1.00	.09	−.38[a]	−.23[a]	−.37[a]	−.36[a]
15. Divorce rate															1.00	.41[a]	−.10	−.12	−.15
16. Central business district (0 = no)																1.00	−.12	.06	.01
17. Median household value																	1.00	.87[a]	.89[a]
18. Average HMDA loan $ per home buyer																		1.00	.99[a]
19. Average CRA HMDA loan $ per home buyer																			1.00
X̄	92.59	8.36	83.85	.12	.03	$47	.04	.08	0	.56	.50	.07	0	.04	.11	.07	$255	$212	$215
SD	106.37	12.89	94.96	.10	.03	$16	.02	.10	1.00	.14	.23	.06	1.00	.04	.03	.26	$92	$63	$66

Source: 2000 Census and HMDA data.
Notes: Means and standard deviations are based on unlogged values.
a. p < .05.

age loan amount per homebuyer increases in neighborhoods, violent and property crime rates decrease ($r = -.43$, $r = -.25$). The relationship is even stronger for average CRA loan amount and crime ($r = -.47$, $r = -.30$). These correlations once again suggest initial support for a mortgage lending–crime relationship.

The relationships between disadvantage and crime and lending and crime can be visually illustrated. Figure 5.1 plots the distributions of disadvantage and crime in Seattle neighborhoods. As can be seen, crimes are not randomly distributed but are clustered primarily in the center of the city. Furthermore, the darkest areas of the map— which indicate those neighborhoods with the highest disadvantage levels—experience the greatest number of crimes.

Figure 5.2 displays the association between home mortgage lending and crime. In this figure, the darkest areas of the map represent the highest crime areas (low: < 73.13 crimes per 1,000; moderate: 73.14–182.05 crimes per 1,000; high: 182.06–443.23 crimes per 1,000; extreme: > 443.24 crimes per 1,000). As Figure 5.2 shows, areas with greater lending activity, where the average home mortgage loan amount per homebuyer is greater, have lower crime rates. Once again, we see support for a lending-crime relationship. At issue, however, is whether the significant negative association between lending and crime will remain after controlling for other community characteristics known to be associated with crime. To determine this, we turn to the regression results.

Table 5.2 displays the 2SLS regression results for the average loan amount per homebuyer and crime, controlling for other community characteristics, as well as adjusting for the reciprocal effect of crime on lending. As expected, disadvantage, residential mobility, the divorce rate, and central business district are all significantly positively associated with violent and property crime rates. More importantly, however, even after controlling for these factors, greater home mortgage lending is significantly associated with lower violent crime levels in Seattle neighborhoods. The standardized coefficient for the relationship between lending and crime is –.215. (This measure can vary from 0, meaning there is no connection between the two variables, to either 1 or –1, indicating a perfect relationship between the two.) Thus, as the average loan amount increases in tracts, the violent crime rate decreases.[7] (See also Table 5.3.)

The effects of lending on crime are even greater for mortgage loans made by CRA-covered institutions. Regression results for average CRA loan amount per homebuyer and crime are displayed

Figure 5.1   Disadvantage and Crime in Seattle Neighborhoods

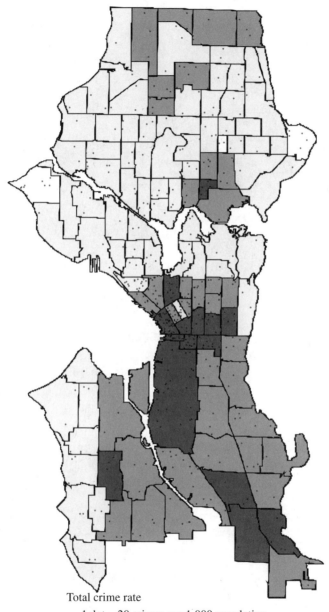

Total crime rate

· 1 dot = 20 crimes per 1,000 population

Disadvantage level

 Low

Moderate

High

Figure 5.2 Home Mortgage Lending and Crime in Seattle Neighborhoods

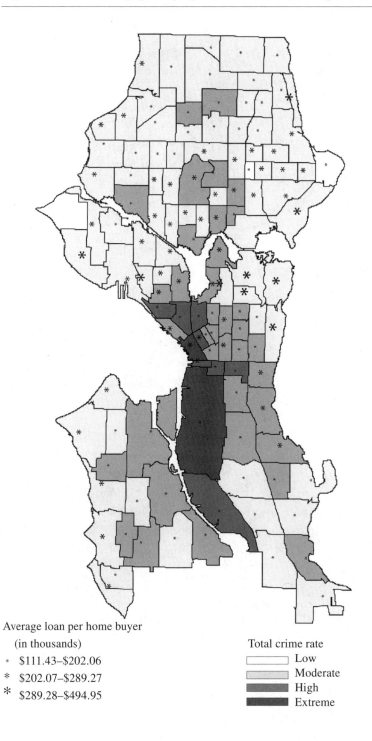

Average loan per home buyer
  (in thousands)

* $111.43–$202.06

* $202.07–$289.27

* $289.28–$494.95

Total crime rate

☐ Low
☐ Moderate
☐ High
☐ Extreme

Table 5.2   2SLS Regression Results for Average HMDA Loan $ per Homebuyer and Crime

Determinants	Total Crime			Violent Crime			Property Crime		
	Beta	Unstand. Coeff.	SE	Beta	Unstand. Coeff.	SE	Beta	Unstand. Coeff.	SE
Disadvantage	.317[c]	.222	.058	.503[c]	.559	.092	.265[b]	.182	.059
Residential mobility	.319[c]	.240	.058	.214[b]	.255	.091	.338[c]	.248	.058
Percent female-headed households	−.136	−.113	.066	.096	.126	.103	−.158	−.127	.066
Divorce rate	.152[b]	3.441	1.270	.126[a]	4.519	1.994	.155[b]	3.410	1.274
Central business district	.287[c]	.761	.195	.222[b]	.934	.307	.292[c]	.756	.196
Median housing value	.062	.049	.089	.123	.154	.139	.046	.036	.089
Average HMDA loan $ amount	−.148	−.392	.290	−.215[a]	−.905	.456	−.134	−.348	.291
Constant	—	5.35[c]	1.393	—	5.76[b]	2.187	—	5.0[c]	1.40
Adjusted R^2		.71			.72			.69	

Sources: 2000 Census and HMDA Data; 1999–2001 Seattle Police Department Annual Report Data.
Notes: a. p < .05.
b. p < .01.
c. p < .001.

in Table 5.4. Once again, average loan amount is negatively associated with violent crime rates (the coefficient is −.301 compared to −.215 for all loans). In addition, for CRA loans, lending is also negatively associated with property crime rates; the coefficient is −.262.[8]

These results demonstrate the association between home mortgage lending and crime. Even after controlling for disadvantage, mobility, housing value, and other important correlates of community crime, and taking into account the reciprocal relationship between lending and crime, average loan amount and particularly average CRA loan amount are significantly associated with lower crime rates in Seattle neighborhoods. Further support for the lending-crime relationship is evident given an increase in the variation in crime explained when the lending variables are included. For example,

Table 5.3　2SLS Regression Results Comparing Effects of Housing Value and Lending on Crime[a]

	Total Crime		Violent Crime		Property Crime	
Determinants	Model 1	Model 2	Model 1	Model 2	Model 1	Model 2
Disadvantage	.317[e]	.320[e]	.504[e]	.519[e]	.266[d]	.267[d]
	.223	.228	.561	.577	.182	.186
	(.058)	(.065)	(.092)	(.093)	(.058)	(.066)
Residential mobility	.315[e]	.294[d]	.207[d]	.222[d]	.335[e]	.310[d]
	.237	.210	.246	.247	.246	.216
	(.058)	(.065)	(.091)	(.092)	(.058)	(.065)
Percent female-headed	−.147[b]	−.007	.076	.139	−.165[c]	−.018
households	−.121	−.005	.099	.170	−.134	−.014
	(.064)	(.070)	(.100)	(.100)	(.064)	(.071)
Divorce rate	.153[d]	.228[e]	.129[c]	.158[d]	.156[d]	.235[e]
	3.466	5.036	4.596	5.432	3.428	5.069
	(1.265)	(1.395)	(1.994)	(1.985)	(1.268)	(1.411)
Central business district	.273[e]	.313[e]	.194[d]	.192[d]	.281[e]	.325[e]
	.723	.843	.813	.807	.728	.856
	(.182)	(.204)	(.287)	(.290)	(.182)	(.206)
Median housing value	—	.046	—	−.028	—	.051
		.036		−.034		.038
		(.052)		(.074)		(.053)
Average HMDA loan	−.098	—	−.115[b]	—	−.096	—
$ amount	−.259		−.484		−.250	
	(.159)		(.251)		(.160)	
Constant	4.7[e]	3.46[e]	3.8[d]	1.48[e]	4.6[e]	3.33[e]
	(.835)	(.305)	(1.316)	(.434)	(.837)	(.308)
Adjusted R^2	.71	.64	.71	.70	.70	.62

Notes: a. Entries are standardized coefficients and unstandardized coefficients followed by standard errors in parenthesis.
　b. $p < .06$.
　c. $p < .05$.
　d. $p < .01$.
　e. $p < .001$.

without the average loan amount variable, the variance explained for total crime is .64; adding the lending variable results in a greater amount of explained variance: .71. The same is true regarding the CRA lending variable. In sum, mortgage lending activity is related to lower crime rates in Seattle communities.

Table 5.4   2SLS Regression Results for Average CRA HMDA Loan $ per Homebuyer and Crime

Determinants	Total Crime			Violent Crime			Property Crime		
	Beta	Unstand. Coeff.	SE	Beta	Unstand. Coeff.	SE	Beta	Unstand. Coeff.	SE
Disadvantage	.329[c]	.226	.058	.511[c]	.564	.092	.277[b]	.186	.058
Residential mobility	.312[c]	.232	.058	.209[b]	.249	.091	.331[c]	.240	.058
Percent female-headed households	−.143	−.116	.065	.095	.124	.103	−.165[a]	−.131	.066
Divorce rate	.151[b]	3.342	1.257	.122[a]	4.327	1.982	.154[b]	3.322	1.263
Central business district	.276[c]	.757	.197	.210[b]	.922	.311	.281[c]	.750	.198
Median housing value	.177	.138	.092	.202	.252	.145	.161	.122	.092
Average HMDA CRA loan $ amount	−.276[a]	−.697	.289	−.301[b]	−1.217	.456	−.262[a]	−.645	.291
Constant		6.7[c]	1.38		7.2[c]	2.177		6.4[c]	1.39
Adjusted R^2		.71			.72			.69	

Notes: a. $p < .05$.
b. $p < .01$.
c. $p < .001$.

Investment, Not Incarceration

Investment matters and policy counts. Where mortgage capital is more readily available, crime rates are lower. This relationship holds even after taking into account those factors that have long been understood to influence crime (e.g., poverty, residential instability, divorce). And the relationship is greater for those loans most influenced by public policy requiring lenders to be responsive to traditionally underserved urban markets. That is, mortgage loans made by lenders under the jurisdiction of the Community Reinvestment Act are more strongly associated with lower crime rates than are mortgage loans generally, which is perhaps another unintended positive effect of the CRA. Just as we found in Chapter 2 that the CRA increases minority access to white neighborhoods, these findings show that the act also ameliorates neighborhood crime.

Table 5.5   2SLS Regression Results Comparing Effects of Housing
Value and CRA Lending on Crime[a]

Determinants	Total Crime		Violent Crime		Property Crime	
	Model 1	Model 2	Model 1	Model 2	Model 1	Model 2
Disadvantage	.326[d]	.320[d]	.508[d]	.519[d]	.274[c]	.267[c]
	.224	.228	.560	.577	.184	.186
	(.058)	(.065)	(.092)	(.093)	(.059)	(.066)
Residential mobility	.304[d]	.294[c]	.200[b]	.222[c]	.324[d]	.310[c]
	.226	.210	.239	.247	.235	.216
	(.058)	(.065)	(.091)	(.092)	(.058)	(.065)
Percent female-headed	−.168[b]	−.007	.067	.139	−.188[b]	−.018
households	−.137	−.005	.087	.170	−.149	−.014
	(.064)	(.070)	(.102)	(.100)	(.064)	(.071)
Divorce rate	.155[c]	.228[d]	.127[b]	.158[c]	.158[c]	.235[d]
	3.448	5.036	4.520	5.432	3.416	5.069
	(1.262)	(1.395)	(1.997)	(1.985)	(1.265)	(1.411)
Central business	.248[c]	.313[d]	.177[b]	.192[c]	.255[d]	.325[d]
district	.679	.843	.780	.807	.681	.856
	(.191)	(.204)	(.303)	(.289)	(.192)	(.206)
Median housing value	—	.046	—	−.028	—	.051
		.036		−.034		.038
		(.052)		(.074)		(.053)
Average HMDA CRA	−.130[b]	—	−.134[b]	—	−.129[b]	—
loan $ amount	−.327		−.542		−.317	
	(.153)		(.242)		(.154)	
Constant	5.1[d]	3.46[d]	4.1[d]	1.48[d]	4.9[d]	3.33[d]
	(.805)	(.305)	(1.274)	(.434)	(.807)	(.308)
Adjusted R^2	.71	.64	.71	.70	.69	.62

Notes: a. Entries are standardized coefficients and unstandardized coefficients followed
by standard errors in parenthesis.
 b. $p < .05$.
 c. $p < .01$.
 d. $p < .001$.

The findings of this chapter have important implications for
social theory, public policy, and future social research. Theoretically,
the findings reinforce, and are reinforced by, the social disorganization perspective. As the theory posits, actions by local residents (e.g.,
supervising neighborhood youth, forming neighborhood watch
groups, and organizing to secure economic resources) contribute to
the quality of life within a community. But maximizing the impact of

such local activity requires tools that can only be provided by institutional actors outside the local community. As Sampson (2001: 109) argues, "policies at the political and macrosocial level are extremely important; recognizing that community social action is possible does not absolve policymakers of the responsibility for seeking equality of opportunities among neighborhoods."

In terms of policy, the findings are also consistent with what many community development professionals have long maintained (Grogan and Proscio 2000). Crime rates are lower in the presence of economic resources, including homeownership, and where poverty rates are low. The stability of the local population, often facilitated by homeownership, and the presence of social capital or networks of reciprocity (e.g., neighborhood associations, political organizations, fraternal societies) contribute to lower crime rates (Putnam 2000: 307–318). Access to mortgage money, and particularly those funds provided by lenders who have an obligation under the CRA to serve low-income communities, reinforces many of these neighborhood characteristics, but more importantly, has an independent effect as well.

The connection between mortgage lending and crime bolsters the arguments of those advocating alternatives to incarceration as a crime prevention strategy. Dina R. Rose and Todd Clear (1998) have demonstrated that increasing incarceration rates above selected thresholds in attempts to reduce neighborhood crime actually increases crime rates in subsequent years. They suggest that this pattern reflects the further withdrawal of vital resources that make any neighborhood work. Offenders are parents and spouses who are trying to raise their children and keep their families intact. They are also workers who contribute to the neighborhood economy. Among the problems confronting former inmates upon their release is finding a place to live and the means to support themselves (Travis et al. 2001), a topic explored at length in the following chapter. A relatively small share of this population may be in a position to purchase a home, but that is not the case with the entire population. Yet many of these individuals return precisely to the communities that have traditionally been underserved by financial institutions. Investment in human capital (e.g., job training, formal education, job placement) is often a critical need for this population. Investment in their communities can also facilitate their reentry.

Community reinvestment advocates have long argued that among the benefits of access to capital for residents of distressed neighborhoods are lower crime rates. Our findings provide preliminary empirical support for this assumption. It is significant, both statistically and substantively, that where availability of mortgage money is greater, crime rates are lower. Equally important is the finding that loans covered by the CRA have an even stronger relationship with crime.

Despite our efforts to control the principal variables that prior research has demonstrated to be associated with crime, there may well be intervening variables that we have been unable to take into account. For example, neighborhood organizations that provide housing counseling or effectively utilize the tools available under the CRA and other fair lending rules may explain, in part, the lending-crime relationship. Similarly, lending may well interact with other formal and informal social organizational factors (e.g., neighborhood supervision and social control, crime watch programs, stability) that are not readily measured. But whether the relationship is more indirect than direct, these findings indicate that mortgage lending is associated with neighborhood crime and that relationship cannot be explained away by other factors commonly associated with crime.

The finding that CRA-covered loans, compared to loans generally, have a stronger relationship with crime rates suggests some important modifications of that critical federal law. Changes in the structure of financial services industries have, over time, limited the impact of the law. As indicated in earlier chapters, the most critical change would be to apply the CRA to those financial institutions not currently covered by the law (e.g., credit unions, independent mortgage companies, insurers) as called for by the proposed Community Reinvestment Modernization Act described in Chapter 4. Whether this proposal receives a serious hearing in Congress remains to be seen.

Finally, the politics and relevant social science findings suggest important avenues for future research. An obvious starting point would be a longitudinal investigation of the lending-crime relationship. Time series analyses would enable researchers to better flesh out the relationship suggested by our two-stage regression models. Additional case studies are also needed, particularly in larger cities and those with higher crime rates. The impact of other forms of investment, both private and public, also needs to be explored. Small business lending data have been publicly available since 1997 and could be analyzed in conjunction with local crime rates. Public investment in schools, transportation, housing, hospitals, police, and elsewhere may well influence selected crimes. Clearly, there are many fruitful directions research could take.

Policy-oriented research is vital because it can provide options for addressing crime. It is very difficult to alter the number of young males in a city or the racial composition of a metropolitan area. But it is possible to alter the number and share of loans going to traditionally underserved neighborhoods, revise school-funding formulas, or hire more police. Ideally, such investments will be based increasingly on solid empirical research findings and decreasingly on "common sense" or political influence.

The benefits of access to capital and the subsequent impact on crime rates are fairly clear to individuals seeking to buy a home. Without a mortgage loan, the vast majority of homeowners today would be renters and would likely live in more dangerous neighborhoods. Homeownership, in addition to providing safe and stable shelter, is also critical for wealth accumulation for most families. As noted previously, half of all homeowners in the United States hold 50 percent or more of their net wealth in home equity (Joint Center for Housing Studies 2002b: 7). But the benefits also accrue to neighborhood residents who did not apply for a loan in any given year or who are not homeowners. Where mortgage loans are more available and homeownership rates are higher, property values tend to be higher as well, including those of homes owned by long-standing residents. In addition, neighborhoods with relatively high levels of homeownership not only have lower crime rates but often have better public services (including public schools), safer streets, and other amenities that all residents share. Homeowners tend to be more satisfied with their communities, more engaged in voluntary organizations and political activities, and generally more committed to their communities (Rohe et al. 2000). Again, others in the community who have not recently taken out a mortgage loan or who are renters benefit from what are in fact neighborhood effects of homeownership. Overall, the impact of capital on crime affects the uneven development of metropolitan areas. But with appropriate policy interventions, credit can be made more available and crime can be reduced in currently distressed neighborhoods, thus ameliorating the uneven development of metropolitan areas generally.

Homeownership, however, is not a universal elixir for urban ills, as discussed in Chapter 3. Families trapped in a high-priced predatory loan from which they cannot escape or in a declining neighborhood where they are unable to sell their home do not benefit, and they often lose considerable financial resources, including their homes, in the worst cases. Renters priced out of the market are often forced to relocate. And racial minorities do not enjoy the same level of benefits due to racial discrimination and its associated costs in urban housing markets. But in general, access to mortgage capital and the home-ownership it brings has important neighborhood as well as individual family effects (Denton 2001).

Clearly, neighborhood characteristics are fundamental to our understanding of crime rates and the quality of life in urban communities for all residents. But that is particularly true for a growing segment of the population, ex-offenders. One of the consequences of the get-tough policies of recent years is that more and more ex-offenders are returning home, generally to socially disorganized, high-crime neighborhoods. Chapter 6 examines the implications of this dynamic for ex-offenders and the communities to which they are returning.

Notes

1. Correlations measure the extent of association between variables. They range from −1 to 1. Correlations closer to 1 mean that variables increase or decrease concurrently. Correlations closer to −1 indicate that as one variable increases, the other decreases. Correlations close to 0 indicate there is little to no relationship.

2. Seattle has 123 tracts, three of which are excluded because they do not have adequate size populations (i.e., they have populations of less than 1,000). This population size requirement allows us to construct reliable rates.

3. Previous community-level studies have had to address problems of multicollinearity among the independent variables. To diagnose potential collinearity, we examined variance inflation factor (VIF) scores, which confirmed the high collinearity between the following disadvantage-related variables (poverty rate, percent on public assistance, median household income, unemployment rate, and percent black) and the following residential mobility variables (residential mobility rate, renters rate, and percent young males). Using these diagnostics and previous research as a guide, we adopted a strategy of confirmatory factor analysis and hypothesized that an interpretable two-factor solution will represent the intercorrelations among indicators of disadvantage and residential mobility. The results supported this hypothesis. For disadvantage, all factor loadings were above .65 (poverty rate = .90, percent households on public assistance = .82, median household income = −.82, unemployment rate = .79, and percent black = .68), and the factor has an eigenvalue of 3.2. For residential mobility, all factor loadings were above .70 (residential mobility rate = .95, renters rate = .93, and percent young males = .73), and the factor has an eigenvalue of 2.3. The disadvantage and residential mobility factors were used along with percent young males, percent female-headed households, divorce rate, central business district, and

the home mortgage lending measures to predict Seattle neighborhood crime rates.

4. Histograms and descriptive statistics indicate that all the variables, excluding percent divorced, were skewed and needed to be logged in the analyses.

5. Two-stage least-squares regression uses instrumental variables that are uncorrelated with the error terms to compute estimated values of the problematic predictor (the first stage) and then uses those computed values to estimate a linear regression model of the dependent variable (the second stage). Since the computed values are based on variables that are uncorrelated with the errors, the results of the two-stage model are optimal.

6. An additional concern in neighborhood research is that of spatial dependence, which has been an issue in some studies. However, previous research on Seattle has indicated that spatial autocorrelation is not a problem in neighborhood crime analyses (Kubrin 2000).

7. One potential concern is the correlation between median housing value and average loan amount (see Table 5.1), as home purchase loans are based on the market value of the property being bought. The correlation between these variables is strong, but collinearity diagnostics indicate that including both variables in the regression analyses does not produce harmful collinearity. The VIFs for median housing value and average loan amount are 5.1 and 4.9, respectively, below the conventional problematic threshold (Kennedy 1992: 183). However, to further test the independent association of lending with crime, we ran additional analyses (see Table 5.3) that explore the relative impact of each variable. Model 1 includes average loan amount but excludes median housing value, whereas Model 2 includes median housing value but excludes average loan amount. The results show that housing value is not significant in any of the models, but lending is significant in the violent crime model, consistent with the basic finding that lending is independently associated with crime. This relationship holds after controlling for several neighborhood factors, including housing value.

8. Again, an examination of the comparative effects of median housing value and average CRA loan amount reveals that loan amount, rather than home value, is the significant variable (see Table 5.5).

6

Residence and Recidivism

Reentry is not just about individuals coming home; it is also about the homes and communities to which ex-prisoners return.
—Dina R. Rose and Todd R. Clear
(quoted in Jeremy Travis and Michelle Waul 2004: 337)

Since the mid-1970s, the US criminal justice system has consistently amplified the use of incarceration. In 1974 approximately 1,819,000 US adults had served time in state or federal prisons, but by 2001, this number had increased threefold to about 5,618,000 men and women. In 2004 alone, over 2 million individuals were incarcerated in prisons and local jails or correctional centers, and for the first time over 100,000 women were housed in prisons (Harrison and Karberg 2004).

Given these figures, more inmates are being released from prison than ever before. About 600,000 individuals, roughly 1,600 a day, will be released any given year to return to their communities (Travis et al. 2001:1). Although the transition from prison to society always has been difficult, current inmates face greater challenges and obstacles than in the past. Today prisoners return home having spent longer terms behind bars. They are less prepared for life on the outside, and they receive less assistance in their reintegration. At the same time, many will return to socially disorganized communities with limited resources, job opportunities, and social services. As a result, prisoner reentry has become one of the most salient issues in criminal justice today, with the central question being, how many of these offenders will reoffend, and why?

Previous research on recidivism has found that men, younger offenders, and those who commit more serious offenses, have priors, are closely supervised during probation/parole, have drug problems, and have little education are more likely to recidivate, controlling for other factors (Benedict and Huff-Corzine 1997; Benedict et al. 1998; Clarke et al. 1988; Gainey et al. 2000; Gendreau et al. 1996; Hepburn and Albonetti 1994; Irish 1989; Listwan et al. 2003; MacKenzie et al. 1999; Schwaner 1998; Spohn and Holleran 2002; Ulmer 2001). Many studies also find that even after controlling for offense and other demographic characteristics, minorities, and particularly African Americans, are more likely to reoffend than whites (Benedict and Huff-Corzine 1997; Clarke et al. 1988; Gendreau et al. 1996; Hanley and Latessa 1997; Listwan et al. 2003; Spohn and Holleran 2002).

Almost none of these studies, however, document the types of neighborhoods prisoners are released into or take into account whether ex-offenders disproportionately return to distressed neighborhoods. As Rose and Clear's quote at the beginning of the chapter implies, "place" is fundamental to our understanding of why people reoffend, yet very little attention has been paid to how ecological characteristics of communities influence the reoffending behavior of prisoners and the opportunity structure they and their neighbors encounter.

This chapter begins to move in that direction. Here we explore the impact of neighborhoods on criminals and the impact of criminals on neighborhoods with respect to a current pressing problem—prisoner reentry. First, we review the key issues surrounding prisoner reentry in a "get tough on crime" era and describe the multiple challenges ex-offenders face upon release. We pay particular attention to the group affected most by these challenges—young black males. As will be shown, the prevalence of incarceration has not been equally distributed among racial groups; black men, especially uneducated young black men, are much more likely to experience prison than other groups (Lynch and Sabol 2001: 12). As a consequence, they face special challenges for reintegration. Equally important, the spread of incarceration throughout black communities—many of which already face multiple disadvantages—poses a unique reentry challenge. Second, we examine trends in reoffending among those released and link rising recidivism levels to current criminal justice policies and practices. Third, we advance previous research by considering how recidivism may be linked to the neighborhoods where prisoners return. As we argue below, neighborhoods vary in their capacity to provide services to ex-offenders, services that facilitate reintegration into society and curb recidivism. As a consequence, recidivism levels may be determined, in part, by the places to which ex-offenders return and the extent to which those places facilitate or subvert successful reentry into the community. Do these neighborhoods offer the services and related economic opportunities ex-offenders need, or do they simply nurture further criminal activity? Finally, in this chapter we examine whether the linkages among residence, privilege, and recidivism may be conditioned by race. In other words, we consider whether higher recidivism rates among blacks may be explained, in part, by the fact that they disproportionately return to (and live in) more economically disadvantaged communities than whites.

Prisoner Reentry in a "Get Tough on Crime" Era

Prisoner reentry is very different than it was just a few decades ago. Today there are many more offenders released from prisons than in the past, and they have served significantly longer prison terms, with only few having received the benefits of extensive rehabilitation or prerelease programs (Seiter and Kadela 2003: 361). These trends reflect, in part, the criminal justice system's transformation in philosophy from that of rehabilitation to punishment. On the state of contemporary crime policy, Kathryn Beckett notes that the two major policy perspectives have been get-tough and managerial approaches. Both are "cynical sides of the same coin," she says, because they are "fundamentally uninterested in the social causes of criminality or in reintegrating offenders and assume instead that punishment, surveillance, and control are the best response to deviant behavior" (Beckett 1997: 107). As a result, more behaviors are now penalized and penalties for crimes have become much harsher, as reflected in criminal justice legislation since the mid-1970s.

Since the early 1980s, criminal justice policy has become increasingly punitive, with each administration calling for tougher penalties, mandatory penalties, lengthier sentences, more prisons, and reduced habeas corpus rights (e.g., the right to due process in criminal proceedings). To illustrate, in 1993, the US Senate passed a $23 billion crime bill that, among other things, made being a member of certain types of gangs a federal offense and expanded the death penalty to cover fifty-two additional offenses. The bill also classified street crimes involving firearms as a federal offense and contained the "three strikes and you're out" provision, which calls for mandatory sentences for persons convicted of three felonies. The war on drugs, with a budget of only $1 billion in 1981 but $13.4 billion in 1993 and nearly $20 billion in 2002, perhaps is the most punitive policy. Between 1980 and 2003, the United States spent more than $300 billion on federal, state, and local antidrug efforts. Mandatory penalties for drug crimes have proliferated and are now the harshest in the nation's history. Collectively, the various laws have had three particularly severe consequences. First, during the past twenty years, the United States experienced a massive boom in incarceration, with the prison population increasing fourfold from 330,000 in 1980 to nearly 1.4 million in 1999. As a result, the United States now incarcerates more of its citizens than any other country in the world (Austin and Irwin 2001: 1; Lynch and Sabol 2001: 4).[1] Second, federal and state budgets have shifted public expenditures from other social services such as education to crime control (Chambliss 1995; Tonry 1995). In California, for example, the 2002 state budget showed that 18 percent of funds were spent on corrections, whereas only 1 percent was spent on higher education (Whitehead et al. 2003). And third, racism and the systematic oppression of minorities, especially young African American men, has been legitimized and institutionalized in the criminal justice system (Chambliss 1995: 236).

Readily available statistics detail the extent to which these policies have adversely affected blacks. Between 1979 and 1990, the percentage of African Americans among those admitted to state and federal prisons grew from 39 to 53 percent. Since 1980 the number of blacks in prison has tripled (Tonry 1995: 49). Black incarceration rates in 1990 (1,860 per 100,000) were nearly seven times higher than white rates (289 per 100,000) (Jankowski 1992: Table 16). And one study reported the following: almost 1 in 3 (32.2 percent) African American men ages twenty to twenty-nine is either in prison, jail, probation, or parole on any given day (Mauer and Huling 1995). Unfortunately, these disparities continue to worsen; the incarceration rate for blacks today (3,437 per 100,000) still far exceeds that for whites (450) (Sourcebook of Criminal Justice Statistics 2002: 500). Projections suggest that these inequalities will continue. Thomas P. Bonczar and Allen J. Beck (1997) estimate that 28.5 percent of black males born in 1991 can expect to enter state or federal prison during their lifetime. For white men, however, the lifetime likelihood is only 4.4 percent.

Even more problematic are arrest and incarceration statistics for drug offenses, fueled by the war on drugs. The absolute number of drug arrests grew from the 1970s to the 1990s, but the percentage of drug arrests for blacks rose most sharply. Between 1985 and 1989, the number of black arrests increased by more than 100 percent, from 210,298 to 452,574, whereas the number of white arrests grew by only 27 percent (Sourcebook of Criminal Justice Statistics, 1985–1989). Drug arrests are a principal reason for the rapid increase in black imprisonment: in 1926, the first year that the race of prison admissions was recorded on a national basis, only 21 percent of all admissions were African American, but by 1970 that figure had grown to 39 percent, and by 1996 it had grown even further to 51 percent (Austin and Irwin 2001: 7).

Not only are more persons, particularly minorities, entering the criminal justice system in greater numbers than ever before, but also they are serving longer sentences as a result of "truth in sentencing" and related policies. Previously, under an indeterminate system, parole boards could release inmates if they showed signs that they were rehabilitated, documented established ties to the community (e.g., housing, family, employment), and provided a "plan" on how they would successfully reenter society. (This discretion, of course, led to racial bias in some cases.) Under these guidelines, offenders would still be remanded back to prison if they violated their release conditions. Many argued this system provided parolees with an incentive both to not reoffend and to develop a transition plan for reentry. With "truth in sentencing" legislation and a shift to determinate sentencing, however, inmates now serve most, if not all, of their sentences. Under the new guidelines, although offenders in most states serve an average of 85 percent of their sentences in prison, about 20 percent of this group serves 100 percent of their allocated sentences. As a result, the average prison term served today is 2.4 years, over seven months longer, on average, than a decade ago. Unfortunately, studies find that longer stays in prison are associated with declining frequency of contact with family members, yet this contact is believed to facilitate reintegration into the community (Lynch and Sabol 2001).[2] Additionally, the likelihood of being divorced increases with time served. Many also argue that with a shift toward determinate sentencing, the incentive for inmates to prepare for release is reduced since they know they cannot achieve an early release date despite following prison rules, attending educational classes, and receiving treatment. Unfortunately, when they do not participate in educational programs or receive other services while incarcerated, offenders reenter communities no more equipped than when they first arrived.

The Challenges of Returning Home

These same offenders eventually return home to communities throughout the United States. In fact, over 95 percent of the more than 2 million inmates who are currently incarcerated will return to their communities. Some cities witnessed particularly high levels of returnees. For example, in 2002, more than 10,000 convicted felons completed their sentences and returned to the streets of Baltimore (Buntin 2003). The volume of offenders released from prison has increased dramatically from 1980 to 2000, from about 170,000 to 585,000 (Lynch and Sabol 2001: 2).

Upon release, a significant number of offenders are in critical "need of help," as a 2005 Urban Institute report noted in its title. Challenges for prisoner reentry include, but are not limited to, substance abuse problems, physical and mental health problems, employability and workforce obstacles, housing issues, and simply overcoming the stigma associated with being an ex-felon. Christy A. Visher and her colleagues (2005: 2) state that among those released in 2004 are a large group of prisoners with serious medical and mental health problems. In their study of eighty-one male prisoners returning to Cincinnati communities, they found the following:

- Prisoners reported long waits to see a doctor and insensitive, uncaring treatment from many of the prison doctors and nurses;
- After release, ex-prisoners said that the lack of information provided to them before release about community services was the biggest obstacle to getting the health care and other services they needed;
- Former prisoners reported that they often had to rely on family, friends, and even the emergency room of the local hospital to obtain the medication they needed after release (3).

Unfortunately, these findings are not limited to one city. Studies of other areas report similar obstacles to the delivery of health care services, both within prison and after release (LaVigne et al. 2004: 29, 37; Travis et al. 2001: 13; Visher et al. 2004).

Health care is arguably most important for those with substance abuse problems, a sizable percentage of inmates today. Studies of inmate populations find that a significant share report extensive, serious involvement with drugs and alcohol. In a study of prisoner reentry in Maryland, for example, the majority of inmates reported some drug (78 percent) or alcohol (61 percent) use prior to prison, with cocaine and heroin topping the list. Moreover, 30 percent reported using cocaine and 41 percent reported using heroin on a daily basis in the six months before entering prison (Visher et al. 2004: 7). In their study of 400 prisoners returning to Chicago communities, Visher and her colleagues (2003: 3) also note that substance abuse was prevalent among their sample, yet very few ex-offenders had received treatment while incarcerated. A 2005 report on prisoner reentry in Texas arrived at a similar finding: among 676 prisoners interviewed shortly before release, it was determined that 80 percent reported illegal drug use prior to their incarceration, yet only 21 percent participated in a treatment program while incarcerated (La Vigne and Kachnowski 2005: 1).

Securing employment constitutes another critical barrier for ex-offenders, particularly in an economy increasingly diverging into a high-skills/high-technology sector and a broad low-skill service economy. Few offenders have promising prospects for advancing out of the bottom rungs of the job ladder, and as Marc Mauer (2005: 609) notes, "What in many cases is a situation of limited connections with the world of work becomes even more problematic with the stigma of imprisonment attached to former offenders."

These challenges and barriers, especially with respect to employment, may be particularly onerous for minorities. The largest share of prisoners released into urban areas is black, and the joint effects of race and a prison sentence as they relate to employer discrimination do not portend well for black ex-prisoners. Indeed, as we reported in Chapter 1, recent research has found that it is easier for a white person with a criminal record to get a job than a black person with no record, even among applicants with otherwise comparable credentials (Pager 2003). One can imagine, therefore, the challenges black ex-offenders face in terms of securing employment after prison.

Not surprisingly, many of these obstacles are related to and compounded by initiatives of the war on drugs, with a seemingly endless series of restrictions placed on people convicted of drug offenses. Depending on the state in which one lives, an eighteen-year-old with even a first-time conviction for felony drug possession now may be barred from receiving welfare benefits for life, prohibited from living in public housing, denied student loans to attend college, permanently excluded from voting, and if not a citizen, deported (Mauer 2005: 610).

The problems ex-offenders face when returning home have begun to receive some attention. But virtually no attention has been given to the challenges communities face as prisoners return home. For communities, the return of released prisoners potentially poses problems for public safety and provisions of social services and challenges for reintegrating neighborhood residents. The increase in the sheer number of offenders returning home, with progressively more serious needs after serving longer sentences, places an insurmountable strain on some urban communities. Discussions about the return and reintegration of ex-prisoners into communities often occur under the presumption that communities want to accept and reintegrate ex-offenders. That may not be a viable assumption. Surveys of residents in local neighborhoods show that public safety is their top concern (e.g., Anderson and Milligan 2001). And given that many offenders have committed serious violent crimes, it is not necessarily the case that neighborhoods want all offenders to return to the places they lived before serving time.

These concerns are exacerbated for the relatively few communities with large concentrations of returning prisoners. Certain neighborhoods—those already facing enormous challenges of poverty, crime, and lack of social services—are particularly burdened by the large influx of prisoners returning home. Released prisoners are concentrated in a few large states (e.g., California, Texas), and the top sixteen states (in terms of the volume of releases) collectively account for 75 percent of all those who leave prison. Of those released in 1998, for example, five states accounted for just under half of the 531,000 offenders released; California alone accounted for 24 percent of the state prison releases (but only 12 percent of the US resident population) (Lynch and Sabol 2001: 15). More importantly, within these states, ex-prisoners are increasingly concentrated in the core counties, or areas that contain the central city of a metropolitan area. Studies further suggest that releases are concentrated within a comparatively few neighborhoods in those cities (Lynch and Sabol 2001: 3; Rose and Clear 1998; Visher et al. 2004).

If ex-offenders returning to their communities create problems for some, they are also assets for others. Their prior removal from those communities can pose equal if not greater problems than the return of many offenders to targeted neighborhoods. High levels of incarceration in some communities may have the unintended consequence of weakening family and community structures as sources of control (Kubrin and Weitzer 2003: 384). Recent work by Rose and Clear examines this dynamic by exploring the effect of incarceration on community organization and the implications for community cohesion and social control. Incarceration of community members may have multiple effects on residents' ability to control crime, particularly in neighborhoods that are already deficient in social ties and social control. If offenders "are resources to some members of the community and if they occupy roles within networks that form the basis for informal social control, their removal is not solely a positive act [in reducing crime], but also imposes losses on those networks and their capacity for strengthened community life" (Rose and Clear 1998: 451).

When a critical mass of community members spend significant time incarcerated, it may (1) disrupt family cohesion and financial resources,[3] (2) reduce the supply of marriageable partners, (3) deplete labor markets, thus undermining the socioeconomic vitality of the neighborhood, (4) decrease the number of adults available to supervise neighborhood youth and intervene in neighborhood problems, and (5) compound neighborhood problems after these incarcerated offenders are released into the community. Incarceration can undermine the ability of released inmates to reestablish positive ties with family members, friends, and neighbors and may make these individuals a liability for their families insofar as they are unable to secure a job. Indeed, one study found that when the number of incarcerated residents reaches a "tipping point," it has the unintended consequence of weakening neighborhood organization and thereby increasing crime (Clear et al. 2003).

The Criminal Justice System's Revolving Door

Given these conditions, it should not be at all surprising that many who leave prison end up returning shortly after release, usually within a year. Mark Souder, a Republican congressman from Indiana, noted that recidivism has turned the US justice system into a revolving door and represents a "massive failure of the penal system to return law-abiding citizens to society" (Elsner 2005). Studies report recidivism levels around 30–35 percent (Benedict and Huff-Corzine

1997; Clarke et al. 1998; Irish 1989), although some report levels as high as 43 percent (Langan and Cunnif 1992). These figures are much higher in studies that measure longer release times; in one large-scale study of 272,111 prisoners released from prisons in 1994, it was noted that 68 percent were rearrested for a new crime in three years (Langan and Levin 2002). Collectively, recidivism studies report differences in reoffending by type of offender population; offenders sentenced to prison have higher recidivism rates and recidivate more quickly than do offenders placed on probation (Spohn and Holleran 2002: 329; see also Clear and Braga 1995 and Petersilia et al. 1986), although recidivism is still fairly common for probationers and parolees. Doris Layton MacKenzie and Spencer De Li (2002: 243) note that probationers and parolees account for a large proportion of the criminal activities in large urban areas, and many of them are rearrested within three years of starting probation or parole. Consider the following statistic. During 1998, there were 170,253 reported parole violators nationwide, representing more than 23 percent of new prison admissions (Beck and Mumola 1999). What accounts for such high levels of reoffending?

As noted earlier, prior studies of recidivism have focused almost exclusively on individual-level characteristics of offenders and their offenses to determine the correlates of reoffending. As already noted, these studies document that those who have committed more serious crimes, have a greater number of prior offenses, or have drug problems, little education, and higher supervision rates during probation/parole are more likely to recidivate. Men and younger offenders also recidivate more often. More importantly, though, many studies find that even after controlling for all these factors, minorities—and particularly blacks—reoffend at a greater rate than whites. Indeed, a meta-analysis of over 130 studies on the predictors of recidivism among adult offenders found race to be one of the strongest predictors (Gendreau et al. 1996: 575).

Notably absent from this long list of studies are measures reflecting the neighborhood contexts in which individuals live. These studies fail to document the types of neighborhoods offenders are released into and thereby treat neighborhood context as constant and therefore irrelevant for understanding recidivism. Yet neighborhoods vary drastically in the amenities or privileges that residents can enjoy. Some communities have low poverty and unemployment levels, ample and quality housing supply, relatively little residential turnover, little crime, and an abundance of services. Others are riddled by crime, poverty, unemployment, and residential instability and offer residents few, if any, services. The studies referenced above make no attempt to determine whether ex-offenders disproportionately return to socially disorganized neighborhoods, which may facilitate recidivism. Individual-level factors do play an important role in predicting who will reoffend versus who will not, but one's immediate environment is also likely to have a significant influence on rates of recidivism, as social disorganization theory predicts.

Social Disorganization and Recidivism

Social disorganization theory, discussed in Chapter 5, provides the framework for understanding how neighborhood structure influences individual behavior. Unlike theories centered on individual-level contributors to crime and recidivism, social disorganization focuses on the effects of places in creating conditions favorable to criminal behavior (Kubrin and Weitzer 2003). To reiterate, this perspective describes how certain features of the urban environment, such as poverty, racial and ethnic heterogeneity, and residential instability, lead to high levels of social disorganization in communities. Neighborhoods that are socially disorganized—that have high levels of poverty, unemployment, family disruption, population turnover, and other social ills—are more likely to experience greater crime and victimization rates, primarily because they have lower levels of informal social control.

A number of social disorganization studies find that crime-related dynamics operate at the neighborhood level that are not reducible to the individual characteristics of neighborhood residents. A basic premise of this research is that individual rates of offending are determined to some extent by social forces in their wider environment and that social disorganization theory provides a basis for identifying these criminogenic conditions. In other words, neighborhood characteristics will have a significant, direct impact on individual rates of offending, even after controlling for individual-level factors such as race, gender, age, socioeconomic status, and others. It is also the case, however, that the relationship between individual-level factors and crime rates may be conditioned by, or vary with, the broader social context (Rountree et al. 1994: 390), constituting an *interaction* between community- and individual-level characteristics.

In recent years, a number of social disorganization studies have examined how neighborhood characteristics directly affect or interact with individual-level factors to influence a variety of outcomes, including victimization (Miethe and McDowall 1993; Rountree et al. 1994; Velez 2001), adolescent development (Elliott et al. 1996), delinquency (Simcha-Fagan and Schwartz 1986; Wikstrom and Loeber 2000), and violence (Sampson et al. 1997; Silver 2000). These findings indicate that even after controlling for individual-level characteristics, neighborhood factors influence the individual likelihood of victimization or offending. This research also finds that certain neighborhood characteristics, such as poverty and unemployment, interact with characteristics of individuals to aggravate victimization and offending rates.

Unfortunately, almost no studies to date have examined these issues for ex-offenders. Poverty, family disruption, joblessness, and residential instability—indicators of neighborhood social disorganization—represent conditions that make readjustment into society and one's neighborhood more difficult and thus contribute to a greater likelihood of reoffending for those just released. As noted earlier, neighborhoods vary in the extent to which they provide residents with job opportunities, employment programs, housing options, community-based substance abuse treatment programs, and other services and programs that address residents' needs. Given that most offenders return home with serious medical, physical, and social problems, these neighborhood services are vital to curb recidivism. Given their situation and needs, ex-offenders' vulnerability to the levels of social disorganization within the neighborhood is heightened.

Ex-offenders also rely on neighborhood resources to be able to comply with the terms of their probation/parole (i.e., being employed, finding stable housing, paying restitution, receiving drug or alcohol treatment, etc.). Frequently offenders are required to hold a job, receive counseling, find housing, and so on as part of their probation/parole.[4] Over the years, the proportion of probationers subject to special conditions, such as residential placement, alcohol and drug abuse treatment, drug testing, mental health counseling, house arrest, day programs, and community service has risen (Clear 1994). The public's more punitive stance, combined with the availability of inexpensive drug testing and a higher number of probationers having substance abuse problems, have contributed to the increased number of conditions imposed. Often offenders must rely on help from the community to successfully comply with the terms of their supervision. Essentially, successful completion of community supervision requires access to services that facilitate compliance with these rules, yet not all neighborhoods offer these services, and some, particularly disorganized communities, offer none at all.

These conditions increase the chances of failure (Petersilia and Turner 1993). Recall the study noted above, which found that in 1998 parole violators represented more than 23 percent of new prison admissions (Beck and Mumola 1999); most notable is the fact that 76.9 percent of these parole violations were for a technical violation only, without the commission of a new felony (Camp and Camp 1998). Most of these ex-offenders will likely return to disadvantaged, socially disorganized neighborhoods.

If, however, prisoners were released into neighborhoods that provided resources facilitating reintegration back into society, they would be less likely to reoffend or violate the conditions of their release. Community reinvestment may be a more effective method than prison construction for reversing these trends. Current policy leads to an ineffective allocation of corrections expenditures. As political reporter Jack Kavanagh charges, "The state of Maryland spends over $600 million a year just on corrections alone. Do you still want to take the approach where you lock them up, let them out and have over a 50 percent recidivism rate? Or do you want to try and invest in some things that might have an impact on recidivism? To me, it's a no-brainer" (Buntin 2003).

Neighborhood context may also explain, in part, why minorities—particularly blacks—reoffend at a greater rate than whites. Minorities more often live in distressed communities, which may influence offending rates above and beyond the individual-level characteristics of the offenders themselves. In other words, the "race effect" found in most studies may be an artifact of what is really a "place effect." Because previous research has not considered that blacks and whites live in drastically different ecological contexts (a point addressed in detail below) that may mitigate or aggravate recidivism, we do not know the extent to which "place" effects account for minorities' increased recidivism levels.

Social disorganization theory recognizes that racial inequality in US cities—as discussed at length in Chapter 1—has created significantly different neighborhood contexts for blacks and whites. Structural factors have created and maintained a system of stratification, giving rise to minority neighborhoods characterized by multiple disadvantages, including poverty, joblessness, and family disruption. The social, political, and economic forces that help to create structural factors include, among other things, redlining and patterns of residential segregation (Squires 1994; Massey and Denton 1993), globalization and de-industrialization (Wilson 1987, 1996), and discrimination (O'Connor et al. 2001, Krysan and Lewis 2004). Scholars argue that the concentrated disadvantage found in many urban African American communities is rarely paralleled in predominantly white neighborhoods, and that in most cities, race is highly correlated with concentrated disadvantage (Morenoff et al. 2001; Sampson and Wilson 1995; Sampson et al. 1997). Robert J. Sampson (1987: 354) argues that racial differences in poverty, family disruption, and joblessness, among other things, are so strong that the "worst" urban contexts in which whites reside are considerably better than the average context of black communities.

Consider, for example, the case of Washington, D.C. According to 2000 census statistics, white median household income ($67,266) is over twice that of black median household income ($30,478), and 25 percent of the black population lives below the poverty line, compared to only 8 percent of the white population. Other measures of social disorganization highlight the disparity between blacks and whites in Washington, D.C., communities. There is a 31 percent difference between the races in the number of female households with no husband present and with children under eighteen (37 percent versus 6 percent). Statistics such as these indicate that black neighborhoods in the city suffer from greater levels of economic disadvantage and social disorganization than do white neighborhoods. This social reality leads to the conclusion that neighborhood context will condition the relationship between race and reoffending levels such that minorities will not have higher rates of recidivism once neighborhood context is taken into account.

In short, when considering the impact of criminals on neighborhoods and the impact of neighborhoods on criminals, social disorganization theory offers a rationale for understanding why current recidivism levels may be so high among ex-offenders and, more specifically, why recidivism rates may be particularly high among minorities.

The Future of Prisoner Reentry

Today more and more Americans are being sent to prison to serve longer sentences. Few of these inmates, however, receive the sort of rehabilitation they need to make it on the outside. As a consequence, recidivism levels remain high, and many are concerned with what they consider to be the revolving door of the criminal justice system. Others are more optimistic; former US attorney general John Ashcroft is hopeful for change. "America is the land of second chances," Ashcroft said in 2004, quoting President George W. Bush's State of the Union Speech. "When the gates of prison open, the path ahead should lead to a better life" (Mills 2004). How true is that statement? A study by the Vera Institute of Justice in New York City identified the myriad issues that confront inmates released from prison (Nelson et al. 1999). Many believe that these challenges make it too easy for ex-prisoners to return to a life of crime.

Opinions about the appropriate policy responses to prisoner reentry vary widely, although almost completely overlooked are initiatives that focus on changing communities. Fixing the extremely disadvantaged communities to which ex-offenders disproportionately return, we argue, would constitute a fruitful approach, an approach that could ultimately help to sever the linkages among race, residence, and privilege. Given the challenges of prisoner reentry, particularly in a "get tough on crime" era, ex-prisoners are more reliant than ever on community services. Although educating inmates and giving them job training for their life after prison undoubtedly is important, these skills matter less if the communities to which ex-offenders return offer few opportunities for success. It is not surprising, therefore, that recidivism rates are as high as they are today. It is also not surprising that even after controlling for all other factors, minorities tend to recidivate at a higher rate than whites. Given that minorities, and blacks in particular, return to disproportionately disadvantaged communities, the effects of place no doubt are stronger for this population.

In an era in which states are beginning to reduce their prison populations and focus more squarely on reentry into the community, policymakers must begin to consider how and to what extent individual behavior is shaped by the surrounding environments. At present, neighborhood factors are absent from recidivism studies, but findings from the social disorganization literature can inform policy on prisoner reentry specifically as it relates to identifying the barriers to successful reintegration of ex-offenders back into society. According to Jeremy Travis, former director of the National Institute of Justice and reentry expert, "Developing a thorough understanding of the characteristics of returning prisoners and the challenges they face in their communities is an important step in shaping public policy toward improving the safety and welfare of all citizens" (Urban Institute

2003). A well-designed, comprehensive reentry system that takes into consideration the characteristics of ex-offenders and the community contexts to which they are returning can enhance public safety, reduce returns to prison, control corrections expenditures, and help prisoners achieve successful long-term reintegration.

If crime has long been a major, if not the most important, challenge confronting urban communities, how to manage a growing prison population that will return home has not received appropriate scrutiny. Yet successful prisoner reentry is essential not just for the welfare of ex-prisoners but for their neighborhoods. And more importantly, neighborhood development is essential for the successful reentry of prisoners. The race-place-privilege nexus is perhaps most explicitly evident in our criminal justice system, as this chapter has shown. Breaking these connections within this context will considerably aid efforts to pursue more balanced, equitable metropolitan development.

Notes

1. The Department of Justice reports that as of November 2004, there were 2.2 million people in US prisons and jails, making its prison system by far the biggest in the world. The United States incarcerates people at a rate five to seven times higher than most other democracies, which last year cost the country $47 billion (Elsner 2005).

2. In one study it was reported that family was a very important source of support for prisoners, both during prison and regarding their expectations for after release. Almost all the prisoners interviewed (94 percent) wanted their families to be involved in their lives during prison (Visher et al. 2003).

3. This may be particularly true regarding children of ex-prisoners. A study of 400 pre-release inmates in Chicago found that six in ten prisoners had children under the age of eighteen (Visher et al. 2003).

4. For offenders granted probation, for example, the court decides what conditions will be included in the probation contract between the offender and the court. It is the judge's responsibility to enumerate the conditions the probationer must abide by in order to remain in the community. The conditions are usually recommended by probation officers. In legal terms, the probation conditions form a contract between the offender and the court. The contract (at least theoretically) states the conditions the offender must abide by to remain in the community. The court requires that the probation officer provide the defendant with a written statement setting forth all the conditions to which the sentence is subject. The offender signs the contract, and the probation officer is the contract's "enforcer," responsible for notifying the court when the contract has been violated (Petersilia 1997).

7

Race, Place, and the Politics of Privilege

Bad neighborhoods defeat good programs.
—Rusk 1993: 121

Who gets what, and why? That is how Gerhard Lenski defined the study of social inequality forty years ago in his classic book *Power and Privilege* (Lenski 1966: 1). If the distribution of privilege today is less determined by ascriptive characteristics and more determined by achieved characteristics than was the case during most of the centuries examined by Lenski, meritocracy is hardly around the corner. This state of affairs has not occurred simply or even largely due to differences among individuals in terms of their skills, abilities, and other attributes. Key determinants of who gets what and why today are social realities associated with place and race. As the previous chapters have shown, these realities reflect policy decisions that have been made at all levels in both public and private institutions. These actions have molded the landscape of housing, crime, and virtually all other features of the good (and not so good) life in US metropolitan areas. But society is not an iron cage. Social realities that have been nurtured by policy can be altered by policy as well.

Knowing what to do constitutes part of the challenge. Equally critical, if not more so, is having a political strategy that will encourage those who need to act to do so in appropriate ways, if the distribution of privilege is to change. Basically, it comes down to understanding self-interests and how they can be molded to alter realities that in many ways currently benefit powerful and privileged interests. Sometimes such interests can be mobilized by organizers who can get seemingly disparate groups to recognize their common ground. On other occasions, litigation and legislation are necessary to force people to do things they would not otherwise voluntarily do. In addition to the specific recommendations offered in previous chapters, below we address a number of strategic issues and propose additional specific tactics for severing the links between place, race, and privilege. We attempt to identify ideas that might actually work and feasible strategies for implementing them. Some have already been implemented and yielded at least some of the intended outcomes. Others are ideas that offer future promise. Clearly, there is no single magic bullet. Therefore, a multipolicy approach is essential. Cities and states can provide "laboratories for democracy." But the federal government, nonprofit organizations, and the private sector all have important roles to play.

Universal Versus Race-Specific Remedies: A False Dichotomy

One of the more unfortunate debates in recent years has been over the question of whether "race-specific" or "universal" remedies are more appropriate for addressing the issues of race and urban poverty. (An even more unfortunate debate, of course, is with those who simply think we have done enough, or perhaps too much, and that neither race nor class remedies are needed.) But the world does not come to us neatly wrapped in race or class packages. Sometimes the issue confronting a mayor, community group, or federal agency is an explicit, neighborhood-level poverty issue, and sometimes it is one of overt racism. All too often, of course, it does indeed involve a combination of race, class, and other fundamental divisions (e.g., gender, ethnicity). The nature of the issue often dictates the appropriate response.

The primary attraction of the universal or class-based approach, according to its proponents, is pragmatism. Recognizing the many common interests of poor and working-class households of any color, supporters argue that the most significant barriers confronting these groups can be addressed with policy initiatives and other actions that do not ignite the hostility often associated with race-based discussions and proposals. Race-neutral policies that assist all those who are working hard but not quite making it reinforce traditional values of individual initiative and the work ethic, thereby providing benefits to people who have earned them, rather than to the so-called undeserving poor. Given the socioeconomic characteristics of racial minorities in general, it is further argued that such approaches will disproportionately benefit these communities, nurturing integration and greater opportunity in a far less rancorous environment than is created with debates over race-specific approaches. Given the "race fatigue" among many whites (and underlying prejudices that persist), class-based approaches are viewed as a more feasible way to address the problems of urban poverty that affect many groups, but particularly racial minorities (Edsall and Edsall 1991; Kahlenberg 1996; Skocpol 2000; Teixeira and Rogers 2000; Warren 2001; Wilson 1999).

Critics of the universal approach argue that although the quality of life for racial minorities has improved over the years, such approaches simply do not recognize the extent to which race and racism continue to shape the opportunity structure in the United States. "Color blindness" is often a euphemism for what amounts to a retreat on race and the preservation of white privilege in its many forms. In a world of scarce resources, class-based remedies dilute available support for combating racial discrimination and segregation. From this perspective, it is precisely the controversy over race that the class-based proponents fear, which demonstrates the persistence of racism and the need for explicitly antiracist remedies including far more aggressive enforcement of fair housing, equal employment, and other civil rights laws. Race-based remedies alone will not resolve all the problems associated with urban poverty, but they must remain front and center as part of the nation's opportunity agenda, according to this perspective (Bonilla-Silva 2003; Edley 1996; Feagin 2000; Fiss 2003; Steinberg 1995).

But this debate presents a false dichotomy. Policy decisions affecting the opportunity structure and quality of life in communities are made every day. Some of them are explicitly associated with economic or class disparities, and others are tied to traditional civil rights or race-specific matters. Decisions in each of these areas influence and are influenced by inequalities of place and race, as shown throughout the previous chapters. That is, "universal" problems and solutions have racial implications, and matters that are addressed through a racial lens have implications for entire regions. The ensuing distribution of privilege, in turn, affects how subsequent problems are defined and decisions are made. Policy responses, some class-based (e.g., building more affordable housing units, making afford-

able credit more widely and equitably available, increasing the minimum wage and earned income tax credit, implementing "living
wage" requirements, providing more effective education and job
training to prison inmates and ex-offenders) and some race-based
(e.g., stricter fair housing and fair lending law enforcement, more
comprehensive affirmative action and related diversity requirements,
stronger prohibitions against racial profiling by police), are essential
if the underlying patterns of privilege are to be altered.

Coalitions that cut across interest groups, including racial groups,
are essential. Many land use planning, housing, and housing finance
proposals, including efforts to revise the CRA and eliminate predatory lending, for example, are generally articulated in color-blind
terms. Fair share housing requirements, tax-based revenue sharing,
and inclusionary zoning (discussed below) are "universal" in character, though they often have clear racial implications. That is, these
proposals are designed to benefit poor and working-class families in
general, though racial minorities would likely benefit disproportionately—a point consistent with Chapter 2's findings regarding the
CRA's impact on black and Latino housing opportunities. Likewise,
efforts aimed at easing the transition from prison to society are likely
to disproportionately benefit minorities, minority communities, and
metropolitan areas generally. Clearly, such proposals are important
parts of an effort to ameliorate spatial and racial inequalities.

But sometimes the issues are racial, and responding in racial
terms cannot be avoided. If African Americans and Hispanics face
discrimination in one out of every four or five visits to a housing
provider, it is difficult to avoid recognizing the need for stronger
enforcement of the federal Fair Housing Act and other state and local
rules prohibiting racial discrimination in housing markets. And such
enforcement works. Since 1990, private, nonprofit fair housing
organizations have generated more than $215 million for plaintiffs
from lawsuits utilizing leverage provided by the federal Fair Housing
Act (National Fair Housing Alliance 2003a, 2005).

Racial minorities constitute "protected groups" targeted by fair
housing law, but it is also the case that communities generally benefit
by ameliorating racial inequality and the ensuing conflict. If Atlanta
does not live up entirely to its slogan as "a city too busy to hate," the
local economy has certainly benefited from the city's ability to alter
its image in the area of race relations in recent decades (Jacoby 1998;
Rutheiser 1996).

Universal and race-based policies are among the essential remedies for challenges posed by inequalities of place and race, and each has implications for the potential success of the other. It is important to overcome the polarization that frames much of this debate. As Christopher Edley Jr. argued, each should have a place in "the opportunity agenda" (Edley 1996: 46). The nature of a particular issue or campaign should dictate the emphasis that will be placed on any particular set of policies. Saul Alinsky famously argued that there are no permanent friends and no permanent enemies. A similar sentiment would appear to apply to the choice of weapons here.

"Pro Place" Versus "Pro People": A Second False Dichotomy

Another unfortunate debate is that between proponents of so-called pro place policies and those who advocate pro people policies. Once again, there is a need for both. And it is also the case that the distinction between policies that focus on improving neighborhoods and those emphasizing individual development is not as great as is often suggested.

Place-oriented policies (e.g., community reinvestment and related efforts to combat redlining and predatory lending practices) in fact benefit both distressed neighborhoods and many of the less privileged households in those neighborhoods (Joint Center for Housing Studies 2002b; Squires 2003b). As indicated previously, enforcement of the Community Reinvestment Act, a federal law passed in 1977 prohibiting redlining, has generated more than $4.2 trillion for underserved urban communities, with low- and moderate-income and minority markets receiving a disproportionately high share of those funds (Joint Center for Housing Studies 2002b; National Community Reinvestment Coalition 2005a: 1). Policies designed to create greater opportunities for individuals and their families (e.g., Moving to Opportunity and other mobility programs) benefit entire communities by reducing the concentration of poverty, segregation, and crime, along with the various social service demands these problems generate (Goering 2005; Goering et al. 2002; Goering and Feins 2003; Rubinowitz and Rosenbaum 2000), though more comprehensive and better managed efforts could yield even greater benefits (Goetz 2004).

One example of a policy that appears to be responding effectively to what is explicitly both a pro place and pro people agenda is HUD's

$5 billion Hope VI program, which began in 1992. The objectives of Hope VI included (1) improving the living environment of residents of severely distressed public housing through demolition, repair, and replacement of those projects; (2) improving neighborhoods around public housing sites; (3) decreasing the concentration of poverty; and (4) building sustainable communities. Preliminary research indicates that Hope VI has successfully demolished many of the nation's most problematic public housing complexes and replaced some of them with higher-quality housing, often in mixed-income communities. Many former residents of the razed projects have been re-housed in their former neighborhoods or provided with housing vouchers that enabled them to find better, safer housing in other communities. One limitation is that many former residents have not yet been successfully relocated, and HUD is taking steps to respond to ongoing needs (Popkin et al. 2004).

It is difficult to disentangle the impact of these two types of policies. But, as with universal and race-specific initiatives, the nature of the problems confronting particular neighborhoods and metropolitan areas in general should dictate the policies of choice. Again, as Edley argued, there is a clear need for both approaches in the "opportunity agenda" (Edley 1996: 46).

Regional Responses to Inequities of Place and Race

A linchpin of spatial and racial inequality is the flight of people, jobs, and other resources to the outlying parts of metropolitan areas, a process subsidized in part by taxpayers throughout the region, who are paying for the roads, schools, and other infrastructure required by the new development. Any effective response must find a way to capture the wealth accumulating at the edge for reinvestment throughout the region. Such regional responses include regional tax-based revenue sharing (in which a portion of the increasing tax revenues from growing commercial and residential property in the outlying suburbs is used for development throughout the region), fair share housing programs or inclusionary zoning (requiring jurisdictions throughout metropolitan areas to provide a reasonable number of affordable housing units for working and poor households), and land use planning initiatives (urban growth boundaries that encourage development in or near the central city and discourage further sprawl) to stimulate balanced development throughout the region (Abbott 2002; Nelson et al. 2004; Orfield 2002).

Regional and metropolitan approaches to government have been long debated, but with some notable exceptions (e.g., Minneapolis/ St. Paul, Indianapolis, Louisville), few communities have taken serious steps in this direction. There are reasons to believe that more may do so in the future. First, the number of voters and jurisdictions who stand to benefit is growing. Many inner-ring suburbs now recognize that they are experiencing problems previously associated with central cities. Myron Orfield has estimated that nationwide, approximately 7 percent of metropolitan area residents live in what he refers to as the "affluent job centers" (Orfield 2002: 171). Even if that 7 percent represents a disproportionately powerful coalition, these numbers should work in favor of more progressive public policy.

Growing income inequality among households and communities, and the increasing number of gated communities that concretely symbolizes that polarization, increasingly have become a subject of public policy debate (Blakely and Snyder 1997; Low 2003). What former labor secretary Robert Reich described as the "secession of the successful" has drained the fiscal capacity of many distressed communities, as well-off families leave cities and move into such communities, where they employ private security forces (thereby relying little on police officers) and private recreational facilities (e.g., country clubs instead of public parks) and send their children to private schools (Reich 1991). In many ways—financially, psychologically, and otherwise—these families withdraw from their surrounding communities, particularly the fiscally strapped central cities of which they were formerly a part. Responding to this demographic and political reality has been a growing concern for public officials at all levels.

Even many of those who presumably are the beneficiaries of sprawl have recognized some of the costs they have begun to pay as well as the benefits of more balanced regional development to mitigate those costs. The congestion and environmental degradation associated with sprawling patterns of development undercut the quality of life that many residents are pursuing. And as indicated earlier, the economic growth of the periphery is not disconnected from what is happening in the central city. Concentrated poverty, the costs of segregation, and uneven development generally undercut prosperity throughout the region.

Uncommon Allies

Many constituencies that traditionally find themselves at odds with each other can find common ground on a range of policies designed to combat sprawl, concentrated poverty, and segregation. Identifying and nurturing such political coalitions is perhaps the key political challenge.

For example, many suburban employers (some of whom may have left their respective cities as part of the sprawling pattern of local development) are unable to find the workers they need, in part because of the high cost of housing in their local communities. Often there are local developers who would like to build affordable housing and lenders who are willing to finance it, but local zoning prohibits such construction. These interests could join with antipoverty groups, affordable housing advocates, civil rights organizations, and others who are generally on the other side of the development table to effectively challenge traditional exclusionary suburban zoning ordinances. Such groups came together in Wisconsin and secured passage of a state land use planning law that provided financial incentives to local municipalities who developed plans for increasing the supply of affordable housing units in their jurisdictions (Squires et al. 1999; Office of Land Information Services 2001).

Welfare reform advocates and affordable housing groups are often on opposing sides of political controversies, yet there are common interests on which they could unite. One objective of welfare reform is to enable people who have been dependent on government services to become economically independent. For many, access to safer neighborhoods where jobs are more readily available can be a critical step to achieving self-sufficiency. In fact, some states have begun to coordinate federal and state housing and welfare services to simultaneously facilitate the entry of former welfare recipients into the workforce and help them find better housing (Sard and Daskal 1998).

Similarly, school choice and fair housing groups—two groups that rarely ally—might recognize that severing the link between the neighborhood in which a family lives and the school their children must attend may well reduce homebuyers' concerns with neighborhood racial composition. Doing so would reduce one barrier to both housing and school segregation while giving students more schooling options (Katz 2003).

In many cities, developers, lenders, community development corporations, environmental groups, local governments, and others are coming together to sponsor transit-oriented development. Such developments create new jobs in locations that are accessible by public transportation, reducing traffic congestion, infrastructure costs, and other disamenities while creating jobs for working families who would not otherwise be able to get to those positions and expanding the pool of potential workers for employers. Increasing such development would yield greater efficiencies in public investment, fewer environmental costs, and more job opportunities for working families (Grady and LeRoy 2006).

This list is hardly meant to be exhaustive. The point is simply that there are some creative political alliances that have begun to be made, and others that are waiting to be made, that can exercise a positive impact on some long-standing and seemingly intractable problems. Sprawl, concentrated poverty, and segregation have many identifiable causes. The confluence of place, race, and privilege becomes less mysterious over time. At least some approaches to reduce uneven development and its many costs are available. Land use planning tools, such as tax-based revenue sharing and the delineation of urban growth boundaries, can be used more extensively to reduce sprawl and some of the associated costs. Community reinvestment initiatives, housing mobility programs, and inclusionary zoning ordinances can be expanded to further diminish the concentration of poverty and its associated costs, most notably, crime. Fair housing law enforcement can be strengthened to reduce racial segregation. With emerging and yet-to-be-discovered political alliances and strategies, what has long been viewed as the seemingly inevitable uneven and inequitable development of metropolitan areas can be ameliorated.

Severing the Connections

When ten-year-old Lafayette Rivers, one of two brothers living in a West Side Chicago public housing complex chronicled in Alex Kotlowitz's award-winning book, *There Are No Children Here*, described his hopes, he began, "If I grow up, I'd like to be a bus driver" (Kotlowitz 1991: x). Children growing up in more privileged neighborhoods often ponder *what* they will do when they grow up, but not *if* they will grow up. The fact that place and race exert such a profound impact on one's future or whether there will even be a future, violates accepted notions of equal opportunity and fair play. The legitimacy of virtually all institutions is challenged when privilege is so unevenly distributed, and for reasons beyond the control of so many individuals.

The costs are not borne by the Lafayette Riverses of the world alone. The security and well-being of every community is threatened when oppositional cultures at such great variance with mainstream norms become as pervasive as they have in many cities today (Anderson 1999; Massey and Denton 1993; Wilson 1996). To paraphrase David Rusk's observation noted earlier, such neighborhoods defeat good programs and good intentions of all kinds, all the time.

By virtually any measure, access to the good life varies dramatically across communities in metropolitan areas today. One constant is the close association between neighborhood and race. But such disparities undermine the quality of life for residents of all areas, and the impacts are not limited to just issues of housing and crime. This threat is compounded when these patterns result from nonmeritocratic factors, such as the neighborhood where people live or the color of their skin. As we observed in Chapter 1, if "Race is woven into the fabric of residential and industrial location choices, of hiring and wage determination, and of the human perceptions that underlie all these processes" (O'Connor 2001: 28), then that is one tapestry that needs to be unraveled. If policy is largely responsible for getting us where we are today, policy can help us pursue a different path tomorrow. It is time to sever the links among race, residence, and privilege.

References

Abbott, Carl. 2002. "Planning a Sustainable City: The Promise and Performance of Portland's Urban Growth Boundary." In *Urban Sprawl: Causes, Consequences, and Policy Responses*, edited by Gregory D. Squires. Washington, DC: Urban Institute.

ACORN. 2004. "Separate and Unequal 2004: Predatory Lending in America." New York: Association of Community Organizations for Reform Now. Available at http://www.acorn.org/index.php?id=1994 (accessed March 18, 2004).

———. 2003a. "Predatory Lending: Press Releases: Congress Considers Preempting All State and Local Laws on Predatory Lending." New York: Association of Community Organizations for Reform Now. Available at http://www.acorn.org/acorn10/predatorylendng/plreleases/ccp.htm (accessed January 29, 2003).

———. 2003b. "ACORN and Household Reach Settlement in Class Action Lawsuit." *ACORN News*, November 25. New York: Association of Community Organizations for Reform Now.

———. 2002. "Separate and Unequal: Predatory Lending in America." New York: Association of Community Organizations for Reform Now. Available at http://www.acorn.org/acorn10/predatorylending/plreports/SU2002/index.php (accessed December 26, 2002).

Agency for Healthcare Research and Quality. 2004. *National Healthcare Disparities Report: Summary* (February). Rockville, MD. Available at http://www.ahrq.gov/qual/nhdr03/nhdrsum03.htm (last accessed on March 28, 2005).

Alba, Richard D., and John R. Logan. 1992. "Assimilation and Stratification in the Homeownership Patterns of Racial and Ethnic Groups." *International Migration Review* 26 (4): 1314–1341.

Alba, Richard D., John R. Logan, and Paul E. Bellair. 1994. "Living with Crime: The Implications of Racial/Ethnic Differences in Suburban Location." *Social Forces* 73 (2): 395–434.

Allard, Scott W., and Sheldon Danziger. 2002. "Proximity and Opportunity: How Residence and Race Affect the Employment of Welfare Recipients." *Housing Policy Debate* 13 (4): 675–700.

American Insurance Association. 1993. *Availability and Use of Homeowners Insurance in the Urban Core of Major American Cities.* Washington, DC: American Insurance Association.

———. N.d. "Credit-Based Insurance Scores: What You Need to Know." Washington, DC: American Insurance Association.

Anderson, Andrea, and Sharon E. Milligan. 2001. "Social Capital and Community Building." Unpublished manuscript for the Aspen Institute Roundtable on Comprehensive Community Building Initiatives for Children and Families. Case Western Reserve University.

Anderson, Elijah. 1999. *Code of the Street: Decency, Violence, and the Moral Life of the Inner City.* New York: W. W. Norton.

Andrews, Edmund L. 2005. "Greenspan Is Concerned About 'Froth' in Housing." *New York Times,* May 21, B1, B4.

Anyon, Jean. 2005. *Radical Possibilities: Public Policy, Urban Education, and a New Social Movement.* New York: Routledge.

———. 1997. *Ghetto Schooling: A Political Economy of Urban Educational Reform.* New York: Teachers College Press.

Austin, James. 2000. "Prisoner Reentry: Current Trends, Practices and Issues." Washington, DC: Institute on Crime, Justice, and Corrections, George Washington University, September.

Austin, James, and John Irwin. 2001. *It's About Time: America's Imprisonment Binge.* Belmont, CA: Wadsworth.

Avery, Robert B., Raphael W. Bostic, Paul S. Calem, and Glenn B. Canner. 1997. "Changes in the Distribution of Banking Offices." *Federal Reserve Bulletin* 83 (September): 707–725.

Avery, Robert B., Raphael W. Bostic, and Glenn B. Canner. 2005. "Assessing the Necessity and Efficiency of the Community Reinvestment Act." *Housing Policy Debate* 16 (1): 143–172.

Avery, Robert B., Glenn B. Canner, and Robert Cook. 2005. "New Information Reported Under HMDA and Its Application in Fair Lending Enforcement." *Federal Reserve Bulletin* 91 (Summer): 344–394.

Badain, David. 1980. "Insurance Redlining and the Future of the Urban Core." *Columbia Journal of Law and Social Problems* 16 (1): 1–83.

Baker, Tom, and Karen McElrath. 1997. "Insurance Claims Discrimination." In *Insurance Redlining: Disinvestment, Reinvestment, and the Evolving Role of Financial Institutions*, edited by Gregory D. Squires. Washington, DC: Urban Institute.

———. 1996. "Whose Safety Net? Home Insurance and Inequality." *Journal of Law and Social Inquiry* 21: 229–264.

Barnekov, Timothy, and Daniel Rich. 1989. "Privatism and the Limits of Local Economic Development Policy." *Urban Affairs Quarterly* 25 (2): 212–238.

Beck, A., and C. Mumola. 1999. *Prisoners in 1998.* Washington, DC: US Department of Justice, Bureau of Justice Statistics.

Becker, Gary S. 1964. *Human Capital: A Theoretical and Empirical Analysis with Special Reference to Education.* New York: Columbia University Press.

Beckett, Kathryn. 1997. *Making Crime Pay: Law and Order in Contemporary America.* New York: Oxford University Press.

Bellair, Paul E. 2000. "Informal Surveillance and Street Crime: A Complex Relationship." *Criminology* 38: 137–167.

Benedict, W. Reed, and Lin Huff-Corzine. 1997. "Return to the Scene of the Punishment: Recidivism of Adult Male Property Offenders on Felony Probation, 1986–1989." *Journal of Research in Crime and Delinquency* 34: 237–252.

Benedict, W. Reed, Lin Huff-Corzine, and Jay Corzine. 1998. "Clean Up and Go Straight: Effects of Drug Treatment on Recidivism Among Felony Probationers." *American Journal of Criminal Justice* 22: 169–187.

Berube, Alan, and William H. Frey. 2002. "A Decade of Mixed Blessings: Urban and Suburban Poverty in Census 2000." Washington, DC: Brookings Institution.

Birnbaum, Birny. 2004. "Results Are In: Insurance Credit Scoring Causes Higher Rates for Poor and Minority Consumers." Austin, TX: Center for Economic Justice.

———. 2003. "Insurer's Use of Credit Scoring for Homeowners Insurance in Ohio: A Report to the Ohio Civil Rights Commission." Columbus: Ohio Civil Rights Commission.

BJS (Bureau of Justice Statistics). 2001. *Sourcebook of Criminal Justice Statistics, 2000.* Washington, DC: US Government Printing Office.

Blakely, Edward J., and Mary Gail Snyder. 1997. *Fortress America: Gated Communities in the United States.* Washington, DC, and Cambridge, MA: Brookings Institution Press and Lincoln Institute of Land Policy.

Blalock, Hubert M., Jr. 1967. *Toward a Theory of Minority-Group Relations.* New York: Wiley.

Blassingame, John W., ed. 1985. *The Frederick Douglass Papers.* New Haven: Yale University Press.

Bluestone, Barry, and Bennett Harrison. 2000. *Growing Prosperity: The Battle for Growth with Equity in the Twenty-First Century.* Boston: Houghton Mifflin.

———. 1982. *The Deindustrialization of America: Plant Closings, Community Abandonment, and the Dismantling of Basic Industry.* New York: Basic Books.

Board of Governors of the Federal Reserve System. 2005. "Banking Agencies Issue Final Community Reinvestment Act Rules." Washington, DC: Board of Governors of the Federal Reserve System (July 19). http://www.federalreserve.gov/BoardDocs/Press/bcreg/2005/20050719/default.htm (last accessed July 21, 2005).

———. 2000. "The Performance and Profitability of CRA-Related Lending." Washington, DC: Board of Governors of the Federal Reserve System.

Bobo, Lawrence D., and Michael P. Massagli. 2001. "Stereotyping and

Urban Inequality." In *Urban Inequality: Evidence from Four Cities*, edited by Alice O'Connor, Chris Tilly, and Lawrence D. Bobo. New York: Russell Sage Foundation.

Bocian, Debbie Gruenstein, and Richard Zhai. 2005. "Borrowers in Higher Minority Areas More Likely to Receive Prepayment Penalties on Subprime Loans." Durham, NC: Center for Responsible Lending.

Bollens, Scott A. 2002. "In Through the Back Door: Social Equity and Regional Governance." *Housing Policy Debate* 13 (4): 631–657.

Bonczar, Thomas P., and Allen J. Beck. 1997. "Lifetime Likelihood of Going to State or Federal Prison." Bureau of Justice Statistics Special Report. Washington, DC: US Department of Justice, NCJ 160092.

Bonilla-Silva, Eduardo. 2003. *Racism Without Racists: Color-Blind Racism and the Persistence of Racial Inequality in the United States*. New York: Rowman and Littlefield.

Bostic, Raphael W., and Breck Robinson. 2002. "Do CRA Agreements Influence Lending Patterns?" Working paper, University of Southern California, Lusk Center for Real Estate.

Bowers, Barbara. 1999. "Redeveloping the Urban Market." *Best's Review* (March): 29–37.

Bowles, Samuel, and Herbert Gintis. 1976. *Schooling in Capitalist America: Educational Reform and the Contradictions of Economic Life*. New York: Basic Books.

Bradbury, Katharine L., Karl E. Case, and Constance R. Dunham. 1989. "Geographic Patterns of Mortgage Lending in Boston, 1982–1987." *New England Economic Review* (September–October): 3–30.

Bradford, Calvin. 2002. "Risk or Race? Racial Disparities and the Subprime Refinance Market." Washington, DC: Center for Community Change.

———. 1979. "Financing Home Ownership: The Federal Role in Neighborhood Decline." *Urban Affairs Quarterly* 14 (3): 313–335.

Bradford, Calvin, and Gale Cincotta. 1992. "The Legacy, the Promise, and the Unfinished Agenda." In *From Redlining to Reinvestment: Community Responses to Urban Disinvestment*, edited by Gregory D. Squires. Philadelphia: Temple University Press.

Brady, James. 1984. "The Social Economy of Arson: Vandals, Gangsters, Bankers, and Officials in the Making of an Urban Problem." *Research in Law, Deviance, and Social Control* 6: 199–242.

Branch, Taylor. 1998. *Pillar of Fire: America in the King Years, 1963–1965*. New York: Simon and Schuster.

———. 1988. *Parting the Water: America in the King Years, 1954–1963*. New York: Simon and Schuster.

Brenner, Lynn. 1993. *The Insurance Information Institute's Handbook for Reporters*. New York: Insurance Information Institute.

Brown, Michael K., Martin Carnoy, Elliott Currie, Troy Duster, David B. Oppenheimer, Marjorie M. Shultz, and David Wellman. 2003. *White-Washing Race: The Myth of a Color-Blind Society*. Berkeley: University of California Press.

Bullard, Robert D. 1996. *Unequal Protection: Environmental Justice and Communities of Color.* San Francisco: Sierra Club Books.

Buntin, John. 2003. "Mean Streets Revisited: Ex-Cons Coming Home in Big Numbers Threaten the Stability of Fragile Inner-City Neighborhoods." Governing.com (August 24). Last accessed at www.governing.com on March 15, 2005.

Bursik, Robert J., and Harold G. Grasmick. 1993. *Neighborhoods and Crime: The Dimensions of Effective Community Control.* New York: Lexington.

Butterfield, Fox. 2003. "With Cash Tight, States Reassess Long Jail Terms." *New York Times,* November 10.

Camp, George M., and Camille Graham Camp. 1998. *The Corrections Yearbook, 1998.* Middletown, CT: Criminal Justice Institute.

Canner, Glenn. 2003. Personal email communication with authors (November 12).

———. 2002. Personal interview with author by telephone (November).

Cashin, Sheryll. 2004. *The Failures of Integration: How Race and Class are Undermining the American Dream.* New York: Public Affairs.

Caskey, John. 2002. "Bringing Unbanked Households Into the Banking System." Washington, DC: Brookings Institution. Available at http://www.brookings.edu/es/urban/capitalxchange/article10.htm (accessed on January 21, 2002).

———. 1994. *Fringe Banking: Check-Cashing Outlets, Pawnshops, and the Poor.* New York: Russell Sage Foundation.

Center for Responsible Lending. 2005a. "Miller, Watt, and Frank Sponsor Anti-Predatory Lending Legislation Based on Landmark North Carolina Solution," Durham, NC: Center for Responsible Lending (March 10).

———. 2005b. "The Ney-Kanjorski Bill: Replaces Effective State Protections Against Predatory Lending with a Weak Federal Standard." Durham, NC: Center for Responsible Lending (March 16).

Chambliss, William. 1995. "Crime Control and Ethnic Minorities: Legitimizing Racial Oppression by Creating Moral Panics." In *Ethnicity, Race and Crime: Perspectives Across Time and Place,* edited by Darnell F. Hawkins. New York: SUNY Press, 235–258.

Cisneros, Henry G. 1993. "Interwoven Destinies: Cities and the Nation." In *Interwoven Destinies: Cities and the Nation,* edited by Henry G. Cisneros. New York: W. W. Norton.

Clarke, Stevens H., Yuan-Huei W. Lin, and W. LeAnn Wallace. 1998. *Probationer Recidivism in North Carolina: Measurement and Classification Risk.* Chapel Hill: University of North Carolina, Institute of Government.

Clear, Todd. 1994. *Harm in American Penology.* Albany: State University of New York Press.

Clear, Todd, and Anthony A. Braga. 1995. "Community Corrections." In *Crime,* edited by James Q. Wilson and Joan Petersilia. San Francisco: Institute for Contemporary Studies.

Clear, Todd, Dina Rose, Elin Waring, and Kristin Scully. 2003. "Coercive Mobility and Crime." *Justice Quarterly* 20: 33–63.

Cloud, Cathy. 2004. Personal interview with author by telephone (January).

Community Action Committee of the Lehigh Valley. 1995. "Homeowners Insurance and the Inner-City Neighborhood." Lehigh, PA: Community Action Committee of the Lehigh Valley.

Community Reinvestment Association–North Carolina, Consumer Federation of America, Consumers Union, National Community Reinvestment Coalition, National Consumer Law Center, and US Public Interest Research Group. Letter to Members of the 107th Congress, October 2, 2002.

Comptroller of the Currency. 2004. "OCC Issues Final Rules on National Bank Preemption and Visitorial Powers; Includes Strong Standard to Keep Predatory Lending out of National Banks." News Release. Washington, DC: Comptroller of the Currency.

———. 2003. "OCC Working Paper: Economic Issues in Predatory Lending." Washington, DC: Comptroller of the Currency.

Conley, Dalton. 1999. *Being Black, Living in the Red: Race, Wealth, and Social Policy in America*. Berkeley: University of California Press.

Crowell, Suzanne, Wanda Johnson, and Tami Trost. 1994. *The Fair Housing Amendments Act of 1988: The Enforcement Report*. Washington, DC: US Commission on Civil Rights.

Crutchfield, Robert D. 1989. "Labor Stratification and Violent Crime." *Social Forces* 68: 489–512.

DeNavas-Walt, Carmen. 2004. Personal communication (September 1).

DeNavas-Walt, Carmen, Bernadette D. Proctor, and Robert J. Mills. 2004. *Income, Poverty, and Health Insurance Coverage in the United States: 2003*. US Census Bureau, Current Population Reports, 60-226. Washington, DC: US Government Printing Office.

Davern, Michael E., and Patricia J. Fisher, US Census Bureau. 2001. "Current Population Reports, Household Economic Studies, Series P70–P71." *Household Net Worth and Asset Ownership: 1995*. Washington, DC: US Government Printing Office.

Deane, Daniela. 2005. "Everybody's an Investor Now." *Washington Post*, May 21, F1, F8.

Dedman, Bill. 1989. "Blacks Turned Down for Home Loans from S and Ls Twice as Often as Whites." *Atlanta Journal-Constitution*, January 22.

———. 1988. "The Color of Money." *Atlanta Journal-Constitution*, May 1–4.

Denton, Nancy. 2001. "Housing as a Means of Asset Accumulation: A Good Strategy for the Poor?" In *Assets for the Poor: The Benefits of Spreading Asset Ownership*, edited by Thomas M. Shapiro and Edward Willf. New York: Russell Sage Foundation, 232–268.

Downs, Anthony. 1999. "Some Realities About Sprawl and Urban Decline." *Housing Policy Debate* 10 (4): 955–974.

———. 1998. "The Big Picture: How America's Cities are Growing." *Brookings Review* 16 (4): 8–11.

Dreier, Peter. 2006. "Katrina and Power in America." *Urban Affairs Review* 41 (4): 528–549.

———. 2003. "The Future of Community Reinvestment: Challenges and Opportunities in a Changing Environment." *Journal of the American Planning Association* 69 (4): 341–353.

Dreier, Peter, John Mollenkopf, and Todd Swanstrom. 2001. *Place Matters: Metropolitics for the Twenty-first Century*. Lawrence: University Press of Kansas.

Edley, Christopher, Jr. 1996. *Not All Black and White: Affirmative Action and American Values*. New York: Hill and Wang.

Edsall, Thomas Byrne, and Mary D. Edsall. 1991. *Chain Reaction: The Impact of Race, Rights, and Taxes on American Politics*. New York: W. W. Norton.

Ellen, Ingrid Gould. 2000. *Sharing America's Neighborhoods: The Prospects for Stable Racial Integration*. Cambridge, MA: Harvard University Press.

Ellen, Ingrid Gould, and Amy Ellen Schwartz. 2000. "No Easing Answers: Cautionary Notes for Competitive Cities." *Brookings Review* 18 (3): 44–47.

Ellen, Ingrid Gould, and Margery Austin Turner. 2003. "Do Neighborhoods Matter and Why?" In *Choosing a Better Life: Evaluating the Moving to Opportunity Experiment*, edited by John Goering and Judith D. Feins. Washington, DC: Urban Institute, 313–338.

———. 1997. "Does Neighborhood Matter? Assessing Recent Evidence." *Housing Policy Debate* 8 (4): 833–866.

Elliehausen, Gregory, and Michel E. Staten. 2003. "An Update on North Carolina's High-Cost Mortgage Law." Washington, DC: McDonough School of Business, Credit Research Center, Georgetown University.

———. 2002. "The Regulation of Subprime Mortgage Products: An Analysis of North Carolina's Predatory Lending Law." Washington, DC: McDonough School of Business, Credit Research Center, Georgetown University.

Elliott, Delbert S., William Julius Wilson, David Huizinga, Robert J. Sampson, Amanda Elliott, and Bruce Rankin. 1996. "The Effects of Neighborhood Disadvantage on Adolescent Development." *Journal of Research in Crime and Delinquency* 33: 389–426.

Elsner, Alan. 2005. "Lawmakers Launch Effort to Help Released Felons." Reuters, February 5. Last accessed at www.reuters.com on March 15, 2005.

Engel, Kathleen C., and Patricia A. McCoy. 2004. "Predatory Lending and Community Development at Loggerheads." Paper presented at the Community Development Finance Research Conference, Federal Reserve Bank of New York, New York, December 10.

———. 2002a. "The CRA Implications of Predatory Lending." *Fordham Urban Law Journal* 29: 1571–1605.

———. 2002b. "A Tale of Three Markets: The Law and Economics of Predatory Lending." *Texas Law Review* 80 (6): 1258–1381.

Ernst, Keith S. 2005. "Borrowers Gain No Interest Rate Benefits from Prepayment Penalties on Subprime Mortgages." Durham, NC: Center for Responsible Lending.

Fainstein, Susan. 2001. *The City Builders: Property Development in New York and London, 1980–2000.* Lawrence: University Press of Kansas.

Fainstein, Susan, and Scott Campbell, eds. 2002. *Readings in Urban Theory.* Oxford: Blackwell.

Farley, Reynolds, and William H. Frey. 1994. "Changes in the Segregation of Whites from Blacks During the 1980s: Small Steps Toward a More Integrated Society." *American Sociological Review* 59: 23–45.

Feagin, Joe R. 2000. *Racist America: Roots, Current Realities, and Future Reparation.* New York: Routledge.

———. 1998. *The New Urban Paradigm: Critical Perspectives on the City.* New York: Rowman and Littlefield.

Federal Financial Institutions Examination Council. 2003a. "Community Reinvestment Act: Interagency Questions and Answers." Available at http://www.ffiec.gov/cra/qnadoc.htm (last accessed August 4, 2003).

———. 2003b. "Home Mortgage Disclosure Act: Who Reports HMDA Data?" Available at http://www.ffiec.gov/hmda/reporter.htm (last accessed September 6, 2003).

———. 2003c. "Reports—Nationwide Summary Statistics for 2002 HMDA Fact Sheet." Washington, DC: Federal Financial Institutions Examination Council.

Federal Trade Commission. 2002. "Citigroup Settles FTC Charges Against the Associates Record-Setting $215 Million for Subprime Lending Victims." Washington, DC: Federal Trade Commission.

Fischer, Mary J. 2003. "The Relative Importance of Income and Race in Determining Residential Outcomes in US Urban Areas, 1970–2000." *Urban Affairs Review* 38 (5): 669–696.

Fisher, Alan. 2005. "The Financial Divide: An Uneven Playing Field." San Francisco: California Reinvestment Coalition.

Fiss, Owen. 2003 *A Way Out: America's Ghettos and the Legacy of Racism.* Princeton: Princeton University Press.

Flippen, Chenoa. 2004. "Unequal Returns to Housing Investments? A Study of Real Housing Appreciation Among Black, White, and Hispanic Households." *Social Forces* 82 (4): 1523–1551.

———. 2001. "Racial and Ethnic Inequality in Homeownership and Housing Equity." *Sociological Quarterly* 42 (2): 121–149.

Ford, Crystal. 2003. "Endorsement for Rep. Gutierrez Bill 'Insurance Credit Score Disclosure and Reporting Act.'" Washington, DC: National Community Reinvestment Coalition.

Frankenberg, Erica, Chungmei Lee, and Gary Orfield. 2003. "A Multiracial Society with Segregated Schools: Are We Losing the Dream?" Cambridge, MA: Civil Rights Project, Harvard University.

Frazier, John W., Florence M. Margai, and Eugene Tettey-Fio. 2003. *Race and Place: Equity Issues in Urban America.* Boulder, CO: Westview Press.

Frey, William H. 2001. "Melting Pot Suburbs: A Census 2000 Study of Suburban Diversity." Washington, DC: The Brookings Institution.

Friedman, Samantha, and Emily Rosenbaum. 2003. "Does Home Ownership Mean Better Housing Conditions? Assessing the Role of Nativity Status and Race/Ethnicity." Unpublished working paper.

Fullilove, Mindy Thompson. 2004. *Root Shock: How Tearing Up City Neighborhoods Hurts America, and What We Can Do About It.* New York: Ballantine.

Fullwood, Sam. 1996. *Waking from the Dream: My Life in the Black Middle Class.* New York: Anchor Books.

Gainey, Randy R., Brian K. Payne, and Mike O'Toole. 2000. "The Relationships Between Time in Jail, Time on Electronic Monitoring, and Recidivism: An Event History Analysis of a Jail-Based Program." *Justice Quarterly* 17: 733–752.

Galster, George, Royce Hanson, Michael R. Ratcliffe, Harold Wolman, Stephen Coleman, and Jason Freihage. 2001. "Wrestling Sprawl to the Ground: Defining and Measuring an Elusive Concept." *Housing Policy Debate* 12 (4): 681–718.

Galster, George, Douglass Wissoker, and Wendy Zimmermann. 2001. "Testing for Discrimination in Home Insurance: Results from New York City and Phoenix." *Urban Studies* 38 (1): 141–156.

Gendreau, Paul, Tracy Little, and Claire Goggin. 1996. "A Meta-Analysis of the Predictors of Adult Offender Recidivism: What Works!" *Criminology* 34: 575–607.

General Accounting Office. 2004. "Consumer Protection: Federal and State Agencies Face Challenges in Combating Predatory Lending." Washington, DC: General Accounting Office.

Goering, John. 2005. "Expanding Housing Choice and Integrating Neighborhoods: The MTO Experiment." In *The Geography of Opportunity: Race and Housing Choice in Metropolitan America*, edited by Xavier de Souza Briggs. Washington, DC: Brookings Institution.

Goering, John, and Judith D. Feins. 2003. *Choosing a Better Life: Evaluating the Moving to Opportunity Social Experiment.* Washington, DC: Urban Institute Press.

Goering, John, Judith D. Feins, and Todd M. Richardson. 2002. "A Cross-Site Analysis of Initial Moving to Opportunity Demonstration Results." *Journal of Housing Research* 13 (1): 1–30.

Goering, John, and Ron Wienk. 1996. *Mortgage Lending, Racial Discrimination, and Federal Policy.* Washington, DC: Urban Institute.

Goetz, Edward G. 2004. "Desegregation Lawsuits and Public Housing Dispersal." *Journal of the American Planning Association* 70 (3): 282–299.

Goldsmith, William W. 2002. "From the Metropolis to Globalization: The Dialectics of Race and Urban Form." In *Readings in Urban Theory*, edited by Susan S. Fainstein and Scott Campbell. Oxford: Blackwell.

Gotham, Kevin Fox. 2002. *Race, Real Estate, and Uneven Development: The*

Kansas City Experience, 1900–2000. Albany: State University of New York Press.

Gottdiener, Marc, and Joe R. Feagin. 1988. "The Paradigm Shift in Urban Sociology." *Urban Affairs Quarterly* 24 (2): 163–187.

Gottfredson, S. D., and Ralph B. Taylor. 1988. "Community Contexts and Criminal Offenders." In *Communities and Crime Reduction*, edited by T. Hope and M. Shaw. London: Her Majesty's Stationery Office, 62–82.

Grace, Martin F., and Robert W. Klein. 1999. "An Analysis of Urban Homeowners Insurance Markets in Texas." Atlanta: Center for Risk Management and Insurance Research, Georgia State University.

Grady, Sarah, and Greg LeRoy. 2006. "Making the Connection: Transit-Oriented Development and Jobs." Washington, DC: Good Jobs First.

Gramlich, Edward M. 2003. Remarks by Edward M. Gramlich at the Texas Association of Bank Counsel Twenty-Seventh Annual Convention, South Padre Island, Texas, October 9.

———. 2002. Remarks by Edward M. Gramlich at the Housing Bureau for Seniors Conference, Ann Arbor, Michigan, January 18.

———. 1998. Remarks by Edward M. Gramlich at Widener University, Chester, Pennsylvania, November 6.

Grogan, Paul S., and Tony Proscio. 2000. *Comeback Cities: A Blueprint for Urban Neighborhood Revitalization.* Boulder, CO: Westview Press.

Guest, Avery. 2000. "Mediate Community: The Nature of Local and Extra-local Ties in Metropolis." *Urban Affairs Review* 36: 603–627.

Haag, Susan White. 2000. "Community Reinvestment and Cities: A Literature Review of CRA's Impact and Future." Washington, DC: Brookings Institution Center on Urban and Metropolitan Policy.

Hagan, John. 1994. "The New Sociology of Crime and Inequality in America." *Studies on Crime and Crime Prevention* 3: 7–23.

Hanley, D. E., and Edward J. Latessa. 1997. "Correlates of Recidivism: The Gender Division." Paper presented at the 1997 annual meeting of the Academy of Criminal Justice Sciences, Louisville, Kentucky, March.

Harrison, Bennett, and Barry Bluestone. 1988. *The Great U-Turn: Corporate Restructuring and the Polarizing of America.* New York: Basic Books.

Harrison, P. M., and J. C. Karberg. 2003. *Prison and Jail Inmates at Midyear 2003.* Washington DC, Department of Justice, Bureau of Justice Statistics.

Hart, Peter D., and Robert M. Teeter. 2002. "Results of the Fannie Mae Foundation Affordable Housing Survey: Summary of Findings." Washington, DC: Fannie Mae Foundation.

Hawley, Amos. 1971. *Urban Society: An Ecological Approach.* New York: Wiley.

Hays, R. Allen. 1995. *The Federal Government and Urban Housing: Ideology and Change in Public Policy.* Albany: SUNY Press.

Heimer, Carol A. 1985. *Reactive Risk and Rational Action: Managing Moral Hazard in Insurance Contracts.* Berkeley: University of California Press.

———. 1982. "The Racial and Organizational Origins of Insurance Redlining." *Journal of Intergroup Relations* 10 (3): 42–60.

Hepburn, John R., and Celesta A. Albonetti. 1994. "Recidivism Among Drug Offenders: A Survival Analysis of the Effects of Offender Characteristics, Type of Offense, and Two Types of Intervention." *Journal of Quantitative Criminology* 10: 159–179.

Herrnstein, Richard, and Charles Murray. 1994. *The Bell Curve: Intelligence and Class Structure in American Life.* New York: Free Press.

Hillier, Amy E. 2003. "Spatial Analysis of Historical Redlining: A Methodological Exploration." *Housing Policy Debate* 14: 137–167.

Hirsch, Arnold. 1998. *Making the Second Ghetto: Race and Housing in Chicago, 1940–1960.* Chicago: University of Chicago Press.

Holzer, Harry J., and Sheldon Danziger. 2001. "Are Jobs Available for Disadvantaged Workers in Urban Areas?" In *Urban Inequality: Evidence from Four Cities,* edited by Alice O'Connor, Chris Tilly, and Lawrence D. Bobo. New York: Russell Sage Foundation.

Horan, Patrick M. 1978. "Is Status Attainment Research Atheoretical." *American Sociological Review* 43 (4): 534–541.

Horn, Martin F. 2000. *Rethinking Sentencing.* Papers from the Executive Sessions on Sentencing and Corrections. Washington, DC: National Institute of Justice, February.

Household International. 2002. "News Release." Prospect Heights, IL: Household International, October 11.

Housing Opportunities Made Equal. 1998. "Jury Hands Down $100,500,000 Verdict Against Nationwide Insurance Company in Housing Discrimination Case." Press release, October 26, Richmond, VA.

Hudson, Michael. 1996. *Merchants of Misery: How Corporate America Profits from Poverty.* Monroe, ME: Common Courage Press.

Hunter, J. Robert, and Miranda Sissons. 1995. "State Legislators and Insurance Conflicts of Interest." Washington, DC: Consumer Federation of America.

Iceland, John, Daniel H. Weinberg, and Erika Steinmetz. 2002a. *Racial and Ethnic Residential Segregation in the United States: 1980–2000.* US Census Bureau, Series CENSR-3. Washington, DC: US Government Printing Office.

———. 2002b. "Racial and Ethnic Residential Segregation in the United States: 1980–2000." Paper presented at the annual meetings of the Population Association of America, Atlanta, May 9–11.

Ihlanfeldt, Keith R. 2004. "Exclusionary Land-Use Regulations Within Suburban Communities: A Review of the Evidence and Policy Prescriptions." *Urban Studies* 41 (2): 261–284.

Illinois Public Action. 1993. "An Analysis of Zip Code Distribution of State Farm and Allstate Agents and Policies in Chicago." Chicago: Illinois Public Action.

Immergluck, Dan. 2004. *Credit to the Community: Community Reinvestment and Fair Lending Policy in the United States.* Armonk, NY: M. E. Sharpe.

Immergluck, Dan, and Geoff Smith. 2004a. "An Econometric Analysis of the Effect of Subprime Lending on Neighborhood Foreclosures." Paper presented at the Thirty-Fourth Annual Meeting of the Urban Affairs Association, Washington, DC.

———. 2004b. "Risky Business: An Econometric Analysis of the Relationship Between Subprime Lending and Neighborhood Foreclosures." Chicago: Woodstock Institute.

Inside Mortgage Financing Publications. 2005. *Mortgage Market Statistical Annual 2005.* 2 Vols. Bethesda, MD: Inside Mortgage Financing Publications.

Insurance Information Institute. 2003. *The Financial Services Fact Book.* New York: Insurance Information Institute.

———. 2002. *The Fact Book 2002.* New York: Insurance Information Institute.

Insurance Research Council. 1997. *Homeowners Loss Patterns in Eight Cities: Chicago, Detroit, Los Angeles, Milwaukee, New Orleans, New York, Philadelphia, St. Louis.* Wheaton, IL: Insurance Research Council.

Irish, James F. 1989. *Probation and Recidivism: A Study of Probation Adjustment and Its Relationship to Post-Probation Outcome for Adult Criminal Offenders.* Mineola, NY: Nassau County Probation Department.

Jackson, Kenneth T. 2000. "Gentleman's Agreement: Discrimination in Metropolitan America." In *Reflections on Regionalism,* edited by Bruce Katz. Washington, DC: Brookings Institution.

———. 1985. *Crabgrass Frontier: The Suburbanization of the United States.* New York: Oxford University Press.

Jacobs, Jane. 1961. *The Death and Life of Great American Cities.* New York: Vintage Books.

Jacoby, Tamar. 1998. *Someone Else's House: Americas Unfinished Struggle for Integration.* New York: Free Press.

Jankowski, Louis W. 1992. *Correctional Populations in the United States, 1990.* Washington, DC: US Department of Justice, Bureau of Justice Statistics.

Jargowsky, Paul. 2003. "Stunning Progress, Hidden Problems: The Dramatic Decline of Concentrated Poverty in the 1990s." Washington, DC: Brookings Institution.

———. 1996. *Poverty and Place: Ghettos, Barrios, and the American City.* New York: Russell Sage Foundation.

Joint Center for Housing Studies of Harvard University. 2004. "Credit, Capital and Communities: The Implications of the Changing Mortgage Banking Industry for Community Based Organizations." Cambridge: Joint Center for Housing Studies of Harvard University.

———. 2002a. "The State of the Nation's Housing 2002." Cambridge: Joint Center for Housing Studies of Harvard University.

———. 2002b. *The Twenty-Fifth Anniversary of the Community Reinvestment Act: Access to Capital in an Evolving Financial Services System.* Cambridge, MA: Joint Center for Housing Studies.

Judd, Dennis R. 1984. *The Politics of American Cities: Private Power and Public Policy*. Boston: Little, Brown.

Kahlenberg, Richard D. 1996. *The Remedy: Class, Race, and Affirmative Action*. New York: Basic Books.

Kain, John. 2004. "A Pioneer's Perspective on the Spatial Mismatch Literature." *Urban Studies* 41 (1): 7–32.

———. 1992. "The Spatial Mismatch Hypothesis: Three Decades Later." *Housing Policy Debates* 3 (2): 371–460.

———. 1968. "Housing Segregation, Negro Employment and Metropolitan Decentralization." *Quarterly Journal of Economics* 82 (2): 175–197.

Katz, Bruce. 2003. Presentation at the Fannie Mae Foundation Annual Housing Conference, "Raising Housing on the Nation's Agenda: Building from the Millennial Housing Commission," Washington, DC, October 9.

Katz, Bruce, and Jennifer Bradley. 1999. "Divided We Sprawl." *Atlantic Monthly*, December, 26–42.

Katznelson, Ira. 1981. *City Trenches: Urban Politics and the Patterning of Class in the United States*. New York: Pantheon Books.

Kennedy, Peter. 1992. *A Guide to Econometrics*. 3rd ed. Cambridge, MA: MIT Press.

Kennedy, Randall. 1997. *Race, Crime, and the Law*. New York: Vintage.

Kest, Steven. 2003. Personal communication (May 13).

Kest, Steven, and Maud Hurd. 2003. "Fighting Predatory Lending from the Ground Up: An Issue of Economic Justice." In *Organizing Access to Capital: Advocacy and the Democratization of Financial Institutions*, edited by Gregory D. Squires. Philadelphia: Temple University Press.

Kilborn, Peter T. 2002. "Easy Credit and Hard Times Bring a Flood of Foreclosures." *New York Times*, November 24.

Kincaid, Mark L. 1994. *Insurance Redlining in Texas: A Preliminary Report*. Austin: Office of the Public Insurance Counsel.

King, Uriah, Delvin Davis, and Keith Ernst. 2005. "Race Matters: The Concentration of Payday Lenders in African American Neighborhoods in North Carolina." Durham, NC: Center for Responsible Lending.

Kingsley, G. Thomas, and Kathryn L. S. Pettit. 2003. "Concentrated Poverty: A Change in Course." Washington, DC: Brookings Institution.

Kington, Raynard S., and Herbert W. Nickens. 2001. "Racial and Ethnic Differences in Health: Recent Trends, Current Patterns, Future Directions." In *America Becoming: Racial Trends and Their Consequences,* Vol. 2, edited by Neil. J. Smelser, William Julius Wilson, and Faith Mitchell. Washington, DC: National Academy Press.

Klein, Robert W. 1997. "Availability and Affordability Problems in Urban Homeowners Insurance Markets." In *Insurance Redlining: Disinvestment, Reinvestment, and the Evolving Role of Financial Institutions*, edited by Gregory D. Squires. Washington, DC: Urban Institute.

———. 1995. *The Impact of Loss Costs on Urban Homeowners Insurance Markets*. Kansas City, MO: National Association of Insurance Commissioners.

Klinenberg, Eric. 2002. *Heat Wave: A Social Autopsy of Disaster in Chicago.* Chicago: University of Chicago Press.

Kling, Jeffrey R., Jens Ludwig, and Lawrence F. Katz. 2005. "Neighborhood Effects on Crime for Female and Male Youth: Evidence from a Randomized Housing Voucher Experiment." *Quarterly Journal of Economics* 120 (1).

Kornhauser, Ruth. 1978. *Social Sources of Delinquency.* Chicago: University of Chicago Press.

Kotlowitz, Alex. 1991. *There Are No Children Here: The Story of Two Boys Growing Up in the Other America.* New York: Doubleday.

Krivo, Lauren J., and Ruth D. Peterson. 1996. "Extremely Disadvantaged Neighborhoods and Urban Crime." *Social Forces* 75 (2): 619–650.

Krugman, Paul. 2002. "For Richer." *New York Times Magazine*, October 20, 62–67, 76, 77, 141, 142.

Kruttschnitt, Candace, Christopher Uggen, and Kelly Shelton. 2000. "Predictors of Desistance Among Sex Offenders: The Interaction of Formal and Informal Social Controls." *Justice Quarterly* 17: 61–88.

Krysan, Maria, and Amanda E. Lewis, eds. 2004. *The Changing Terrain of Race and Ethnicity.* New York: Russell Sage Foundation.

Kubrin, Charis E. 2000. "Racial Heterogeneity and Crime: Measuring Static and Dynamic Effects." *Research in Community Sociology* 10: 189–218.

Kubrin, Charis E., and Ronald Weitzer. 2003a. "New Directions in Social Disorganization Theory." *Journal of Research in Crime and Delinquency* 40: 374–402.

———. 2003b. "Retaliatory Homicide: Concentrated Disadvantage and Neighborhood Culture." *Social Problems* 50: 157–180.

LaFalce, John. 2000. "Open Forum: Predatory Lending 'Epidemic.'" *National Mortgage News*, April 24, 4.

Langan, Patrick A., and Mark A. Cunniff. 1992. *Recidivism of Felons on Probation, 1986–1989.* Washington, DC: Bureau of Justice Statistics.

Langan, Patrick A., and David J. Levin. 2002. "Recidivism of Prisoners Released in 1994." Bureau of Justice Statistics Special Report. Washington, DC: US Department of Justice.

Lanza-Kaduce, Lonn, Karen F. Parker, and Charles W. Thomas. 1999. "A Comparative Recidivism Analysis of Releasees from Private and Public Prisons." *Crime and Delinquency* 45: 28–47.

La Vigne, Nancy G., and Vera Kachnowski. 2005. *Texas Prisoners' Reflections on Returning Home.* Washington, DC: Urban Institute.

La Vigne, Nancy G., and Samuel J. Wolf, with Jesse Jannetta. 2004. *Voices of Experience: Focus Group Findings on Prisoner Reentry in the State of Rhode Island.* Washington, DC: Urban Institute.

Leadership Conference on Civil Rights. 2002. "Building Healthy Communities." Washington, DC: Leadership Conference on Civil Rights.

Lee, Bill Lann. 1999. "An Issue of Public Importance: The Justice Department's Enforcement of the Fair Housing Act." *Cityscape* 4 (3): 35–56.

Lenski, Gerhard E. 1966. *Power and Privilege: A Theory of Social Stratification*. New York: McGraw-Hill.

Leonhardt, David. 1997. "Two Tier Marketing." *Business Week*, March 17, 82–90.

LeRoy, Greg. 2005. *The Great American Jobs Scam: Corporate Tax Dodging and the Myth of Job Creation*. San Francisco: Berrett-Koehler Publishers.

———. 1997. *No More Candy Store: States and Cities Making Job Subsidies Accountable*. Chicago: Federation for Industrial Retention and Renewal and Grassroots Policy Project.

LeRoy, Greg, Sara Hinkley, and Katie Tallman. 2000. *Another Way Sprawl Happens: Economic Development Subsidies in a Twin Cities Suburb*. Washington, DC: Institute on Taxation and Economic Policy.

Lewis, Karen. 2002. "Smart Borrowing Group's Goal." *Richmond Times-Dispatch*, October 27.

Lewis Mumford Center. 2001a. "Ethnic Diversity Grows; Neighborhood Integration Lags Behind." Available at http://mumford1.dyndns.org/cen2000/WholePop/WPreport/page1.html (accessed September 18, 2002).

———. 2001b. "Metropolitan Racial and Ethnic Change—Census 2000." Albany: Lewis Mumford Center.

Levitt, Steven D. 1997. "Using Electoral Cycles in Police Hiring to Estimate the Effect of Police on Crime." *American Economic Review* 7 (3): 270–290.

Li, Wei, and Keith S. Ernst. 2006. *The Best Value in the Subprime Market: State Predatory Lending Reforms*. Durham, NC: Center for Responsible Lending.

Lindblom, Charles E. 1977. *Politics and Markets: The World's Political Economic System*. New York: Basic Books.

Listwan, Shelley Johnson, Jody L. Sundt, Alexander M. Holsinger, and Edward J. Latessa. 2003. "The Effect of Drug Court Programming on Recidivism: The Cincinnati Experience." *Crime and Delinquency* 49: 389–411.

Litan, Robert E., Nicolas P. Retsinas, Eric Belsky, Gary Fauth, Paul Leonard, and Maureen Kennedy. 2001. *The Community Reinvestment Act After Financial Modernization: A Final Report*. Washington, DC: US Department of the Treasury.

Logan, John R. 2004. "Resegregation in American Public Schools? Not in the 1990s." Albany: Lewis Mumford Center.

———. 2003. "Life and Death in the City: Neighborhoods in Context." *Contexts* 2 (2): 33–40.

———. 2002a. "The Suburban Advantage." Working paper. Albany: Lewis Mumford Center.

———. 2002b. "Separate and Unequal: The Neighborhood Gap for Blacks and Hispanics in Metropolitan America." Working paper. Albany: Lewis Mumford Center.

Logan, John R., and Harvey Molotch. 1987. *Urban Fortunes.* Berkeley: University of California Press.

Logan, John R., Brian J. Stults, and Reynolds Farley. 2004. "Segregation of Minorities in the Metropolis: Two Decades of Change." *Demography* 41 (1): 1–22.

Long, James, and Steven Caudill. 1992. "Racial Differences in Home Ownership and Housing Wealth: 1970–1986." *Economic Inquiry* 30: 83–100.

Long, Larry E. 1988. *Migration and Residential Mobility in the United States.* New York: Russell Sage Foundation.

Low, Setha. 2003. *Behind the Gates: Life, Security, and the Pursuit of Happiness in Fortress America.* New York: Routledge.

Lunt, Penny. 1993. "Banks Make Check-Cashing Work." *ABA Banking Journal* (December): 51–52.

Luquetta, Andrea. 2002. Personal communication (March 29).

———. 2000. Personal communication with Gregory D. Squires (September 20).

Luquetta, Andrea, and Deborah Goldberg. 2001. "Insuring Investment." *Shelterforce* 23 (6): 12–15.

Lynch, James P., and William J. Sabol. 2001. "Prisoner Reentry in Perspective." *Crime Policy Report,* Vol. 3. Washington, DC: Urban Institute Justice Policy Center.

Lynch, Robert G. 2004. *Rethinking Growth Strategies: How State and Local Taxes and Services Affect Development.* Washington, DC: Economic Policy Institute.

Lynch, William H. 1997. "NAACP v. American Family." In *Insurance Redlining: Disinvestment, Reinvestment, and the Evolving Role of Financial Institutions,* edited by Gregory D. Squires. Washington, DC: Urban Institute.

MacDonald, Heather I. 1998. "Mortgage Lending and Residential Integration in a Hypersegregated MSA: The Case of St. Louis." *Urban Studies* 35 (11): 1971–1993.

MacKenzie, Doris L., K. Browning, S. B. Skroban, and D. A. Smith. 1999. "The Impact of Probation on the Criminal Activities of Offenders." *Journal of Research in Crime and Delinquency* 36: 423–453.

MacKenzie, Doris Layton, and Spencer De Li. 2002. "The Impact of Formal and Informal Social Controls on the Criminal Activities of Probationers." *Journal of Research in Crime and Delinquency* 39: 243–276.

Malveaux, Julianne. 2003. "'Banking While Black' Hurts Homeowners." *USA Today,* December 12.

Markowitz, Fred E., Paul E. Bellair, Allen E. Liska, and Jianhong Liu. 2001. "Extending Social Disorganization Theory: Modeling the Relationships Between Cohesion, Disorder, and Fear." *Criminology* 39: 293–319.

Massey, Douglas S. 2001. "Residential Segregation and Neighborhood Conditions in US Metropolitan Areas." In *America Becoming: Racial Trends and Their Consequences,* edited by Neil J. Smelser, William

Julius Wilson, and Faith Mitchell. Washington, DC: National Academy Press.

———. 1995. "Getting Away with Murder: Segregation and Violent Crime in Urban America." *University of Pennsylvania Law Review* 143 (5): 1203–1232.

———. 1985. "Ethnic Residential Segregation: A Theoretical Synthesis and Empirical Review." *Sociology and Social Research* 69: 315–350.

Massey, Douglas S., Gretchen A. Condran, and Nancy A. Denton. 1987. "The Effect of Residential Segregation on Black Social and Economic Well-Being." *Social Forces* 66 (1): 29–56.

Massey, Douglas S., and Nancy Denton. 1993. *American Apartheid: Segregation and the Making of the Underclass*. Cambridge, MA: Harvard University Press.

———. 1988. "The Dimensions of Residential Segregation." *Social Forces* 67: 281–315.

———. 1987. "Trends in the Residential Segregation of Blacks, Hispanics, and Asians." *American Sociological Review* 52: 802–825.

Massey, Douglas S., and Mary J. Fischer. 1999. "Does Rising Income Bring Integration? New Results for Blacks, Hispanics, and Asians in 1990." *Social Science Research* 28: 316–326.

Mauer, Marc. 2005. "Thinking About Prison and Its Impact in the Twenty-First Century." *Ohio State Journal of Criminal Law* 2: 607–618.

Mauer, Marc, and Tracy Huling. 1995. *Young Black Americans and the Criminal Justice System: Five Years Later*. Washington, DC: Sentencing Project.

Mazier, E. E. 2001a. "Minority Agent Support Still Has a Ways to Go." *National Underwriter*, October 29.

———. 2001b. "Minority Intern Program Launched." *National Underwriter*, October 29.

McKinnon, Jesse. 2003. "The Black Population in the United States: March 2002." Washington, DC: US Census Bureau.

McWhorter, John H. 2000. *Losing the Race: Self-Sabotage in Black America*. New York: Free Press.

Mead, Lawrence. 1992. *The New Politics of Poverty: The Nonworking Poor in America*. New York: Basic Books.

Merton, Robert K. 1968. *Social Theory and Social Structure*. New York: Free Press.

Metzger, John T. 2001. "Clustered Spaces: Racial Profiling in Real Estate Investment." Paper presented at the International Seminar on Segregation and the City, Lincoln Institute of Land Policy, Cambridge, MA, July 26–28.

Meyer, Laurence H. 1998. Remarks Before the 1998 Community Reinvestment Conference of the Consumer Bankers Association, Arlington, VA, May 12.

Meyer, Stephen Grant. 2000. *As Long as They Don't Move Next Door: Segregation and Racial Conflict in American Neighborhoods*. Lanham, MD: Rowman and Littlefield.

Miethe, Terance D., and David McDowall. 1993. "Contextual Effects in Models of Criminal Victimization." *Social Forces* 71: 741–759.

Millen, John C., and Constance K. Chamberlain. 2001. "Agreement Reached That Will Benefit Homeowners Throughout the Country." Press release announcing settlement agreement between Nationwide Insurance and Housing Opportunities Made Equal (April 24).

Miller, Lisa L. 2000. "Taking It to the Streets: Reframing Crime Prevention Through Race and Community." *Studies in Law, Politics, and Society* 20: 207–238.

Mills, C. Wright. 1958. *The Causes of World War Three*. New York: Ballantine.

Mills, Lila J. 2004. "Ashcroft Touts Efforts to Help Ex-prisoners Re-enter Society." *Plain Dealer* (September 9). Last accessed at www.cleveland.com on March 15, 2005.

Morenoff, Jeffrey D., Robert J. Sampson, and Stephen W. Raudenbush. 2001. "Neighborhood Inequality, Collective Efficacy, and the Spatial Dynamics of Urban Violence." *Criminology* 39: 517–559.

Moskowitz, Erik. 1995. "One-Stop Shops Offer Check Cashing and More." *Christian Science Monitor*, August 23, 9.

Munnell, Alicia, Geoffrey M. B. Tootell, Lynn E. Browne, and James McEneaney. 1996. "Mortgage Lending in Boston: Interpreting HMDA Data." *American Economic Review* 86 (1): 25–53.

Murray, Charles. 1984. *Losing Ground: American Social Policy, 1950–1980*. New York: Basic Books.

Myers, Samuel, and C. Chung. 1996. "Racial Differences in Home Ownership and Home Equity Among Preretirement-Aged Households." *Gerontologist* 36: 350–360.

National Association of Independent Insurers. 1994. *An Analysis of Crime and Fire Statistics, Dwelling Characteristics, and Homeowners Insurance Losses for Selected Urban Areas*. Washington, DC: National Association of Independent Insurers.

National Commission on Neighborhoods. 1979. *People Building Neighborhoods: Final Report to the President and Congress of the United States*. Washington, DC: US Government Printing Office.

National Community Reinvestment Coalition. 2005a. *CRA Commitments*. Washington, DC: National Community Reinvestment Coalition.

———. 2005b. "NCRC Disappointed by Federal Ruling Weakening CRA." Washington, DC: National Community Reinvestment Coalition.

———. 2003. *The Broken Credit System: Discrimination and Unequal Access to Affordable Loans by Race and Age*. Washington, DC: National Community Reinvestment Coalition.

———. 2002a. "Anti–Predatory Lending Toolkit." Washington, DC: National Community Reinvestment Coalition.

———. 2002b. *CRA Commitments*. Washington, DC: National Community Reinvestment Coalition.

———. 2001a. "Home Loans to Minorities and Working Class Populations

Increase, but Policymakers Do Not Address Remaining Credit Gaps: A Review of National Data Trends from 1993–2000." Washington, DC: National Community Reinvestment Coalition.

———. 2001b. "NCRC Press Release: Better Home Loan Data Critical For Anti-Discrimination in Indian Country." Washington, DC: National Community Reinvestment Coalition, April 16.

National Fair Housing Alliance. 2005. "$215,000,000 and Counting." Washington, DC: National Fair Housing Alliance.

National Fair Housing Alliance. 2003a. "$190,000,000 and Counting." Washington, DC: National Fair Housing Alliance.

———. 2003b. "Fair Housing Trends Report." Washington, DC: National Fair Housing Alliance.

National Fair Housing Alliance, Inc. v. Travelers Property Casualty Corporation, Aetna Casualty and Surety Company, and Citigroup, Inc. 2000. US District Court for the District of Columbia, Case Number 1:00CV01506.

National Inspection Company. 1958. "Report on Negro Areas of Chicago." Chicago: National Inspection Company.

National Training and Information Center. 2002. "This Old Reg: The Community Reinvestment Act Needs Renovation." Chicago: National Training and Information Center.

———. 1999. "Preying on Neighborhoods: Subprime Mortgage Lending and Chicago Land Foreclosures." Chicago: National Training and Information Center. Available at http://www.ntic-us.org/preying/preying.html, March 27, 2006.

Neighborhood Reinvestment Corporation. 1997. *The Neighbor Works Network and Neighborhood Reinvestment Corporation 1997 Annual Report*. Washington, DC: Neighborhood Reinvestment Corporation.

———. 1995. *Pathways to Partnership*. Washington, DC: Neighborhood Reinvestment Corporation.

Nelson, Arthur C., Casey J. Dawkins, and Thomas Sanchez. 2004. "Urban Containment and Residential Segregation: A Preliminary Investigation." *Urban Studies* 41 (2): 423–439.

Nelson, M., P. Deess, and C. Allen. 1999. *The First Month Out: Post-Incarceration Experiences in New York City*. New York: Vera Institute of Justice.

Newman, Kathe, and Elvin K. Wyly. 2004. "Geographies of Mortgage Market Segmentation: The Case of Essex County, New Jersey." *Housing Studies* 19 (1): 53–83.

Nyden, Philip, John Lukehart, Michael T. Maly, and William Peterman. 1998. "Neighborhood Racial and Ethnic Diversity in US Cities." *Cityscape* 4 (2): 1–18.

Ochs, Phil. 1965. "Love Me, I'm a Liberal." Barricade Music.

O'Connor, Alice. 2001. "Understanding Inequality in the Late Twentieth-Century Metropolis: New Perspectives on the Enduring Racial Divide." In *Urban Inequality: Evidence from Four Cities*, edited by Alice

O'Connor, Chris Tilly, and Lawrence D. Bobo. New York: Russell Sage Foundation.

O'Connor, Alice, Chris Tilly, and Lawrence D. Bobo, eds. 2001. *Urban Inequality: Evidence from Four Cities.* New York: Russell Sage Foundation.

Office of Land Information Services, Department of Administration, State of Wisconsin. 2001. "Wisconsin's Comprehensive Planning Legislation." Madison: State of Wisconsin. Available at http://www.doa.state.wi.us/dhir/documents/compplanstats.pdf (last accessed June 18, 2004).

Oliver, Melvin L., and Thomas M. Shapiro. 1995. *Black Wealth/White Wealth: A New Perspective on Racial Inequality.* New York: Routledge.

Orfield, Gary, and Susan E. Eaton. 2003. "Back to Segregation." *Nation*: 5, March 3.

Orfield, Myron. 2002. *American Metropolitics: The New Suburban Reality.* Washington, DC: Brookings Institution.

———. 1997. *Metropolitics: A Regional Agenda for Community and Stability.* Washington and Cambridge: Brookings Institution Press and the Lincoln Institute of Land Policy.

Orzechowski, Shawna, and Peter Sepielli. 2003. "Current Population Reports, Household Economic Studies, Series P70–P88." *Net Worth and Asset Ownership of Households: 1998 and 2000.* US Census Bureau. Washington, DC: US Government Printing Office.

Pager, Devah. 2003. "The Mark of a Criminal Record." *American Journal of Sociology* 108: 937–975.

Paltrow, Scott J. 1998. "A Matter of Policy: How a State Becomes Popular with Insurers." *Wall Street Journal*, January 14.

Parent, Dale, Dan Wentwork, Peggy Burke, and Becky Ney. 1994. *Responding to Probation and Parole Violations.* Washington, DC: US Department of Justice, National Institute of Justice.

Pattillo-McCoy, Mary. 1999. *Black Picket Fences: Privilege and Peril Among the Black Middle Class.* Chicago: University of Chicago Press.

Pennington-Cross, Anthony. 2002. "Subprime Lending in the Primary and Secondary Markets." *Journal of Housing Research* 13 (1): 31–50.

Peters, Alan, and Peter Fisher. 2004. "The Failures of Economic Development Incentives." *Journal of the American Planning Association* 70 (1): 27–36.

Petersilia, Joan. 1997. "Probation in the United States." *Crime and Justice* 22: 149–200.

Petersilia, Joan, and Susan Turner. 1993. "Intensive Probation and Parole." In *Crime and Justice: A Review of the Research*, vol. 17, edited by Michael Tonry. Chicago: University of Chicago Press.

Petersilia, Joan, Susan Turner, and Joyce Peterson. 1986. *Prison Versus Probation in California: Implications for Crime and Offender Recidivism.* Santa Monica, CA: Rand.

Peterson, Ruth D., and Lauren J. Krivo. 1993. "Racial Segregation and Black Urban Homicide." *Social Forces* 71(4): 1001–1026.

Polikoff, Alexander. 2006. *Waiting for Gautreaux: A Story of Segregation,*

Housing, and the Black Ghetto. Evanston, IL: Northwestern University Press.

Popkin, Susan J., Bruce Katz, Mary K. Cunningham, Karen D. Brown, Jeremy Gustafson, and Margery Austin Turner. 2004. "A Decade of Hope VI: Research Findings and Policy Challenges." Washington, DC: Urban Institute and Brookings Institution.

Powers, D. J. 1997. "The Discriminatory Effects of Homeowners Insurance Underwriting Guidelines." In *Insurance Redlining: Disinvestment, Reinvestment, and the Evolving Role of Financial Institutions*, edited by Gregory D. Squires. Washington, DC: Urban Institute Press.

President's National Advisory Panel on Insurance in Riot-Affected Areas. 1968. *Meeting the Insurance Crisis of Our Cities.* Washington, DC: US Government Printing Office.

Pulido, Laura. 2004. "Environmental Racism and Urban Development." In *Up Against the Sprawl: Public Policy and the Making of Southern California,* edited by Jennifer Wolch, Manuel Pastor Jr., and Peter Dreier. Minneapolis: University of Minneapolis Press.

Putnam, Robert D. 2000. *Bowling Alone: The Collapse and Revival of American Community.* New York: Simon and Schuster.

Quercia, Roberto G., Michael Stegman, and Walter R. Davis. 2005. "The Impact of Predatory Loan Terms on Subprime Foreclosures: The Special Case of Prepayment Penalties and Balloon Payments." Chapel Hill: Center for Community Capitalism, University of North Carolina.

———. 2003. "The Impact of North Carolina's Anti-Predatory Lending Law: A Descriptive Assessment." Chapel Hill: Center for Community Capitalism, University of North Carolina.

Rae, Douglas W. 2003. *City: Urbanism and Its End.* New Haven, CT: Yale University Press.

Raphael, Steven, and Michael A. Stoll. 2002. "Modest Progress: The Narrowing Spatial Mismatch Between Blacks and Jobs in the 1990s." Washington, DC: Brookings Institution.

Reddy, Anitha. 2002. "Lending Case to Cost Citigroup $215 Million." *Washington Post,* September 20.

Reed, Adolph, Jr. 2005. "Classifying the Hurricane." *Nation,* October 3. Available at http://www.thenation.com/doc/20051003/reed (last accessed September 26, 2005).

———. 1988. "The Black Urban Regime: Structural Origins and Constraints." *Comparative Urban Research* 12: 140–187.

Reich, Robert B. 1991. *The Work of Nations.* New York: Alfred A. Knopf.

Renuart, Elizabeth. 2002. *Stop Predatory Lending: A Guide for Legal Advocates.* Washington, DC: National Consumer Law Center.

Ritter, Richard J. 1997. "Racial Justice and the Role of the US Department of Justice in Combating Insurance Redlining." In *Insurance Redlining: Disinvestment, Reinvestment, and the Evolving Role of Financial Institutions,* edited by Gregory D. Squires. Washington, DC: Urban Institute.

Rohe, William M., Shannon Van Zandt, and George McCarthy. 2000. *The*

Social Benefits and Costs of Homeownership: A Critical Assessment of the Research. Chapel Hill: Center for Urban and Regional Studies, University of North Carolina at Chapel Hill.

Rose, Dina R., and Todd Clear. 1998. "Incarceration, Social Capital, and Crime: Implications for Social Disorganization Theory." *Criminology* 36: 441–479.

Rosenbaum, James E., and Susan Popkin. 1991. "Employment and Earnings of Low-Income Blacks Who Move to Middle-Income Suburbs." In *The Urban Underclass,* edited by Christopher Jencks and Paul E. Peterson. Washington, DC: Brookings Institution, 342–356.

Rosenbaum, James E., Stefanie DeLuca, and Tammy Tuck. 2005. "New Capabilities in New Places: Low-Income Black Families in Suburbia." In *The Geography of Opportunity: Race and Housing Choice in Metropolitan America,* edited by Xavier de Souza Briggs. Washington, DC: Brookings Institution.

Ross, Stephen L., and John Yinger. 2002. *The Color of Credit: Mortgage Discrimination, Research Methodology, and Fair-Lending Enforcement.* Cambridge, MA: MIT Press.

Rountree, Pamela Wilcox, Kenneth C. Land, and Terance D. Miethe. 1994. "Macro-Micro Integration in the Study of Victimization: A Hierarchical Logistic Model Analysis Across Seattle Neighborhoods." *Criminology* 32: 387–414.

Rubinowitz, Leonard S., and James E. Rosenbaum. 2000. *Crossing the Class and Color Lines: From Public Housing to White Suburbia.* Chicago: University of Chicago Press.

Ruquet, Mark E. 2001. "Carriers Help with Diversity Training." *National Underwriter,* October 29.

Rusk, David. 2001. "The 'Segregation Tax': The Cost of Racial Segregation to Black Homeowners." Washington, DC: Brookings Institution.

———. 1999. *Inside Game Outside Game: Winning Strategies for Saving Urban America.* Washington, DC: Brookings Institution.

———. 1993. *Cities Without Suburbs.* Baltimore: Johns Hopkins University Press.

Rutheiser, Charles. 1996. *Imagineering Atlanta: The Politics of Place in the City of Dreams.* New York: Verso.

Saadi, Michel. 1987. *Claim It Yourself: The Accident Victim's Guide to Personal Injury Claims.* New York: Pharos Books.

St. John, Craig. 2000. "Racial Residential Segregation by the Level of Socioeconomic Status." *Social Science Quarterly* 81 (3): 701–715.

Sampson, Robert J. 2001. "Crime and Public Safety: Insights from Community-level Perspectives on Social Capital." In *Social Capital and Poor Communities,* edited by Susan Saegert, Phillip J. Thompson, and Mark R. Warren. New York: Russell Sage, 89–114.

———. 1987. "Urban Black Violence: The Effect of Male Joblessness and Family Disruption." *American Journal of Sociology* 93: 348–382.

———. 1986. "Crime in Cities: The Effects of Formal and Informal Social

Control." In *Communities and Crime*, edited by A. J. Reiss and Michael Tonry. Chicago: University of Chicago Press, 271–311.

Sampson, Robert J., and W. Byron Groves. 1989. "Community Structure and Crime: Testing Social-Disorganization Theory." *American Journal of Sociology* 94: 774–802.

Sampson, Robert J., Jeffrey D. Morenoff, and Thomas Gannon-Rowley. 2002. "Assessing 'Neighborhood Effects': Social Processes and New Directions in Research." *Annual Review of Sociology* 28: 443–478.

Sampson, Robert J., Stephen W. Raudenbush, and Felton Earls. 1997. "Neighborhoods and Violent Crime." *Science* 277: 918–924.

Sampson, Robert J., Gregory D. Squires, and Min Zhou. 2000. *How Neighborhoods Matter: The Value of Investing at the Local Level.* Washington, DC: American Sociological Association.

Sampson, Robert J., and William Julius Wilson. 1995. "Toward a Theory of Race, Crime, and Urban Inequality." In *Crime and Inequality*, edited by John Hagan and Ruth D. Peterson. Stanford, CA: Stanford University Press, 37–54.

Sard, Barbara, and Jennifer Daskal. 1998. "Housing and Welfare Reform: Some Background Information." Washington, DC: Center on Budget and Policy Priorities.

Sawyer, Noah, and Kenneth Temkin. 2004. "Analysis of Alternative Financial Service Providers." Washington, DC: Fannie Mae Foundation and the Urban Institute.

Schill, Michael H. 2002. "Legislative and Regulatory Efforts to Promote Community Reinvestment and Fair Lending." Unpublished working paper.

Schill, Michael H., and Samantha Friedman. 1999. "The Fair Housing Act of 1988: The First Decade." *Cityscape* 4 (3): 57–78.

Schultz, Jay D. 1997. "Homeowners Insurance Availability and Agent Location." In *Insurance Redlining: Disinvestment, Reinvestment, and the Evolving Role of Financial Institutions*, edited by Gregory D. Squires. Washington, DC: Urban Institute.

———. 1995. "An Analysis of Agent Location and Homeowners Insurance Availability." *Journal of Insurance Regulation* 14 (1): 65–89.

Schuman, Howard, Charlotte Steeh, Lawrence Bobo, and Maria Krysan. 1997. *Racial Attitudes in America: Trends and Interpretations.* Cambridge, MA: Harvard University Press.

Schwaner, Shawn L. 1998. "Patterns of Violent Specialization: Predictors of Recidivism for a Cohort of Parolees." *American Journal of Criminal Justice* 23: 1–17.

Schwartz, Alex. 1998a. "Bank Lending to Minority and Low-Income Households and Neighborhoods: Do Community Reinvestment Agreements Make a Difference?" *Journal of Urban Affairs* 20 (3): 269–301.

———. 1998b. "From Confrontation to Collaboration? Banks, Community Groups, and the Implementation of Community Reinvestment Agreements." *Housing Policy Debate* 9 (3): 631–662.

Seiter, Richard P., and Karen R. Kadela. 2003. "Prisoner Reentry: What Works, What Does Not, and What Is Promising." *Crime and Delinquency* 49: 360–388.

Shapiro, Thomas M. 2004. *The Hidden Cost of Being African American: How Wealth Perpetuates Inequality.* New York: Oxford University Press.

Shipler, David K. 2004. *The Working Poor: Invisible in America.* New York: Alfred A. Knopf.

Shlay, Ann. 1999. "Influencing Agents of Urban Structure: Evaluating the Effects of Community Reinvestment Organizing on Bank Residential Lending Practices." *Journal of Urban Affairs* 35 (2): 247–278.

Shonkoff, Jack P., and Deborah A. Phillips, eds. 2000. *From Neurons to Neighborhoods: The Science of Early Child Development.* Washington, DC: National Academy Press.

Sidney, Mara S. 2003. *Unfair Housing: How National Policy Shapes Community Action.* Lawrence: University Press of Kansas.

Silver, Eric. 2000. "Extending Social Disorganization Theory: A Multilevel Approach to the Study of Violence Among Persons with Mental Illnesses." *Criminology* 38: 1043–1073.

Silver, Josh. 2001. "Strengthening the CRA." *Shelterforce* 120 (November–December): 27.

Simcha-Fagan, Ora, and Joseph E. Schwartz. 1986. "Neighborhood and Delinquency: An Assessment of Contextual Effects." *Criminology* 24: 667–699.

Skocpol, Theda. 2000. *The Missing Middle: Working Families and the Future of American Social Policy.* New York: W. W. Norton.

Smith, Shanna L., and Cathy Cloud. 1997. "Documenting Discrimination by Homeowners Insurance Companies Through Testing." In *Insurance Redlining: Disinvestment, Reinvestment, and the Evolving Role of Financial Institutions,* edited by Gregory D. Squires. Washington, DC: Urban Institute.

Snyder, David F. 2003. "The Consumer Benefits of Credit-Based Insurance Scoring: Ohio Civil Rights Commission." Washington, DC: American Insurance Association.

Sourcebook of Criminal Justice Statistics. 1985–1989; 2002. *Prisoners in 1985, 1986, 1987, 1988, 1989, 2002.* Washington, DC: US Department of Justice, Bureau of Justice Statistics.

South, Scott J., and Kyle D. Crowder. 1998a. "Leaving the 'hood: Residential Mobility Between Black, White, and Integrated Neighborhoods." *American Sociological Review* 63: 17–26.

———. 1998b. "Housing Discrimination and Residential Mobility: Impacts for Blacks and Whites." *Population Research and Policy Review* 17 (4): 369–387.

———. 1997a. "Residential Mobility Between Cities and Suburbs: Race, Suburbanization, and Back-to-the-City Moves." *Demography* 343: 525–538.

————. 1997b. "Escaping Distressed Neighborhoods: Individual, Community, and Metropolitan Influences." *American Journal of Sociology* 102: 1040–1084.

South, Scott J., and Glenn D. Deane. 1993. "Race and Residential Mobility: Individual Determinants and Structural Constraints." *Social Forces* 72: 147–167.

Spohn, Cassia, and David Holleran. 2002. "The Effect of Imprisonment on Recidivism Rates of Felony Offenders: A Focus on Drug Offenders." *Criminology* 40: 329–357.

Squires, Gregory D. 2004. *Why the Poor Pay More: How to Stop Predatory Lending*. Westport, CT: Praeger.

————, ed. 2003a. *Organizing Access to Capital: Advocacy and the Democratization of Financial Institutions*. Philadelphia: Temple University Press.

————. 2003b. "The New Redlining: Predatory Lending in an Age of Financial Service Modernization." *Sage Race Relations Abstracts* 28 (3–4): 5–18.

————, ed. 2002. *Urban Sprawl: Causes, Consequences, and Policy Responses*. Washington, DC: Urban Institute.

————, ed. 1997. *Insurance Redlining: Disinvestment, Reinvestment, and the Evolving Role of Financial Institutions*. Washington, DC: Urban Institute.

————. 1994. *Capital and Communities in Black and White: The Intersections of Race, Class, and Uneven Development*. Albany: SUNY Press.

Squires, Gregory D., and Sally O'Connor. 2001. *Color and Money: Politics and Prospects for Community Reinvestment in Urban America*. Albany: SUNY Press.

————. 1998. "Fringe Banking in Milwaukee: The Rise of Check-Cashing Businesses and the Emergence of a Two-Tiered Banking System." *Urban Affairs Review* 34 (1): 126–149.

Squires, Gregory D., Sally O'Connor, Michael Grover, and James Walrath. 1999. "Housing Affordability in the Milwaukee Metropolitan Area: A Matter of Income, Race, and Policy." *Journal of Affordable Housing and Community Development Law* 9 (1): 34–73.

Squires, Gregory D., Sally O'Connor, Josh Silver. 2001. "The Unavailability of Information on Insurance Unavailability: Insurance Redlining and the Absence of Geocoded Disclosure Data." *Housing Policy Debate* 12 (2): 347–372.

Squires, Gregory D., and William Velez. 1987. "Neighborhood Racial Composition and Mortgage Lending: City and Suburban Differences." *Journal of Urban Affairs* 9 (3): 217–232.

Squires, Gregory D., William Velez, and Karl Taeuber. 1991. "Insurance Redlining, Agency Location, and the Process of Urban Disinvestment." *Urban Affairs Quarterly* 26 (4): 567–588.

Stearns, Linda Brewster, and John Logan. 1986. "The Racial Structuring of the Housing Market and Segregation in Suburban Areas." *Social Forces* 65: 28–42.

Stegman, Michael A., Marta Rocha, and Walter Davis. 2004. "The Accessibility of Self-Service Banking Technology to Low-Income and Minority Communities: Preliminary Results from a Spatial Analysis of Automated Teller Machines in the United States." Presented at the Community Development Finance Research Conference, Federal Reserve Bank of New York.

Steinberg, Stephen. 1995. *Turning Back: The Retreat from Racial Justice in American Thought and Policy*. Boston: Beacon Press.

Stoll, Michael A., and Steven Raphael. 2000. "Racial Differences in Spatial Job Search Patterns: Exploring the Causes and Consequences." *Economic Geography* 76 (3): 201–228.

Stuart, Guy. 2003. *Discriminating Risk: The US Mortgage Lending Industry in the Twentieth Century*. Ithaca, NY: Cornell University Press.

Suttles, Gerald D. 1968. *The Social Order of the Slum: Ethnicity and Territory in the Inner City*. Chicago: University of Chicago Press.

Teixeira, Ruy, and Joel Rogers. 2000. *America's Forgotten Majority: Why the White Working Class Still Matters*. New York: Basic Books.

Texas Department of Insurance. 2004. "Use of Credit Information by Insurers in Texas." Austin: Texas Department of Insurance.

Thomas, Paulette. 1999. "Selling Big Insurers on Inner-City Policies." *Wall Street Journal*, May 6, B1, B12.

Thurow, Lester. 1987. "A Surge in Inequality." *Scientific American* 256 (5): 30–37.

Tiebout, Charles. 1956. "A Pure Theory of Local Expenditures." *Journal of Political Economy* 64: 416–424.

Tilly, Chris, Philip Moss, Joleen Kirschenman, and Ivy Kennelly. 2001. "Space as a Signal: How Employers Perceive Neighborhoods in Four Metropolitan Labor Markets." In *Urban Inequality: Evidence from Four Cities*, edited by Alice O'Connor, Chris Tilly, and Lawrence D. Bobo. New York: Russell Sage Foundation.

Toledo Fair Housing Center v. Farmers Insurance Groups of Companies. 1999. Common Pleas Court of Lucas County, Case No. CI0199901339.

Tonry, Michael. 1995. *Malign Neglect: Race, Crime, and Punishment in America*. Oxford: Oxford University Press.

Trapp, Shel. 2004. *Dynamics of Organizing: Building Power by Developing the Human Spirit*. Chicago: Shel Trapp.

Travis, Jeremy. 2000. "But They All Come Back: Rethinking Prisoner Reentry." Sentencing and Corrections—Issues for the Twenty-First Century Brief No. 7. Washington, DC: Urban Institute.

Travis, Jeremy, Amy L. Solomon, and Michelle Waul. 2001. "From Prison to Home: The Dimensions and Consequences of Prisoner Reentry." Report from the Justice Policy Center, Urban Institute, Washington, DC.

Travis, Jeremy, and Michelle Waul, eds. 2003. *Prisoners Once Removed: The Impact of Incarceration and Reentry on Children, Families, and Communities*. Washington, DC: Urban Institute.

Turner, Margery, and Stephen L. Ross. 2005. "How Racial Discrimination Affects the Search for Housing." In *The Geography of Opportunity: Race and Housing Choice in Metropolitan America*, edited by Xavier de Souza Briggs. Washington, DC: Brookings Institution.

Turner, Margery Austin, Fred Frieberg, Erin Godfrey, Carla Herbig, Diane K. Levy, and Robin R. Smith. 2002a. *All Other Things Being Equal: A Paired Testing Study of Mortgage Lending Institutions.* Washington, DC: Urban Institute.

Turner, Margery Austin, Stephen L. Ross, George C. Galster, and John Yinger. 2002b. *Discrimination in Metropolitan Housing Markets: National Results from Phase I HDS 2000.* Washington, DC: Urban Institute.

Turner, Margery Austin, and Felicity Skidmore, eds. 1999. *Mortgage Lending Discrimination: A Review of Existing Evidence.* Washington, DC: Urban Institute.

Ulmer, Jeffrey T. 2001. "Intermediate Sanctions: A Comparative Analysis of the Probability and Severity of Recidivism." *Sociological Inquiry* 71: 164–193.

Urban Institute. 2003. "New Initiative Aims to Strengthen Community Strategies for Prisoners Returning to Society." Urban Institute Press Release (April 16). Last accessed at www.urban.org on March 15, 2005.

US Census Bureau. 2003. Table DP-1. Profile of General Demographic Characteristics, 2000. Available at http://censtats.census.gov/data/ WA/1605363000.pdf (last accessed March 27, 2006).

———. 2002a. "American Housing Survey for the United States: 1999." Table 3-1 and Table 3-14. Available at www.census.gov/hhes/www/ housing/ahs/ahs99/tab31.html and www.census.gov/hhes/www/ housing/ahs/ahs99/tab314.html (last accessed March 27, 2006).

———. 2002b. *Census 2000 Summary File 3 Technical Documentation.* Washington, DC: US Government Printing Office.

———. 2001. "Population Estimates of Metropolitan Areas, Metropolitan Areas Inside Central Cities, Metropolitan Areas Outside Central Cities, and Nonmetropolitan Areas by State for July 1, 1999 and April 1, 1990 Population Estimates Base." Available at http://www.census .gov/population/estimates/metro-city/ma99-06.txt (last accessed April 26, 2001).

———. 2000. "Selected Characteristics of Households and Families by Quintile." Available at http://ferret.bls.census.gov/macro/032000/quint/ toc.htm (last accessed March 27, 2006).

———. 1999. *Money Income in the United States: 1998.* Washington, DC: US Government Printing Bureau.

US Department of Housing and Urban Development. 2000a. *The State of the Cities 2000.* Washington, DC: US Department of Housing and Urban Development.

———. 2000b. *Unequal Burden: Income and Racial Disparities in Subprime Lending in America.* Washington, DC: US Department of Housing and Urban Development.

————. 1997. *The State of the Cities 1997*. Washington, DC: US Department of Housing and Urban Development.

US Department of Justice. 2001. *Criminal Victimization 2000: Changes 1999–2000 with Trends 1993–2000*. Washington, DC: US Department of Justice.

————. 1999. *Criminal Victimization and Perceptions of Community Safety in 12 Cities, 1998*. Washington, DC: US Department of Justice.

Velez, Maria. 2001. "The Role of Public Social Control in Urban Neighborhoods." *Criminology* 39: 837–863.

Venkatesh, Sudhir Alladi. 2000. *American Project: The Rise and Fall of a Modern Ghetto*. Cambridge: Harvard University Press.

Visher, Christy A., Nancy G. LaVigne, and Jill Farrell. 2003. "Illinois Prisoners' Reflections on Returning Home." Washington, DC: Urban Institute Justice Policy Center (September 9).

Visher, Christy A., Vera Kachnowski, Nancy LaVigne, and Jeremy Travis. 2004. "Baltimore Prisoners' Experiences Returning Home." Washington, DC: Urban Institute.

Visher, Christy A., Rebecca L. Naser, Demelza Baer, and Jesse Jannetta. 2005. *In Need of Help: Experiences of Seriously Ill Prisoners Returning to Cincinnati*. Washington, DC: Urban Institute.

Von Hoffman, Alexander. 2003. *House by House, Block by Block: The Rebirth of America's Urban Neighborhoods*. New York: Oxford University Press.

Von Zielbauer, Paul. 2003. "Initiatives Aim to Halt Cycle of Felons Returning to Jail." *New York Times*, August 4.

Warner, Barbara D., and Pamela Wilcox Rountree. 1997. "Local Social Ties in a Community and Crime Model: Questioning the Systemic Nature of Informal Social Control." *Social Problems* 44: 520–536.

Warren, Mark R. 2001. *Dry Bones Rattling: Community Building to Revitalize American Democracy*. Princeton: Princeton University Press.

Weitzer, Ronald. 1999. "Citizen's Perceptions of Police Misconduct: Race and Neighborhood Context." *Justice Quarterly* 16: 819–846.

Wertheim, Carla. 2002. Telephone interview (October 24).

White, Michael. 1986. "Segregation and Diversity Measures in Population Distribution." *Population Index* 52 (2): 198–221.

Whitehead, John T, Jocelyn M. Pollock, and Michael C. Braswell. 2003. *Exploring Corrections in America*. Cincinnati, OH: Anderson.

Wikstrom, Per-Olof H., and Rolf Loeber. 2000. "Do Disadvantaged Neighborhoods Cause Well-Adjusted Children to Become Adolescent Delinquents? A Study of Male Juvenile Serious Offending, Individual Risk and Protective Factors, and Neighborhood Context." *Criminology* 38: 1109–1142.

Williamson, Thad, David Imbroscio, and Gar Alperovitz. 2002. *Making a Place for Community: Local Democracy in a Global Era*. New York: Routledge.

Willis, Gary. 2003. "Insurance Scoring: A New Form of Redlining?" Paper presented at the Thirty-Third Annual Meeting of the Urban Affairs Association, Cleveland, Ohio (March 27).

Wilson, William J. 1999. *The Bridge over the Racial Divide: Rising Inequality and Coalition Politics.* Berkeley: University of California Press.

———. 1996. *When Work Disappears: The World of the New Urban Poor.* New York: Alfred A. Knopf.

———. 1987. *The Truly Disadvantaged: The Inner City, the Underclass, and Public Policy.* Chicago: University of Chicago.

Wissoker, Douglas, Wendy Zimmermann, and George Galster. 1998. "Testing for Discrimination in Home Insurance," Washington, DC: Urban Institute.

Wolff, Edward N. 2001. "Recent Trends in Wealth Ownership, from 1983 to 1998." In *Assets for the Poor: The Benefits of Spreading Asset Ownership*, edited by Thomas M. Shapiro and Edward N. Wolff. New York: Russell Sage Foundation.

———. 1995. *Top Heavy: A Study of the Increasing Inequality of Wealth in America.* New York: Twentieth Century Fund Press.

Yaspan, Robert. 1970. "Property Insurance and the American Ghetto: A Study in Social Irresponsibility." *Southern California Law Review* 44: 218–274.

Yinger, John. 1995. *Closed Doors, Opportunities Lost: The Continuing Costs of Housing Discrimination.* New York: Russell Sage Foundation.

Index

African American communities, concentrated disadvantage in, 132. *See also* Minority communities

African American male criminals: drug arrests/incarceration of, 123; incarceration rates of, 122; recidivism of, 120; and reintegration into community, 120, 125

American Family Mutual Insurance Company, case settlement provisions, 86-87

Association of Communities Organized for Reform Now (ACORN), 65

Banking system: fringe bankers in, 61-62; and households lacking bank accounts, 62; and redlining prohibitions, 88; regulation, 32. *See also* Fringe bankers; Predatory lenders; Subprime lenders

Black homeownership: comparative rate of, 7; and discrimination against homebuyers, 10; property insurers' discriminatory guidelines, 82, 83

Black household income: comparative rates of, 7-8; and wealth disparity explanations, 8-10

Black infant mortality rate, 11

Black/white segregation, moderate decline in, 6-7

Capital access: and community crime rates, 96, 115-116; and policy-oriented research, 115

Central city, concentration of public housing in, 20

Citigroup, prosecution of, 65

Community Reinvestment Act (CRA), 63, 64; and banking regulation, 32; and credit access, 95; "innovative" lending and, 52; legislation, 31, 32; lending assessment and, 51-52; limited enforcement of, 32-33; and minority credit access, 26; and minority housing access to white neighborhoods, 42-48; minority/low-income lending impacts of, 26-27, 34; and neighborhood crime rates, 112; passage of, 67; performance-oriented regulation of, 32-33, 34; politics and, 50; redlining and, 26, 31, 88; and regulatory change, 32-34; scope of, 51; spatial emphasis of, 26-27, 33; third-party challenges to, 32; white homebuyers and, 45-46

Community reinvestment: current policy debates over, 51-52; movement, and minority access to white neighborhoods, 26-28

About the Book

In the United States today, quality of life depends heavily on where one lives—but high levels of racial segregation in residential communities make it frustratingly difficult to disentangle the effects of place from those of race. Gregory Squires and Charis Kubrin tackle these issues head-on, exploring how inequities resulting from the intersection of race and place, coupled with the effects of public policy, permeate and shape structures of opportunity in the United States.

Gregory D. Squires is professor of sociology at George Washington University. His publications include *Color and Money: Politics and Prospects for Community Reinvestment in Urban America* and *Capital and Communities in Black and White: The Intersections of Race, Class, and Uneven Development.* **Charis E. Kubrin** is associate professor of sociology at George Washington University. She is coeditor of *Crime and Society* (2nd edition) and has published numerous articles on race and crime.